ELEMENTS

of

INFLUENCE

ELEMENTS

of

INFLUENCE

The Art of Getting Others to
Follow Your Lead

TERRY R. BACON

AMACOM
AMERICAN MANAGEMENT ASSOCIATION
New York • Atlanta • Brussels • Chicago • Mexico City • San Francisco
Shanghai • Tokyo • Toronto • Washington, D.C.

Bulk discounts available. For details visit:
www.amacombooks.org/go/specialsales
Or contact special sales:
Phone: 800-250-5308
E-mail: specialsls@amanet.org
View all the AMACOM titles at: www.amacombooks.org

This publication is designed to provide accurate and authorita-tive information in regard to the subject matter covered. It is sold with the understanding that the publisher is not engaged in rendering legal, accounting, or other professional service. If legal advice or other expert assistance is required, the services of a competent professional person should be sought.

Library of Congress Cataloging-in-Publication Data

Bacon, Terry R.
  Elements of influence : the art of getting others to follow your lead / Terry R. Bacon.
     p. cm.
  Includes index.
  ISBN-13: 978-0-8144-1732-4 (hbk.)
  ISBN-10: 0-8144-1732-9 (hbk.)
  1. Influence (Psychology) 2. Leadership. I. Title.
  BF774.B23 2012
  658.4'092—dc22

                              2011003902

About AMA
American Management Association (www.amanet.org) is a world leader in talent development, advancing the skills of individuals to drive business success. Our mission is to support the goals of individuals and organizations through a complete range of products and services, including classroom and virtual seminars, webcasts, webinars, podcasts, conferences, corporate and government solutions, business books, and research. AMA's approach to improving performance combines experiential learning—learning through doing—with opportu-nities for ongoing professional growth at every step of one's career journey.

Printing number

10 9 8 7 6 5 4 3 2 1

PERMISSIONS AND CREDITS

Part I: Cover photo © Ilya Terentyev/iStockphoto.com.

Chapter 1: Sitting dog (photo © Brenda A. Carson/iStockphoto.com), jumping dog (photo © Happyborder/iStockphoto.com).

Part II: Cover photo © Valentin Casarsa/iStockphoto.com.

Chapter 3: Albert Einstein (Library of Congress—Oren Jack Turner/Getty Images); Ruth Bader Ginsburg (photo by Bloomberg via Getty Images); *Animal Farm* by George Orwell (Copyright © George Orwell, 1945) by permission of Bill Hamilton as the Literary Executor of the Estate of the Late Sonia Brownell Orwell and Secker & Warburg Ltd. For US print rights contact Harcourt Brace.; Excerpts from ANIMAL FARM by George Orwell, copyright 1946 by Harcourt, Inc. and renewed 1974 by Sonia Orwell, reprinted by permission of Houghton Mifflin Harcourt Publishing Company.

Chapter 4: Kenneth R. Feinberg (photo by Mark Wilson/Getty Images); Vince Lombardi (photo by Marvin E. Newman/Sports Illustrated/Getty Images).

Chapter 6: Peter Drucker (photo by George Rose/Getty Images); George H. W. Bush, Dick Cheney, and Colin Powell (photo by Jerome Delay/AFP/Getty Images); Excerpt from *The Paper Chase* © 1973 courtesy of Twentieth Century Fox. Written by James Bridges. All rights reserved. Used by permission.

Chapter 7: Mia Hamm (photo by Richard Schultz/WireImage/Getty Images); Ashley Olsen with Tommy Hilfiger (photo by Jamie McCarthy/Getty Images).

Part III: Cover photo © Valentin Casarsa/iStockphoto.com.

Chapter 10: Bernard Madoff (photo by Timothy A. Clary/AFP/Getty Images).

Chapter 11: Jeffrey Skilling (photo by Dave Einsel/Getty Images); Andrew Fastow (photo by Bloomberg via Getty Images).

CONTENTS

PREFACE

I have been studying leadership for the better part of my professional life, and I've become convinced that leadership—true leadership, authentic leadership—is never an act of control, coercion, or dominance. Leadership arises from the core of who a leader is. It's an act of influence. Authentic leaders do not seek to compel; they seek to inspire. They do not impose their will on others; rather, they live according to core beliefs and principles that attract others; they initiate change because they envision a better way, and others follow that path because they believe it is a better way.

To be sure, countless people have masqueraded as leaders: Adolf Hitler, Joseph Stalin, Mao Zedong, Benito Mussolini, Idi Amin, Samuel Doe, Pol Pot, Suharto, Saddam Hussein, Nicolae Ceaușescu, Erich Honecker, Slobodan Milošević, Ratko Mladic, Jean-Claude Duvalier, Manuel Noriega, Augusto Pinochet, Kim Il Sung, Kim Jong-il, Robert Mugabe, Ferdinand Marcos, Muammar Gaddafi, Omar al-Bashir, Fidel Castro, David Koresh, Jim Jones, and other despots have claimed to be leaders. All vested themselves with godlike authority, exalting in the glory of self-congratulation, but used their power to trick, bribe, enslave, or terrorize others into submission. To call this leadership is to call cheating on exams an act of scholarship.

I've also come to believe that management, albeit a noble and necessary profession, should not be confused with leadership. Management is a by-product of organization; it arises from the need to control the elements, people, and processes of an organization in an efficient and effective way. Managers control those reporting to them by virtue of the authority vested in their positions, and although this legitimate authority gives them the right to command others and to control the operations and budgets in their areas of responsibility, it does not make them leaders. To be sure, managers may also be leaders, but leaders are not necessarily managers. In fact, authentic leadership often emerges in individuals who lack formal authority. It may even be that having formal authority stymies leadership development in people who might otherwise emerge as leaders but are instead seduced by the siren call of positional power and never learn to lead through their authentic selves. Management is a noble and necessary profession, but leadership is to management as painting is to painting by numbers.

Despots coerce; managers control; leaders influence.

What has intrigued me most about leadership is not why leaders choose to lead, but why followers choose to follow. As I've studied leaders in history or in the organizations I've worked with, I've asked myself, "Why would anyone follow this person? What is it about this person that is compelling, interesting, attractive, or inspirational?" Naturally, there are different reasons to explain why people follow a leader. A brilliant leader may inspire through his knowledge, and followers may, in essence, say to themselves, "I can learn something from him." A well-networked leader may build a followership through the energy of social connection, her followers wanting to be as engaged and connected as she is. A powerful, well-positioned leader may draw followers who are ambitious and want to hitch their wagons to a rising star. Sometimes, followers are simply inspired by who the leader is or what the leader represents (think of Bill Gates in technology innovation and entrepreneurship, Martin Luther King Jr. in civil rights, Calvin Klein in fashion, or Germaine Greer in feminism).

As I studied successful leaders, I realized that what is fundamental to all of them is that they are powerful in some ways. They may be powerful because of what they know or can do, how well they can communicate, how attractive or likable they are, what role they play, how much information they control, how well networked they are, how well people regard them, or what people think of their character. I explored these and other sources of power in my previous book, *The Elements of Power: Lessons on Leadership and Influence*. Building a base of power is a prerequisite to leading or influencing anyone. Without power, there is no leadership or influence. With power, people have the *capacity* to lead or influence but will not do so until they act, until they do something that causes other people to follow their lead. This book is about the things leaders do to influence others.

A number of books on influence have appeared in the past few decades, but many of them focus on how marketers, advertisers, and retailers influence consumers. Although their insights are valuable, most people don't write marketing copy, design ad campaigns, determine product prices, or develop sales strategies. Most people have more typical influence and leadership challenges: They want to know how to persuade potential donors to contribute money to a cause, how to convince the boss to give them a raise, how to compel people to vote for the candidate they favor, how to get a teenager to keep her room clean, and so on. This book is about these kinds of everyday influence challenges. No matter who you are, where you work, or what you do in life, how do you get others to follow your lead?

A WORD ABOUT PRONOUNS AND COMPANY NAMES

When offering illustrative examples in this book, as much as possible, I have avoided the awkward use of dual pronouns: he or she, his or her, him or her, and himself or herself. Although these constructions are meant to be inclusive, they are a clumsy use of English. Instead, when I am speaking hypothetically or illustratively, I either have used the plural forms of these pronouns, which do not signify gender, or have varied my pronoun usage, sometimes referring to someone as *he* and sometimes as *she*. My pronoun choices are random and are meant to illustrate that the gender of my hypothetical subjects is irrelevant.

In this book, I also refer, variously, to Lore, Lore International Institute, Korn/Ferry International (and its thought leadership arm, the Korn/Ferry Institute), and Lominger. Korn/Ferry International is the parent company. Korn/Ferry began as an executive search firm but has been expanding into leadership and talent consulting through internal growth and acquisition. It acquired Lore International Institute in November 2008 and Lominger several years earlier. All these companies are now part of Korn/Ferry, but if earlier work had been done under an original company name, I use that name for the sake of accuracy.

GLOBAL RESEARCH STUDY ON POWER AND INFLUENCE

In appendix B, I describe a research study I conducted at Lore on global power and influence. That research began in 1990 and continues today. It is based on a proprietary 360-degree assessment, the Survey of Influence Effectiveness. During the past twenty years, our database has grown to more than 64,000 subjects and over 300,000 respondents, and it has given me and my colleagues insight into the strength of people's power sources, how frequently they use different influence techniques, how effectively they use them, how appropriate those techniques are for their culture, and how skilled they are in twenty-eight areas related to leadership and influence effectiveness. Because this study was global, it has allowed us to identify differences in the uses of power and influence in forty-five countries around the world. For more information on my findings from the global research, see www.theelementsofpower.com.

ACKNOWLEDGMENTS

Many people helped me during the creation of this and my previous book on power, and I deeply appreciate their contributions. First, I would like to thank my colleagues at Korn/Ferry International for their assistance. Bruce Spining helped with my research at various points during the project. Joey Maceyak managed the Survey of Influence Effectiveness (SIE) database and built the programs that helped me extract and analyze the data. Susan Kuhnert kept me organized and assisted me with research and management of the project, and David Gould created the figures that appear in this book. I am also indebted to Donna Stewart for her cross-cultural research and to Jade Masterson for her tenacious and successful pursuit of permissions. Many thanks to these fine people.

I would also like to thank Ellen Kadin, my longtime editor at the American Management Association, as well as Erika Spelman, who is an author's dream as editor. Book publishing is a collaboration between the author and the publisher, and I appreciate everything Ellen, Erika, and their colleagues did on behalf of *Elements of Influence*.

Finally, I would like to thank my wife, Debra, for her love and understanding throughout a seemingly endless writing process. Book writing is a passion that people who don't write may not fully comprehend. Debra understands, although she's a photographer, not a writer, and she grants me my occasional fits and allows me to disappear into my cave and sit in front of a keyboard until the tap is opened. Thanks to her for a lifetime's worth of patience.

ELEMENTS

of

INFLUENCE

INTRODUCTION

We human beings are social creatures, and our world works because of the many ways we interact with and influence one another. We get our way with others by developing bases of power—which derive from a number of personal and organizational sources—and using that power to influence how others think, feel, and act. We succeed in business as well as in life when we learn how best to influence others to do our bidding, accept our point of view, follow our lead, join our cause, feel our excitement, or buy our products and services.

We should be clear about one thing from the start: Influence is not some magic power only a few people have. Every person on the planet exercises influence all the time. Influencing is what all of us seek to do whenever we want someone else to do something, to agree with us, to believe something, to choose something, to think in a particular way, to accept our perspective, or to behave differently. Even the simple act of greeting other people is an act of influence (you are trying to persuade them that you are friendly and not hostile, and you want to influence them to treat you in a friendly, nonhostile manner in return). A baby tries to influence its mother when it cries. Children try to influence their parents when they ask if they can watch a television program or go outside and play. Teachers try to influence their students; salespeople try to influence their customers; employees try to influence their boss; advisers try to influence their clients; lobbyists try to influence elected officials; advertisers try to influence consumers; leaders try to influence their followers; and authors, like me, try to influence readers.

We tend to think that power and influence belong only to those who are very powerful and influential—to kings and presidents, government officials, generals, billionaires, movie stars, renowned athletes, and others among the rich and famous—but this is a fallacy. Influence is so common and so much a part of the fabric of daily life that we usually fail to recognize it when it happens. In virtually every human interaction, there will be multiple attempts at influence, some verbal and some nonverbal. The person I'm speaking to nods her head (wanting me to believe that she agrees with what I've said or at least understands it). I ask for her opinion (this is an influence attempt called consulting). She tells me what she thinks and indicates why she thinks it is true (another influence attempt, since she is trying to persuade me to accept her idea of truth). I suggest we meet with someone else (an influence attempt) to discuss the matter further. She agrees but wants to bring along an expert who can validate her perspective (another influence attempt).

Round and round we go, each one of us trying to influence the other so we can shape the outcome—and this is what human interactions are: a continuous negotiation for agreement or acceptance as we all attempt to exert our will, point of view, or interests. In English, the word *influence* can have negative connotations, as in *influence peddling* in Washington or one person exerting *undue influence* on another. But these negative examples of influence give a bad name to what is actually a ubiquitous and, for the most part, ethical human practice. The fact is that you could not get along in the world if you were not able to influence others *and if you were not willing to be influenced by them* on a nearly continuous basis. As other authors have noted, "No one escapes psychological 'axwork,' the constant reconfiguring of our beliefs, attitudes, intentions, and behavior by unrelenting and ubiquitous forces. . . . Persuasion is constantly remaking us into persons who are measurably changed. Sometimes imperceptibly—ofttimes dramatically."[1]

Influence is part of nearly every communication and occurs in virtually every human interaction. Influence is crucial to business, too. It is so fundamental to leadership that there could be no leadership without it.

So what is influence? *Webster's* dictionary defines influence as "the act or power of producing an effect without apparent exertion of force or direct exercise of command," or "the power or capacity of causing an effect in indirect or intangible ways." The research on power and influence shows, however, that while it may happen without an *apparent* exertion of force, influence can also be overt and quite tangible, as when a merchant offers a customer free shipping if the customer will accept the price being stated (an influence technique called exchanging) or when a product developer says to a colleague, "I need your help on a project" (an influence technique called stating).

Influence is the art of getting others to take your lead— to believe something you want them to believe, think in a way you want them to think, or do something you want them to do.

ETHICAL INFLUENCE

When influence is ethical, the person being influenced (the *influencee*) consents to be influenced, although most of the time that consent is implicit and unstated. A friend asks me for a favor, and I agree to it. A colleague calls me and suggests that we meet to talk about an urgent business opportunity, and I move other appointments on my calendar so that we can meet right away. I am listening to a debate between two presidential candidates. They are discussing the economy and one of them seems to have a better grasp of the issues and a better solution to the problems—and I decide to vote for that candidate. During an annual physical, my doctor tells me that my cholesterol level is too high and advises me to see a nutritionist who can help me learn to eat healthier foods—and I make an appointment with the nutritionist as soon as I leave the clinic. In each of these cases, I am not being coerced. I have a choice. I could decide to say no to each of these influence attempts, so I am, in effect, consenting to be influenced.

If I have no choice, however, then the influence attempt is coercive or manipulative and therefore unethical. A man points a gun at me and demands that I give him my wallet. A solicitor tells me that my generous gift to the nonprofit she represents will aid people in a developing country, but in fact she is pocketing many donations as part of her "management fee." An angry man pushes his way to the front of the line at my service counter, demanding that I serve him first and give him what he wants or he'll report me to my supervisor.

My boss tells me not to worry about some charges on his expense account that he doesn't have receipts for. In the same breath, he says it's too bad about the recent layoffs and I should feel lucky I still have a job. A customer will agree to accept my proposal only if I pay a consulting fee to an agent in his country—who happens to be the customer's cousin. In these cases, I am being pressured, coerced, or lied to, and saying no could have negative consequences for me.

Threats, coercion, manipulation, and intimidation are forms of influence, and they often succeed—at least in the short term—because they are expedient. As every school yard bully knows, the quickest way to get other kids to do what you want is to pound them into submission, or threaten to. But physical coercion comes with a price. The other kids may comply, but they learn to fear the bully, and what they fear they avoid or hate. They may appreciate what the bully can do to them if they don't submit, but they don't respect the bully. Bullying, like other unethical forms of influence, usually destroys the relationship between influencer and influencee—and invites retaliation at some future point. So while these methods are expedient, they are rarely practical long-term solutions, particularly in business and normal daily life.

INFLUENCE AND AUTHORITY

Influence without willing consent can be ethical if the influencer has the legitimate authority to ask or demand that people do what he wants. We live and work in social structures of various kinds—families, clans, communities, states and nations, companies, teams, departments, business units, and so on. In each of these social institutions, we vest some people with the legitimate authority to lead the group, organize efforts, make decisions, assign tasks, represent the group to outsiders, adjudicate disputes, enforce rules and norms, maintain the group's values, and so on. These people have legitimate authority over us by virtue of their roles or positions, and while we may not always want to accede to that authority and do what they want us to do, we frequently comply because of the price we might pay for noncompliance. (In my previous book, *The Elements of Power,* I call this legitimate authority *role* power.) A police officer pulls up behind my car and signals for me to pull over. I comply, listen while the officer lectures me about bringing my car to a complete stop at a stop sign, and stoically accept the traffic ticket that is going to cost me money. I don't want the lecture or the ticket and may feel I don't deserve it, but the officer's legitimate social authority enables her to influence me in ways I may feel are coercive but nonetheless accept.

One of the common ways people try to influence others is to borrow legitimate authority (an influence attempt called legitimizing). Legitimizing is often effective but can backfire when it is overused, particularly with people who resist authority. Throughout history, leaders and rulers of various kinds have used legitimate authority to compel their subjects or followers to heed them, and the command-and-control methods originated centuries ago by churches, states, and militaries evolved from the institutional authority societies vested in their leaders. However, times are changing. People today, particularly in the developed countries, are more resistant to legitimate authority, even when they recognize its validity. This is especially true in business. As Harvard's John Kotter notes, "Trying to control others solely by directing them and on the basis of the power associated with one's position simply will not work—first, because managers are always dependent on some people over whom they have no formal authority, and second, because virtually no one in modern organizations will passively accept and completely obey a constant stream of orders from someone just because [that person] is the 'boss.'"[2]

Until the Industrial Revolution, most people were farmers or worked in agriculture in some way. They were brown-collar workers. By the late nineteenth and early twentieth centuries, as industry grew in the developed world and more people moved from rural areas to cities, most people had become blue-collar workers, laboring in factories and shops and building the infrastructures that support industrialization. By the late twentieth century, however, as the developed world moved from an industrial to an information economy, a white-collar workforce of better-educated, more professional workers emerged. Peter Drucker labeled them "knowledge workers," and knowledge workers want to be led; they don't want to be told. So, influencing *with* authority does not work very well with knowledge workers. They may comply, but they will eventually resent the imposition of authority. And, in today's war for talent, they don't have to keep working for authoritarian bosses or their companies. They can leave. Even though their bosses may have the legitimate authority to use command-and-control methods, these kinds of workers prefer to be influenced *without* authority.

As Jay Conger noted in an article published in *Harvard Business Review*, "Gone are the command-and-control days of executives managing by decree. Today businesses are run largely by cross-functional teams of peers and populated by baby boomers and their Generation X offspring, who show little tolerance for unquestioned authority."[3] Today, as Conger suggests, most of a leader's work is done through influence rather than authority, through collaborative rather than coercive methods, by inspiring commitment rather than demanding compliance. In this flatter and more global world of the twenty-first century, leaders in global businesses, as well as managers and professionals who work across borders, must be facile at influencing without authority.

THE RESEARCH ON GLOBAL POWER AND INFLUENCE

Since 1990, I have been conducting research on power and influence for Lore International Institute, which is now part of Korn/Ferry International. Based on literature reviews, client interviews, and preliminary surveys, I created a framework of power and influence whose items appeared to be mutually exclusive and collectively exhaustive, which means that the framework should be able to describe every kind of power base and every act of influence. This framework became the basis for a 360-degree assessment called the Survey of Influence Effectiveness (SIE), which we began using with Fortune 500 clients in 1991.[4]

The SIE is a powerful instrument. It assesses not only how frequently people use ten positive or ethical influence techniques, but also how effectively they use them and how appropriate those techniques are in their culture. Those ten influence techniques, which are discussed in depth in this book, are logical persuading, legitimizing, appealing to relationship, socializing, consulting, appealing to values, modeling, exchanging, stating, and alliance building. As you will see, these are ten common ways in which people try to influence others ethically. There are also four negative or unethical influence practices: avoiding, manipulating, intimidating, and threatening. The SIE also measures how frequently people in different cultures use those techniques.

Another part of the SIE measures the sources of a person's power. In our framework there are eleven sources of power—five organizational sources, five personal sources, and one meta-source. The organizational sources are role, resources, information, network, and reputation. The personal sources are knowledge, expressiveness, attraction, character, and history with the influencee (or degree of familiarity). The meta-source of power is *will*. It's important to understand how people develop and use these sources of power, and I explored that topic in my previous book, *The Elements of Power: Lessons on Leadership and Influence*. In this book, I describe how people use the ten positive influence techniques, as well as the four negative or "dark side" techniques.

CAN INFLUENCE BE LEARNED?

Can you become better at influencing others? Can you learn how to influence people more effectively in other cultures? If I didn't believe the answer to these questions was "yes," I would not have written this book. Influence is a skill like any other. Each of us learns influencing skills as we develop from childhood to adulthood, but few of us are masters at influencing. Although some people are born with an innate capacity to influence others—just as some people are born with musical, mathematical, or linguistic genius—even their gifts need to be nourished and developed.

Most people do not naturally excel at influencing, in part because influencing effectively requires a great deal of adaptability, perceptiveness, and insight into other people, and in part because influence has cultural variations, and we learn to influence almost exclusively from within our own cultural lens. If we are fortunate to have lived in many different cultures during our childhood, we may have grasped that power and influence differ tremendously from one culture to the next, and we may have learned to adapt accordingly. But few people have this advantage. Many of us are steeped in our culture, barely aware that others may see the world differently, and we tend to become judgmental rather than accepting of other cultures. We assume that others see the world as we do, react as we do, interpret experience as we do, and therefore use power and influence the way we do. But this is not the case.

Can you become better at influencing others? Yes, of course, if you are open to alternative ways of seeing the world, and if you do not assume that others should or will value what you value and assume what you assume. Influencing effectively requires an adaptive mindset, and influencing effectively across cultures requires a global mindset. To some extent, a global mindset is a product of your psychology, your willingness to accept others as they are instead of wishing them to be more like yourself. And it is a product of both self-acceptance and acceptance of others. Those who are best at influencing globally accept others who are different from themselves in a curious and benign fashion. They accept and even cherish differences instead of presuming that every "normal" person would think and behave like themselves. Can this global mindset be learned? Yes, if you are willing. Yes, if you are open. Influencing is a skill. It can be learned. You can influence others more effectively, including people in other cultures.

This book is going to show you how. For the reader's convenience, each chapter ends with a summary of the key concepts found in that chapter, followed by a list of challenges for readers. These challenges are written as questions intended to stimulate reflection and discussion of the ideas and research found throughout the book. Good luck. Bonne chance. Buena suerte. Viel glueck. Καλή τύχη. Buona fortuna. 행운을 빕니다. Goed geluk. Boa sorte. Удача.

KEY CONCEPTS

1. Influence is not some magic power only a few people have. Every person on the planet exercises influence all the time. Influence is part of nearly every communication. It occurs in virtually every human interaction. It is so fundamental to leadership that there could be no leadership without it.

2. Influencing across cultures is challenging because people in different cultures have different sets of beliefs and values and use different influence conventions. What works for you in your country will not necessarily work—or work the same way—in another culture.

3. At the simplest level, influence is the art of getting others to take your lead—to believe something you want them to believe, think in a way you want them to think, or do something you want them to do.

4. Influence can be ethical or unethical. When it is ethical, the influencee consents to be influenced, although most of the time that consent is implicit and unstated. When influence attempts are coercive or manipulative, the influence is unethical. Unethical influence is expedient, but it usually destroys the relationship between the influencer and influencee.

5. Until recently, it was common for leaders to influence with authority, but with the rise of knowledge workers, people are more resistant

to such command-and-control methods. Today, most of a leader's work is done through influence rather than authority, through collaborative rather than coercive methods, by inspiring commitment rather than demanding compliance.

6. Influencing is a skill. It can be learned. You can become better at influencing others, even across cultures. Influencing effectively requires an adaptive mindset, and influencing effectively across cultures requires a global mindset.

CHALLENGES FOR READERS

I argued in this introduction that influence is ubiquitous, that it occurs in virtually every communication and human interaction, and that we are all subjected to hundreds, if not thousands, of influence attempts every day. Because influence is part of the fabric of our lives, we are mostly unaware of all the times someone or something attempts to influence us. As an exercise, try to become more consciously aware. For an hour in your office or place of work, or during your train ride into the city, or for an hour at home during the evening, try to identify every time someone or something tries to influence you.

1. Can you recall when someone has tried to influence you in an unethical way? Lied to you? Coerced you? Intimidated you? Threatened you? How did you respond? Did you give in to the influence attempt or resist it? How did you feel about that person afterward? More important, how did you feel about yourself?

2. Have you ever tried to influence someone else by manipulating them or coercing them? If we're honest with ourselves, most of us would admit that, yes, sometimes we have used unethical influence methods. Sometimes, it is quicker and easier to tell a little lie to get people to go along with something they might not otherwise go along with. If and when you have bent the truth a little or deliberately intimidated someone, were you successful in influencing that person? Did it ever come back to haunt you? Did using an unethical influence technique affect your relationship with that person?

3. If you are in a position of authority, do you ever use that authority to get others to do what you want? In other words, do you boss them around? How well does that work? How do they feel about being subjected to your authority?

4. Does your boss or anyone else with authority over you ever use authority to get you to do something? Do you ever feel bossed around? How does that feel? Are you eager to do what the other person demands? Are you willingly compliant? Or do you feel some resentment at the imposition of authority?

© Ilya Terentyev/iStockphoto.com

PART I

GETTING OTHERS TO FOLLOW YOUR LEAD

If leadership means getting things done through and with the help of other people, then the art of leadership is getting others to follow your lead. Accomplishing that means *influencing* them in a variety of ways. You might do it by appealing to their values and inspiring them to follow you in the pursuit of lofty goals. Or you might set an example they are inclined to follow. Or you might explain why the course of action you want them to take is the logical and reasonable thing to do. Or you might give them something in return for your cooperation. These approaches to influencing others will succeed some of the time with some people, but they are unlikely to succeed all of the time with all people for the simple reason that people differ in how they respond to attempts to influence them, and they may find one approach more compelling or persuasive than others.

People who are very effective at influencing others are skilled at the full range of influence techniques and know how and when to use them. They are good at reading people and responding—in the moment—to what they are seeing and hearing as they interact with the people they are trying to influence. In the first part of this book, I explain the fundamentals of influence and describe the ways and means of influencing others. Knowing the fundamentals is a prerequisite to developing your influence skills and your ability to get others to follow your lead.

CHAPTER 1

FUNDAMENTALS OF INFLUENCE

Some books claim that if you follow their principles you can influence anyone to do anything. According to these authors, you can get anyone to like you, love you, and find you irresistibly attractive. Wow! They assert that you can take control of *any* situation, win at *every* competition, and gain the upper hand *every* time. One book, written for men wanting to pick up women, boasts that by following its mystery methods you can get beautiful women into bed. Another boldly proclaims that you can get anyone to say yes in eight minutes or less. When I read claims such as these, I am reminded of a saying attributed to Abraham Lincoln: "You can fool some of the people all of the time, and all of the people some of the time, but you cannot fool all of the people all of the time."

Are there secrets that will make you irresistibly attractive to whomever you want? Is it possible to influence people to do *anything* you want? If these claims were true, then surely some pro-life advocates would have discovered these principles by now and used them to convert all their pro-choice opponents to their position (or vice versa). If it were that easy to influence people, to influence *anyone* to do *anything*, then why hasn't the conflict in the Middle East been resolved? Why haven't conservatives influenced all liberals to adopt their conservative philosophy and agenda (or vice versa)? For that matter, why hasn't some influential cook persuaded all other cooks to proclaim that her recipe makes the absolute best authentic Texas chili?

Apparently people aren't reading these books or aren't following the advice—or the claims are simply nonsense, and it's not actually possible to get anyone to do whatever you want in eight minutes or less. In the real world, you cannot influence some people all of the time. Nor can you influence all of the people some of the time, and you certainly cannot influence all of the people all of the time. People are more complicated than that, generally think for themselves, and may have many valid reasons for not doing what you want them to do or thinking the way you want them to think.

The next time someone promises you that by following his secrets you can influence *anyone* to do *anything,* beware: He's trying to sell you snake oil. In fact, if you have a choice between buying his advice or buying real snake oil, buy the snake oil. It probably has some useful purpose.

INFLUENCE ATTEMPTS AND THE RANGE OF POSSIBLE OUTCOMES

This chapter addresses the fundamentals of influence—what you need to know to understand how power and influence actually work, in life as well as in business. These principles are universal. They apply in China and India as well as in Poland, Canada, Peru, France, and everywhere else around the globe. They apply in families, teams, clubs, and clans as well as in corporations and in one-on-one situations. A first, important fundamental is that influence attempts do not have binary (yes/no) outcomes. When you try to influence someone, the outcome is not simply "yes, she was influenced" or "no, she wasn't." In fact, there is a range of possible outcomes to every influence attempt, as illustrated in figure 1-1.

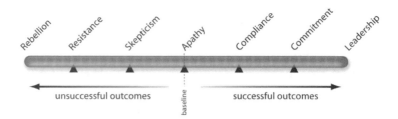

► Figure 1-1. Every influence attempt can have a wide range of outcomes.

The Baseline

The baseline refers to the fact that all of us are headed down our own path—doing what we are doing, thinking what we are thinking, and believing what we believe. We will continue on our own path unaware of you and unaffected by you until you try to influence us to do, think, or believe something different. Once you do try to influence us, we may still not be influenced one way or the other. We may remain apathetic or indifferent toward you or what you are proposing—and we may not even consciously recognize your presence. One possible outcome of an influence attempt, then, is no influence. We remain unmoved or unaffected and perhaps even unaware of you.

Each of us is subjected to hundreds if not thousands of influence attempts every day. We talk to others, we see other people, we read books, watch television or listen to the radio, see or hear advertisements, read newspapers or magazines, open e-mails, participate in meetings, work with people, are approached by solicitors, call on customers, and so on. We may be influenced by people we see, talk to, meet with, or read about—or we may not. If we were moved by every influence attempt we experience daily, we would be tossed willy-nilly from one direction to the next and have no constancy in or control of our lives. So an important part of the human experience is deciding (mostly subconsciously) whether to be influenced by something we experience. I see the ad for some product but am not moved to buy it. I see the latest fashions displayed in a department store window but continue walking by. I hear someone complaining about a corporate decision but don't care. I receive brochures from suppliers but don't need or am not interested in what they are selling, so I put the brochures in the recycle bin.

I am unmoved. I have not been influenced. I have not changed direction. The baseline is the norm. It's what exists before an influence attempt and often what exists afterward.

Compliance, Commitment, and Leadership

If an influence attempt succeeds, the most likely outcome is simple consent, agreement, or compliance. The person complies with your request, agrees with your suggestion, or does what you want. You try to persuade a potential customer to look at a demo of your product, and the customer is willing to do so. You ask a colleague to give you feedback on a report you've just written, and the colleague agrees. You tell your teenage son that you'd like help cleaning up the kitchen after dinner, and he helps you—begrudgingly perhaps, but he helps. These are examples of compliance. The person you are trying to influence goes along with what you want. He deviates from the path he was on and consents to do or think what you would like.

Sometimes you want more than compliance; you want commitment. You want the person not simply to agree with you but to agree wholeheartedly, to be enthusiastic and engaged, to consent not merely with the head but also with the heart. Compliance usually implies rational consent. If I were asked why I complied with someone's request, I would most often explain my decision in logical terms: "It made sense. I had no reason to say no." However, commitment means to be emotionally impelled, to assume an obligation, to be swept up in an emotional current and be willingly engaged. If asked why I became committed to someone or something, I would usually explain my decision in emotional terms: "Because I believed. Because it was the right thing to do. Because it moved me to tears." One reason Barack Obama won the 2008 U.S. presidential election and John McCain, his Republican opponent, did not is that Obama spoke to people's emotions and inspired them to believe in hopeful change, whereas McCain offered rational reasons why he should be president. ("Vote for me," he said, "because I know how to confront our enemies.") In essence, McCain asked for compliance and Obama inspired commitment. Whether President Obama has delivered on his promises is another issue. My point here is that candidate McCain's rhetoric was not as compelling to as many American voters as candidate Obama's rhetoric. McCain wanted people's votes; Obama wanted their hearts and minds.

Figure 1-2 illustrates the difference between compliance and commitment. The lab on the left is compliant. It is poised dutifully, obeying its master's commands to sit and stay. Collar around its neck, tethered to a leash, watchful, it waits to be released. In contrast, the dog on the right is committed. Leaping for the ball, it is as far off the ground as it can get. Ears flying, mouth open, this dog is committed because it is doing something it loves to do. Anyone who's ever played ball with a dog knows the boundless joy the dog experiences. You are usually worn out before the dog is. These photos illustrate an important distinction between compliance and commitment. Animals and people who comply with an influence attempt often do so because it feels compulsory or required either by the person making the influence attempt or by the situation. They comply because they must, or because they have no reason to disagree, or because it's what they've

► Figure 1-2. The difference between compliance (left) and commitment (right).

been trained to do or have become accustomed to doing. They commit when what they're being asked to do fills them with joy, engages them emotionally, is rewarding in some way, or is what they love doing anyway.

Beyond commitment, another possible outcome of an influence attempt is leadership. Here, the person is not merely influenced to become committed to the cause but goes beyond that and assumes a leadership role, taking the mantle from the influencer and advancing the cause even further. Throughout history, many people have been influenced to the point of leadership. Ronald Reagan inspired legions of Reaganite fiscal conservatives in the United States and abroad. Mohandas Gandhi moved hundreds of millions of Indians to nonviolent protest and noncooperation with British authorities, which led to India's independence, and he influenced a number of political protégés to assume greater leadership roles, including Jawaharlal Nehru, who became India's first prime minister. Prominent figures in the African-American civil rights movement—W.E.B. DuBois, Malcolm X,

Rosa Parks, and Martin Luther King Jr., to name a few—influenced many followers to take leadership roles, among them Jesse Jackson, Julian Bond, Robert Moses, James Meredith, and Andrew Young. A common goal of inspirational leaders is not merely to induce commitment but to inspire others to assume leadership and carry forward the aims of a movement that the inspirational leader could not accomplish alone.

As you will read later in the discussion of each of the influence techniques, some techniques are more likely to result in compliance than commitment or leadership. Logical persuading, legitimizing, exchanging, and stating, if they are successful, generally result in compliance or simple agreement. On the other hand, socializing, appealing to relationship, alliance building, and consulting have the potential to cause commitment, and appealing to values and modeling may result in leadership. This is not to say that you can't use logic, for instance, to inspire others to assume leadership, but logical persuading is far less likely to have that effect than appealing to values or modeling.

Skepticism, Resistance, and Rebellion

What are the possible outcomes when an influence attempt is unsuccessful? As figure 1-1 shows, the least undesirable outcome, from the influencer's perspective, is skepticism, which indicates doubt or distrust. Like most people, I receive unsolicited calls now and then from high-pressure salespeople who believe that their unrelenting barrage will convince me to send them money. Regardless of what they are selling and whether I need their product or service, I am so put off by their approach that I am more than unmoved and uninfluenced; I am annoyed and even angry. You could argue that apathy is also an unsuccessful outcome, and it is, but skepticism is more than someone simply being unmoved; skepticism plants the seeds of doubt and distrust in the influencee's mind and makes it more difficult for the influencer to successfully influence that person in the future.

Even stronger negative reactions to an influence attempt are resistance, where the influencee either actively or passively resists what the influencer wants, and beyond that, rebellion, where the influencee takes the lead in resisting the influencer and tries to enlist others in a rebellion against what the influencer seeks. For instance, imagine I have a colleague who comes to me with a proposal to outsource what I believe is an important part of our core business. She tries to persuade me that we can save money and improve service and quality by outsourcing. However, I don't buy it. I'm skeptical and give her reasons why I don't think it's a good idea. Not only did she fail to influence me, she has created doubt in my mind, and I will be less inclined to agree with her in the future unless she returns with far more compelling arguments.

But I might also respond to her influence attempt with active or passive resistance. If I actively resist, I might do some research on outsourcing in this area, compile evidence against the idea, and circulate a report to that effect. My aim is to counter her by trying to influence others against her idea. Or I may passively resist by failing to support her, by voicing my skepticism in private meetings with others, and by working harder to ensure that the area she wants to outsource is performing well. But an even stronger negative reaction would be for me to rebel by taking up the anti-outsourcing cause, visibly and enthusiastically opposing outsourcing, building an alliance of managers who oppose the idea, and waving the flag at the executive level to not only resist her idea but crush it.

The outcomes shown on both sides of the baseline in figure 1-1 are, in effect, opposites. Skepticism is the opposite of compliance, resistance is the opposite of commitment, and rebellion is the opposite of leadership. Of course, reality is not as neat as this figure suggests. How people respond, positively or negatively, to an influence attempt varies tremendously, but the essential point is that with any influence attempt there can be no outcome (the baseline), a positive/successful outcome for the influencer, or a negative/unsuccessful outcome—and these outcomes can vary in the intensity of the reaction. Why is this important? Because a number of personal, organizational, and cultural factors affect how people will respond to you when you try to influence them. Understanding the possible outcomes and what you can do to manage them is crucial if you are going to be more successful at influencing others, especially across cultures.

An important fundamental of influence, then, is that every influence attempt has a range of possible outcomes. To be most effective at influencing others, you need to know how to achieve the successful outcomes and avoid the unsuccessful ones.

THE TEN LAWS OF INFLUENCE

There are ten more fundamentals of influence, which I call "the ten laws of influence."

Law 1:
Influence Attempts May Fail for Many Legitimate Reasons

As I said earlier, the idea that you can influence anyone to do anything is nonsense. There are many reasons why people may not be moved by or even aware of your influence attempt. In his book *John P. Kotter on What Leaders Really Do,* John Kotter explores why people may not respond to a manager's influence attempts: "Some people may be uncooperative because they are too busy elsewhere, and some because they are not really capable of helping. Others may well have goals, values, and beliefs that are quite different and in conflict with the manager's and may therefore have no desire whatsoever to help or cooperate."[1] Additionally, the people you are trying to influence may not care about what you want them to support. They may disagree with your opinion, idea, suggestion, proposal, or point of view. They may not need what you are selling, or accept your line of reasoning, or be inspired by what you are saying. Or they may be distracted. Or they may not have enough regard for you or your team or company to pay attention to your message.

Consider this. In business, salespeople spend more time studying and practicing the techniques of influence than any other group in a company, and even the very best of them cannot sell their products or services to every customer all the time. Why? Because as skilled and influential as they may be, there are many valid reasons why they cannot and will not persuade some customers—and those reasons often have more to do with the customers and the situation than with the salespeople. In the real world, many factors affect a buying decision, and even skilled salespeople may not be aware of, and may not be able to change, factors that lead buyers to choose another provider or buy nothing at all.

Law 2:
Influence Is Contextual

People will not consent to be influenced unless the situation and environment are conducive to them saying yes. Agreement is built on the foundations of latitude, interests, and disposition.

By this, I mean that the person you want to influence must have the latitude to say yes, that your request or direction should not be contrary to the person's interests and values, and the person must be disposed to say yes to you.

LATITUDE—Of these foundations of agreement, latitude is most important. Is the influencee able to say yes? Does the person have the freedom to agree if he wants to? I saw a cartoon recently in which a pollster in ancient times is talking to a peasant in front of a grass hut. The pollster is asking whether the peasant would say that Attila the Hun is a very good leader, a good leader, a poor leader, or a very poor leader. This is darkly humorous because the peasant's life may be at stake if he gives the wrong answer. He doesn't have the latitude to render an honest opinion about Attila's leadership.

Why wouldn't people have the latitude to be influenced? Maybe they don't have the authority to say yes. Rules, regulations, laws, standards, or guidelines may prohibit it. Or the person you are trying to convince to buy your product doesn't have the authority to buy it because of her position in her company. Or the person may already have committed to another course of action and needs to honor that commitment or believes that an authority figure in his life (like a parent, teacher, or boss) would not approve. Or, like offering a cocktail to a recovering alcoholic, you may be asking a man to do something he has vowed not to. The constraints he faces may be internally or externally imposed, and you may not ever know what they are. So a first question to ask yourself when you are trying to influence a customer, manager, colleague, partner, or anyone else is this: Does this person have the latitude to say yes?

If not, you are trying to influence the wrong person. Or else it is not the right time (maybe the person will have more latitude later). Or maybe this influence attempt with this person will never succeed.

INTERESTS—Second, ask whether your request is aligned with the person's interests and values. If not, then the person's interests would not be well served by going along with you and, in this situation, most people most of the time will not willingly consent to be influenced. An example is Eric Liddell, the "Flying Scotsman," a sprinter in the early twentieth century. Representing Great Britain in the 1924 Olympics, he is portrayed in the film *Chariots of Fire*. A devout Christian, Liddell refused to run on the Sabbath, which took him out of contention for the 100-meter race, his best event. In the film, members of the British Olympic committee, led by the Prince of Wales, are trying to influence Liddell to run the 100-meter trials "for king and country." He adamantly refuses, and the head of the committee accuses him of being impertinent. Liddell angrily replies that what is impertinent is trying to influence a man to deny his beliefs.

As this example illustrates, you will meet with resistance if you try to persuade people to do something that is not in their best interests or is inimical to their values or beliefs. So you need to understand what is important to them and avoid directly confronting their values. Does this mean that you can never get people to deviate from their values or beliefs, however slightly? No, but experience shows that you must approach them cautiously and must not directly confront, deny, or invalidate their belief system. As the authors of the book *Yes!* write, "The best way to ride a horse is in the direction that the horse is going. Only by first aligning to the direction the horse is going is it possible to then slowly and deliberately steer it where you'd like to go."[2] This makes sense. If you try to change the horse's direction too quickly, you'll likely be thrown off the horse. Similarly, you are likely to fail if you try to influence people to deviate from their deeply held values and beliefs and if what you are asking is not in their best interests.

DISPOSITION—Finally, people may not respond to an influence attempt simply because they are not in the right frame of mind. I had a client, whom I'll call Donna, who was very temperamental. From one call to the next, you never knew whether she would be friendly and collaborative or combative and disagreeable. In my years of working with her, I could never predict which Donna would answer the phone. So I learned that influencing her required patience and perseverance. I had to wait for her foul moods to pass before once again bringing up a point I'd raised earlier, and sometimes I just had to weather the storm and wait until the next call, when she might be more receptive. I've never met anyone more mercurial than Donna, but even the most reasonable and receptive of people are occasionally testy. I would venture that all of us get up on the wrong side of the bed now and then and are disagreeable for a time.

Some people may not be in a cooperative frame of mind because they are distracted, busy, or secretive by nature or profession. A scene in the film *All the President's Men* is illustrative. Early in the film, during the arraignment of the five men caught trying to bug Democratic national headquarters, reporter Bob Woodward (played by Robert Redford) enters the courtroom and sits behind a country club lawyer named Markham (played by Nicolas Coster). Woodward asks if he's there in connection with the Watergate burglary, and the lawyer replies that he's not there. Realizing how ludicrous that sounds, he adds that he's not the lawyer for the accused burglars. After directing Woodward to the right attorney, Markham refuses to answer more questions and leaves the room. Undaunted, Woodward follows him into a hallway and asks Markham how he got there so soon, because the burglars hadn't yet made a phone call since their arrest, the implication being that someone other than the burglars arranged for private counsel. Markham avoids answering the question and returns to the courtroom. Woodward again pursues him, where, upon further questioning, Markham reveals that he met one of the burglars at a social occasion. What Woodward learns from Markham raises his suspicion that what happened at the Watergate is not a commonplace burglary.

In this scene, Woodward is trying to influence a source to provide information. For various reasons, the source is not disposed to cooperate, but persistence on Woodward's part eventually yields some nuggets that aid in his investigation by convincing him that there is much more to the story. Sometimes, the people you are trying to influence may be uncooperative because they fear you, are suspicious of you, or don't like who you are or what you represent. Or they may be prejudiced against you for some reason, and you may never know why. All these factors can raise their resistance and lower their receptivity. For people to consent to your influence attempt, they must be disposed to be cooperative.

THE SIMPLE TEST—An easy way to gauge how responsive someone might be to an influence attempt is to use this simple test: Ask yourself, *Why would this person say yes or no?* Asking this question puts you in the other person's shoes. It forces you to see the situation from the influencee's perspective. Assume that you want to ask a friend to donate money to a college scholarship fund, and what you are asking for would be a sizable donation for him. Why would he say yes or no?

REASONS HE MIGHT SAY YES:

1. He likes you.
2. He knows the college scholarship fund is important to you.
3. He's an alumnus and the college is important to him.
4. He hasn't given much to charity this year and feels guilty about it.
5. He will do so expecting you to support his favorite charity later.
6. He's just come into some extra money and is feeling magnanimous.

REASONS HE MIGHT SAY NO:

1. He likes you but has felt some distance growing between you.
2. He is friendly toward you but really doesn't consider you a close friend and feels no obligation to support your causes.
3. He has no particular allegiance to this college.
4. He doesn't have the money or is not the charitable sort.
5. He has already given to charity and doesn't feel that he can contribute more now.
6. He is willing to contribute, but not the amount you are asking for— and he's annoyed that you are asking for so much.
7. He's already given to the college scholarship fund and doesn't want to give more.
8. You did not contribute to his favorite charity when he asked you to, and now he feels no obligation to reciprocate.
9. He's received some bad news recently and is not in a giving mood.
10. He's worried about losing his job (or already knows he's going to be laid off) and can't spare the cash.

This simple test is a useful exercise even though you can't divine everything in your friend's mind. You won't be aware of all the reasons he might say yes or no, but it is still useful to try to predict them ahead of time. It may help you choose the right influence technique and frame your arguments in the right way. In short, it helps to know what people find persuasive and what they don't. It helps to know whether they have the latitude to say yes, and if not, why not. It helps to know their interests and values, and it helps to know whether they will be in the right frame of mind to cooperate with you.

Of course, as you are trying to influence your friend, his reactions and responses will reveal information you can use to reframe your arguments in the moment. What you don't know ahead of time you can learn as you are talking to him, and that will give you more insight into why he is saying no and what he might need to say yes. Then the art of influencing involves being adaptive as well as discerning whether you risk damaging the relationship if you persist. Sometimes, it is wisest to stop while you're ahead and come back later if you think his circumstances may change or he may change his mind after he reflects on what you are requesting.

Law 3:
Influence Is Often a Process Rather Than an Event

As already noted, you may not be able to influence people the first time and in the first way you approach them. Influence is often a process rather than an event. People may not be in the right frame of mind when you first approach them. Or they may be resisting initially because they need to think it over. Introverts, for example, often need some private reflection before they can agree to a proposal. They need to consider the idea, perhaps talk to a confidant, and think through the notion before they buy into it. Or maybe they need more or different evidence. Or, if they don't know you well, they may need to become comfortable with you before they consent. Some people may feel that agreeing to something too readily could make them appear to be pushovers. Other people are inherently resistant to influence and will push back initially almost regardless of who is doing the influencing.

Sometimes, the influence technique you are using is not one they respond well to. If you keep trying the same approach, you may create greater and greater resistance. A common failing of people who are extremely logical, for instance, is to assume that everyone else is as logical and will be convinced by well-reasoned, logical arguments. When they try this technique, and it fails, they typically resort to more logic, more facts, more evidence—even in the face of mounting resistance. So an important lesson about influencing is that when the technique you are using isn't working, it's best to try something else. Don't keep hammering away, thinking you can wear people down. Browbeating people into submission only makes you annoying, and if they give in, it will likely be under duress, which is unethical and likely to damage your relationship.

If the influence technique you are using is not working, don't keep doing the same thing. Try something else.

Law 4:
Influence Is Cultural

What works in Mexico may not work as well in Malaysia, just as the openness and informality typical in Australia, even in business settings, may not be as acceptable in Germany or the Netherlands (in fact, it could cause suspicion). Influence effectiveness depends in part on the conventions, values, and beliefs prevalent in every culture. Throughout much of this book and the related websites (www.terryr bacon.com and www.theelementsofpower.com), I explore how power and influence differ around the world. My benchmark for examining culture is the GLOBE study of sixty-two societies, the most recent and comprehensive analysis of global cultural differences.[3] This study identifies eight dimensions of cultural difference: performance orientation, future orientation, gender egalitarianism, assertiveness, individualism and collectivism, power distance, humane orientation, and uncertainty avoidance.

The GLOBE authors define assertiveness as "the degree to which individuals in organizations or societies are assertive, confrontational, and aggressive in social relationships."[4] In the GLOBE study, Hungary, Germany, Hong Kong, and Austria were among the countries ranked highest in use of assertiveness practices. Sweden, New Zealand, Switzerland, and Japan were among those ranked lowest. My research on global power and influence shows that people in the countries ranked lowest on assertiveness practices have the following influence characteristics:

- ► They are more likely to build and use a network of supporters rather than trying to influence by themselves. In short, they build more alliances.
- ► They are less likely to be perceived as threatening in their behavior.
- ► They are more likely to build close friendships with others and try to influence by appealing to those relationships.
- ► They are more likely to take the lead and show others how to do things. In other words, they are more likely to act as mentors, coaches, or teachers.
- ► They are higher rated in terms of using attraction as a power source, which means they are more likely to have qualities people seem to like. (See *The Elements of Power* for a fuller discussion of this power source.)

In contrast, people in those countries ranked highest in assertiveness have these characteristics:

► They are more likely to legitimize their requests by appealing to some form of authority.

► They are more likely to speak boldly and without hesitation and to use strong gestures to make their points.

► They are likely to be more creative in finding alternatives or solutions.

► They are likely to be more expressive and have a broader network of contacts inside and outside their organization.

It should be apparent from these lists that trying to influence people in high- and low-assertiveness cultures presents different challenges and that some influence techniques will work better or worse in each country depending on this cultural difference alone. If I were trying to influence a customer in Germany, for instance, I would expect the customer to be more responsive to hierarchy and authority, to be direct and perhaps bold in stating her position, and to expect me to respond when she refers to authorities to substantiate her points. But if I then traveled to Japan for a customer meeting, I would expect that customer to involve others in the decision making, to seek consensus around the buying decision, to spend more time socializing before getting down to business, and to value building a closer relationship as a prerequisite to doing business. Moreover, I would understand that my Japanese customer would be confounded and perhaps even embarrassed for me if I were to interact with him the same way I interacted with my German customer. He might interpret my boldness, expressiveness, and directness as impolite and even aggressive. And while these observations may appear to reinforce cultural stereotypes, they are in fact supported by the research on how Germans and Japanese differ in their approaches to power and influence.

Law 5:
Ethical Influence Is Consensual and Often Bilateral

I noted in the introduction that ethical influence is consensual, which means that the person being influenced goes along with the influencer willingly, without real or imagined coercion—although, when the person is responding to someone who has the legitimate authority to ask for or demand compliance, such as when a police officer signals for a driver to stop his car, the person may feel pressured to comply but nonetheless submits to the authority because that authority is socially sanctioned. Influence by authority represents a special case of influencing, to be explored in much more detail in chapter 3.

In ethical influence without authority, the person being influenced is open to the influence and has the right to say no. So the influencee is aware of the influence attempt as well as the motives of the person behind it. It is ethical if an investment manager advises me to invest in a stock and she earnestly believes the stock will do well in the future. It is unethical if she advises me to buy the stock because she receives a commission based on the sale even though she has evidence, which she hides from me, that the stock is about to fall, and she knows that I risk losing much of my investment. When influence is done with integrity, the influencee chooses to be persuaded, having complete knowledge of the facts, but is fully aware of the option to say, "No, I'm not convinced," or "No, not at this time."

Finally, ethical influence is inherently bilateral, which means the influencer is open to being influenced in return. An ethical manager, even while giving instructions and assigning responsibilities to her subordinates, remains open to being influenced if her subordinates have better ideas or suggestions about how to complete assignments more efficiently or effectively. Ethical influence may involve give-and-take as the parties negotiate an agreement or understanding, and the consent to be influenced goes both ways.

Law 6: Unethical Influence May Succeed— but Always at a Cost

Throughout human history, tyrants, dictators, and thugs have known that people can control others and impose their will—sometimes over millions of people—through force, brutality, intimidation, and murder. In *The Prince,* Machiavelli said that "it is better to be feared than loved, if you cannot be both." Centuries later, Mao Tse-tung asserted that "political power grows out of the barrel of a gun." It would be naïve to assume that destructive influence tactics don't work. Clearly, they do. Mao tortured and murdered his opponents, reigned over China for decades, became a cult figure, and died in his sleep. Stalin and Hitler prevailed for a time and murdered millions of people. At Jonestown, Jim Jones convinced 900 people to drink the Flavor Aid. And Bernie Madoff bilked thousands of investors out of billions of dollars before his house of cards came tumbling down.

The dark side clearly does work, which is why it is so appealing to those among us with no scruples, but the destruction it causes wreaks havoc not only upon the victims but ultimately upon the victimizer, if not in body at least in name. Machiavelli also wrote, "The new ruler must determine all the injuries that he will need to inflict. He must inflict them once and for all." In the epic landscape of national politics, this philosophy of power is most evident in tragedies like Cambodia's killing fields, but it is also played out, on a much smaller scale, by executives who abuse their power, managers who try to motivate by fear instead of inspiration, and others who try to gain advantage by manipulating the truth. In the end, these tactics destroy trust, damage relationships, and are rarely worth their perceived short-term gains. Nonetheless, they are appealing to those who don't give a damn—and to other psychopaths among us.

Law 7:
People Respond Best to the Influence Techniques They Use Themselves

People tend to assume that what they like, everyone else will like; that what works well for them will also work for others. This is the case because, by and large, most people believe that they are normal and that their view of reality is shared by most other people. As Martin G. grew up, for instance, he discovered that he made more friends and had greater influence among his friends when he was outgoing and funny. This became a social pattern for him, and he began associating with other people who were outgoing and funny. Their acceptance of him reinforced his behavior. As he entered the workplace, he was attracted to positions and companies where being outgoing and funny was rewarded. Like all people, Martin works best within his comfort zone, so he tries to influence others by using his strengths, by socializing. Not surprisingly, then, he responds best when others socialize with him. Today, he is a successful salesman with a thick address book and a broad network of customers and contacts.

In contrast, Akiko N. grew up in a family of high ideals, and she attended a school named after a revered national hero. She took pride in her accomplishments and those of her friends and family, and dreamed of a better world where the injustices and inequalities she saw no longer existed. Among her friends and colleagues at work, she is known as an idealist and a dreamer. She often tries to influence people by inspiring them, by appealing to their values and ideals, and this is what she responds to as well. Logical arguments resonate less with her than appeals to her heart.

These examples illustrate an important insight about influence. If people try to influence you through logical persuasion, then they will likely be responsive to logic themselves. If they try to bargain or negotiate with you, then they will probably also respond to exchanging. If they legitimize by appealing to authority, then they probably respect authority and will respond to it as well. Whatever influence techniques people use most often are probably the ones they will find most influential.

Law 8:
If You Are Observant,
People Will Reveal What They Find Most Influential

I think this one of the most profound insights about influence. In many cases, you don't have to guess what people will find most influential. If you are observant, if you listen to other people and observe their behavior and the environments they create for themselves, you can discover how best to influence most people. In Martin G.'s case, the moment you meet him you see someone who is extroverted and forthcoming. His office is full of mementos from customers as well as samples of his company's products. There are family and vacation photos on his walls and on the shelves of his bookcase. His environment invites you to ask about his life and find some connection with him. He loves doing business at lunch and is quick to share the latest joke he's heard. It is abundantly clear that he can be influenced by socializing.

It takes a little longer to get to know Akiko, who is a more private person, but when she opens up you learn that she volunteers at the Humane Society and that she values tradition and has a strong sense of place. She is as concerned about *why* you would do something as *what* you would do. She admires inspirational leaders and listens to new age and classical music. Everything about her suggests that she'll respond best if you appeal to her values.

People who respond best to logical persuading will show you that they think logically, respect facts and evidence, and are often intolerant of cognitive sloppiness. People who respond best to the consulting influence technique will show that they want to be involved, that they have ideas to share, and that they need to feel a part of the solution. And so on. If you are observant, people will reveal how they like to be influenced, and knowing that will make you much more effective at influencing others.

Law 9:
Influence Usually Involves a Mix of Techniques

In education and training programs where I have taught others how to influence more effectively, I have observed thousands of exchanges where one person is attempting to influence another. An interesting observation, which I've seen confirmed many times, is that it is rare for people to use only one influence technique. Typically, influence involves a mixture of techniques. For example, the influencer begins by trying to explain why she believes X is the right approach or strategy. The influencee pushes back. The influencer tries logic again, offering more evidence or another line of reasoning. When that is inconclusive, she switches to an appeal to values, which creates a spark of interest but still does not succeed. So she tries consulting—asking questions to draw the other person in. This succeeds to a greater extent, even more than she'd hoped. Emboldened, she again tries to seal the deal with logic but is rebuffed. So she legitimizes, gets a strong negative reaction, and goes back to appealing to values, which makes a good connection. To gain final agreement, she offers an exchange, which is accepted.

This is often how successful influence attempts proceed. The initial attempt either is not convincing or is greeted with skepticism, so the influencer tries something else, exploring and adapting as she learns more from the influencee's reactions and responses. When people stubbornly stick with the technique they started with, they often fail because the influencee's resistance stiffens. If the influencer persists, despite evidence that it's not working, the influencee may become annoyed or angry, and the situation devolves into a contest of wills. If you are a parent and have tried to get your children to clean up their bedrooms, you know how it goes. For this reason, I strongly recommend that if what you are attempting isn't working, try something else.

Law 10:
The More Power You Have, the More Influential You Will Be

Power is the force that governs how influential you can be. The more power you have, the more potential influence you can wield. Some authors treat power and influence as the same concept, but this muddies an important distinction. You can have great power but choose not to exercise as much direct influence as you could. Gandhi is an example. As a moral exemplar and political giant in the India of his time, he had tremendous power and could have used it in nearly whatever manner he chose, but he channeled his power in ways he believed were spiritually and morally correct (and his moral stance increased his power within India and around the world). However, Gandhi may be the exception to the aphorism that power corrupts and absolute power can corrupt absolutely. Many people with great power cannot restrain themselves from exercising it, often in ways that harm or inhibit others; others, like Gandhi, have the spiritual and moral fortitude to prevent power from corrupting them. In any case, the more power someone has, the greater potential influence he can exert on the lives, fortunes, thoughts, actions, and ideals of others.

Where does power come from? I answered that question in my previous book, *The Elements of Power: Lessons on Leadership and Influence.* Here, suffice it to say that there is a direct correlation between the amount of power you have and how much leadership and influence you can wield.

KEY CONCEPTS

1. No matter how capable an influencer you are, the idea that you can influence anyone to do anything is nonsense. Influence attempts may fail for many legitimate reasons.

2. Influence attempts do not have binary (yes/no) outcomes. They may result in no influence. If successful, the most likely outcome is compliance, but influence attempts may also result in commitment or leadership. If unsuccessful, they may provoke a negative reaction in the influencee, including skepticism, resistance, or rebellion.

3. People will not consent to be influenced unless the situation and environment are conducive to them saying yes. The foundations of agreement are latitude, interests, and disposition. For you to successfully influence people, they must have the latitude to say yes, saying yes must be aligned with their interests and values, and they must be disposed to say yes.

4. To gauge how responsive someone might be to an influence attempt, use the simple test. Ask yourself, *Why would this person say yes or no?*

5. Influence is often a process rather than an event. Sometimes, people may not be influenced the first time you approach them. You may need to keep trying. However, if the influence technique you are

using is not working, don't keep doing the same thing. Try something else.

6. Influence is cultural. People in different countries and cultures may differ in how they respond to the different influence techniques. To influence effectively in different cultures, you need to understand how power and influence are used in that culture and adapt accordingly.

7. Ethical influence is consensual and often bilateral. Unethical influence may succeed—but always at a cost.

8. People respond best to the influence techniques they use themselves; and if you are observant, people will reveal what they find most influential.

9. Influence usually involves a mix of techniques.

10. The more power you have, the more influential you will be.

CHALLENGES FOR READERS

1. Consider some of your most recent attempts to influence others at work or in your life. Reflect on three or four influence attempts that succeeded. What were you trying to do and, more important, why were you successful?

2. Now reflect on three or four influence attempts that failed. What were you trying to do in these cases, and why weren't the people influenced as you had hoped? What could or should you have done differently? What might have made the difference?

3. Reflect on how other people have influenced you in the past. Has someone ever been so influential with you that you became *committed* to that person's ideas or course of action? Have you ever been moved to assume a *leadership* role? How did the influencer accomplish that? What was so compelling for you?

4. Conversely, has someone ever tried to influence you, and your reaction was to actively or passively *resist* or to instigate a *rebellion*? If so, what prompted your reaction? What did the person do or say that exacerbated the situation? What should the person have done differently?

5. Has anyone ever tried to influence you to do something that was contrary to your interests or values? What was your response?

6. One of the foundations of agreement is disposition. Think about the times someone has tried to influence you, and you didn't cooperate

simply because you weren't in a cooperative frame of mind. When is the best time to approach you? When would conditions be most favorable? Now think about your boss or a peer. When is the best time to approach that person? When is the worst time? What does this suggest about influencing anyone?

7. Apply the simple test to someone you need to influence about something important: *Why might this person say yes? And why might she say no?* In light of your answers, how should you approach this person to ensure success?

8. Have you worked cross-culturally? Or worked with people from different countries in your own culture? What differences do you perceive in how power and influence work in different cultures? Consider some influence approaches you have made that did not work as you expected with people from other cultures. Why were those approaches ineffective?

9. People respond best to the influence techniques they use themselves. Consider your boss and the three or four other people you work with most closely. How do they try to influence others? What techniques do they use? Logic? Authority? Inspiration? Familiarity? Consulting? Next, consider some customers you work with frequently. How do they attempt to influence you or others? What techniques do they prefer?

10. Remember, if you are observant, people will reveal what they find most influential. Think about some of the people you work most closely with. What are the best ways to influence them, and what cues do they give that reveal the best ways to influence them? What about you? What is the best way for someone else to influence you? What do you do or say that reveals that? What about your office or home environment suggests the ways you are able to be influenced?

CHAPTER 2

THE WAYS AND MEANS OF
INFLUENCE

What is remarkable about the ways and means of influencing others is that there are so many of them. The English language contains numerous verbs whose meaning connotes influencing people to think or act differently or otherwise do something the influencer wants: *activate, actuate, admonish, affect, align, animate, appeal, argue, arouse, ask, bait, bargain, barter, beckon, beg, beguile, bewitch, bias, cajole, captivate, catalyze, charm, coach, coax, convert, convince, debate, demand, develop, dicker, dispose, drive, egg on, enchant, encourage, enlist, entice, exchange, excite, explain, foment, galvanize, goad, haggle, impel, impress, incline, induce, inspire, instigate, inveigle, lead, mediate, mobilize, motivate, move, negotiate, offer, persuade, plead, preach, precipitate, prevail upon, prod, prompt, proselytize, provoke, pull, push, quicken, seduce, shock, solicit, spur, stimulate, stir, suborn, suggest, sway, teach, tempt, touch, urge, wheedle, win over,* and *woo.* Most of these verbs connote positive or ethical means of influencing others, although some, like inveigle or seduce, might also imply deceitful ways of influencing people to do something against their better judgment.

However, if we add to our list means of influencing that virtually everyone would agree are unethical, we would add verbs like *assault, attack, blackmail, browbeat, bully, cheat, con, cow, deceive, defraud, delude, fleece, fool, frighten, harm, hoodwink, impose upon, intimidate, lie to, manipulate, menace, mislead, scare, terrify, threaten, trick,* and *victimize.* The language has a plethora of words describing diverse means of exerting influence because, as I argued in chapter 1, influencing others is such a fundamental part of human interaction. People try to influence each other all the time, in different ways, so in our various languages we have created many ways of describing it. Fortunately, we can boil down these ways and means into a simple framework, as shown here, for understanding how people influence others ethically.

INFLUENCE STRATEGIES	INFLUENCE TECHNIQUES
Explaining or telling (rational approaches)	Logical persuading Legitimizing Exchanging Stating
Finding common ground (social approaches)	Socializing Appealing to relationship Consulting Alliance building
Finding inspiration (emotional approaches)	Appealing to values Modeling

One of the most frequent strategies people use to try to influence others is to explain what they want or why they want it, or to simply tell others what they want. It's a rational approach to influencing. When people offer an explanation, it can take two forms: It can be based on logical reasoning or on authority. Either someone says, "I think we should do this because it's logical to do so," or "I think we should do this because an authority (such as a boss) wants us to do it." *Logical persuading* is the most frequent influence technique used by people around the world and is unquestionably the influence technique of choice in business; however, sometimes it's not the most effective way to influence others, particularly if you are trying to inspire commitment or leadership. *Legitimizing* (appealing to authority) is used much less frequently. There are dozens of ways to appeal to authority, but they have mixed success because some people are inherently resistant to authority or may resist particular authorities.

Exchanging and *stating* are also rational approaches to influence, but in these cases the explanation is usually implied. You can influence by offering an exchange or incentive for cooperation. Bartering and negotiating are forms of exchanging; you offer to do a favor for someone if that person does a favor for you. This is a rational approach to influencing because the influencee weighs the pros and cons of the exchange, either explicitly by negotiating the terms of the exchange or implicitly by deciding whether it's worth doing what the influencer is asking for or proposing. Stating is an influence technique in which the influencer simply states what he wants or intends to do. Typically, stating is an implied appeal to authority. If your boss says, "I'd like you to submit your report to accounting by three o'clock today," he is stating what he wants, and behind his influence attempt is the legitimate authority of his role as your boss. He doesn't have to specifically cite his authority. That is implied. I discuss logical persuading and legitimizing in chapter 3, and exchanging and stating in chapter 4.

Another strategy for influencing others is to find common ground, to establish similarity with the person you are trying to influence or to increase the other person's liking for you. These are social approaches to influencing. Research shows that we are more likely to say yes to people we like or feel a connection with. *Socializing* is an influence technique in which influencers seek to socialize with the people they wish to influence—by introducing themselves, making connections, sharing information, finding similar interests or values, and building upon the common human need to bond with others. *Appealing to relationship* means influencing by asking people we already know for help, assistance, support, or agreement. This is typically a very effective influence technique because people who know each other are already inclined to be helpful, friendly, and supportive.

Consulting is influencing either by asking questions that stimulate the other person to draw insights or by engaging the other person in the approach to solving a problem. When people participate in the solution to a problem, they are more likely to support it. Finally, *alliance building* is an influence technique in which the influencer builds support for what she wants by finding other supporters and then using that support when she approaches the person she's trying to influence. Alliance building also occurs when groups agree on ground rules or operating principles and the influencer uses that agreement to influence others to adhere to the social norms of the group. This approach to influence is based on social proof or peer pressure ("If others are supporting this idea, then I suppose I should, too"). I discuss socializing and appealing to relationship in chapter 5, and consulting and alliance building in chapter 6.

A third strategy for influencing others is to motivate or inspire them using emotional approaches. If the explaining strategy is an appeal to the head, then the inspiring strategy is an appeal to the heart. When *appealing to values,* influencers are trying to convince people to go along with them because it feels good or feels right—it energizes them emotionally or enlivens or engages their spirit. Politicians, religious leaders, executives, marketers, advertisers, writers, poets, and public speakers of all kinds have long used this technique to engage audiences and move them to action by appealing to their emotions. A more subtle means of influence is to *model* what you want others to do or to model a way of living, thinking, or being that others may want to emulate. Teachers, coaches, managers, leaders, parents, and others are role models all the time. Whether or not they consciously use modeling as an influence technique, they are constantly behaving in ways that may influence others to follow their example—good or bad. I discuss appealing to values and modeling in chapter 7.

WHAT MAKES INFLUENCE EFFECTIVE?

In my previous book, *The Elements of Power,* I described the eleven sources of power that people can develop. (For a brief explanation of these sources of power, see appendix A.) Unless you build a power base you will not be influential. The greater your power base, the more influence you will be capable of exerting. A knowledgeable, well-educated, eloquent, attractive person of good character in a senior role in an organization, someone with a broad network, good command of information and resources, and an excellent reputation, will be substantially more influential than a person embodying the opposite characteristics. When you try to influence people, you are applying your power in order to accomplish a goal. Imagine two influencing situations: In one case, I am trying to persuade my spouse to go to a particular restaurant I like, and in another instance, I'm trying to persuade a colleague to join me in a meeting with an important new customer. My success in these situations will depend on a number of factors, some of which I can control and others that I cannot. The factors I can control are shown in this formula:

TOPS = **influence effectiveness**

where

T = my choice of influence technique
O = my organizational power sources
P = my personal power sources, including will power
S = the skill with which I use the influence technique

In the first situation, I will be more likely to succeed if I have good history and attraction power with my spouse and if I am skillful at appealing to our relationship. However, if I clumsily rely on my position as president of a company (role power) and my extensive network of business connections and try to persuade her by stating my request ("This is where we're going"), then I may appear overbearing and authoritative and will probably fail (actually, in my marriage that would fail catastrophically). In the second situation, I'll be more likely to influence my colleague to join me in the customer meeting if I use techniques like logical persuading, socializing, appealing to values, or exchanging, and draw upon my strongest sources of power, which are knowledge, attraction, character, information, network, and reputation.

The factors in influence effectiveness that I can't control are the ones cited previously in chapter 1: the influencee's latitude, interests, and disposition. My spouse would have the latitude to say yes, and it presumably would not conflict with her values or interests, but she may not be disposed to agree with me on the choice of restaurant. She might be angry with me at the moment and not inclined to agree with anything I suggest, or she may have had another restaurant in mind, in which case we might influence each other by exchanging ("Let's go to your choice of restaurant tonight and my choice another night"). My colleague may not have the latitude (she may have another customer commitment), the interest (my meeting could be outside her area of expertise or company responsibility), or the disposition (she might be competing with me for the next promotion and doesn't want to help me).

There's a simple way to test for effectiveness before you try to influence someone, which I described in chapter 1. Simply ask: *Why would this person say yes and why would she say no?* If I know my spouse is angry with me, it may not be the opportune moment to influence the choice of restaurant (I may be taking my supper in the doghouse). If that particular colleague is competing with me for a promotion, then perhaps I should try to find someone else to join me in this customer meeting. If the situation is favorable, however—that is, if the influencee does have the latitude to be influenced and is disposed to do so—I will be most likely to succeed if I choose the right techniques, have the right power sources, and am skilled in the right ways.

INFLUENCE AND LEADERSHIP

Earlier I argued that there can be no leadership without influence, because influencing is how leaders lead. In their classic book on leadership, Warren Bennis and Burt Nanus echo this point. "There is a profound difference between management and leadership," they wrote, "and both are important. 'To manage' means 'to bring about, to accomplish, to have charge of or responsibility for, to conduct.' 'Leading' is 'influencing, guiding in direction, course, action, opinion.'"[1] They add that "an *essential* factor in leadership is the capacity to influence."[2]

Managers also use influence, of course, because only a fraction of managerial work can actually be accomplished through control and the use of authority. The aim of both managers and leaders is to accomplish an organization's goals. Managers do it through plans, organization, processes, task assignments, measurements, and so on, but they must also direct people and manage their performance, and you can't manage people solely through command-and-control methods. People are human beings, not machines, mechanical parts, or assembly lines. They respond best when they are treated like human beings, they work best when they have a voice in how the work is done, and they remain loyal and engaged when they feel respected, trusted, well informed, and cared for. That's why the best managers also lead, and they lead through the social and emotional approaches to influencing, not just the rational approaches.

Leaders lead by mobilizing people around a compelling vision of the future, by inspiring them to follow in the leader's footsteps. They show people what's possible and motivate them to make those possibilities real. They energize and focus people in ways that fulfill their dreams, give them a sense of purpose, and leave them with a profound sense of accomplishment when the work is done. Leaders lead by modeling ways of thinking or acting and by encouraging new ways of looking at situations, and by so doing they give people the words and the courage to make those new ways their own. The best leaders are teachers, mentors, and role models—and they accomplish the vast majority of their work through influence, not authority.

In many cases, leaders and managers are one and the same. The division vice president who leads a team of people to accomplish what they might not have thought possible is also a manager. The manager who oversees a team's task performance but also looks after the team members' career planning and coaches them on developing their skills is also a leader. The art of management and leadership is to know when to act as a manager and when to act as a leader, when to use authority and when to use influence, when to ask and when to tell, when to take over and when to let go. In every case, it is crucial for leaders and managers to understand the range of influence techniques they can use, know when and how to use them, build their power bases so that they have the capacity to be influential, and sharpen their skills so that they can influence people effectively.

WHAT THE RESEARCH TELLS US ABOUT INFLUENCE TECHNIQUES

My research on global power and influence reveals some interesting facts about the frequency and effectiveness of the ten influence techniques. First, across the world, in nearly every culture, five of these techniques (which I call the *influence power tools*) are used significantly more often than the other five. I measured influence frequency on a seven-point scale. The ratings indicate how frequently each of the people we assessed used a particular influence technique.

As table 2-1 shows, the five influence power tools—*logical persuading, socializing, stating, consulting,* and *appealing to relationship*—had frequency averages in the 5s, while the remaining techniques averaged in the 4s. The gap between these groups of influence techniques is significant. By and large, then, no matter which culture you are living or working in, people will be most apt to use one of the five power tools when they try to influence others. People generally begin by offering logical reasons for their request or proposal. The default mode, so to speak, is logical persuading. Depending on the situation and the influencee, they may supplement logical persuading with a social form of influence—socializing (if they don't know the influencee well) and/or appealing to relationship (if they do know the person)—and they might try to gain cooperation by asking for the influencee's ideas through the consulting technique. Mixed with logical and social ways of influencing may be direct statements of their position or need.

Generally, the less frequently used influence techniques are reserved for special situations. Influencers may use appealing to values when they are trying to influence a large group of people or when the topic or need has an emotional or value component (e.g., when someone is soliciting funds for a charitable cause). They would use exchanging during negotiations or when the best way to gain someone's

INFLUENCE TECHNIQUE	AVERAGE FREQUENCY RATING
Logical persuading	5.91
Socializing	5.52
Stating	5.43
Consulting	5.39
Appealing to relationship	5.28
Legitimizing	4.79
Appealing to values	4.77
Modeling	4.77
Alliance building	4.76
Exchanging	4.47

► Table 2-1. Global averages for influence technique frequency.

cooperation is to bargain or trade for it. Alliance building is probably used less frequently because it is time-consuming and is best done when influencers have few other good options for swaying someone's opinion or gaining people's cooperation. Legitimizing (or appealing to authority) is best reserved for situations where an influencer needs quick compliance, whereas modeling is done when the influencer has a lot of time and can influence people slowly.

Table 2-2 shows the global average ratings for the effectiveness (as well as the frequency) of the ten influence techniques. As this table indicates, all the techniques have effectiveness ratings in the 5s except for legitimizing, which is substantially lower. People are generally less effective at legitimizing because it can be challenging to appeal to authority without appearing heavy-handed (as I discuss in more depth in chapter 3). What is more notable from this table is that three of the influence techniques—logical persuading, stating, and legitimizing—have higher frequency ratings than effectiveness ratings. For consulting, frequency and effectiveness are nearly equivalent. But for the remaining six techniques, the average frequency rating is less than the average effectiveness rating. These differences suggest that people around the world use logical persuading, stating, and legitimizing more often than they should. These techniques are overused. Conversely, people tend to use socializing, appealing to relationship, appealing to values, modeling, alliance building, and exchanging less often than they should. These techniques are underused.

INFLUENCE TECHNIQUE	AVERAGE EFFECTIVE- NESS RATING	AVERAGE FREQUENCY RATING
Logical persuading	5.68	5.91
Socializing	5.61	5.52
Appealing to relationship	5.55	5.28
Consulting	5.41	5.39
Modeling	5.39	4.77
Stating	5.35	5.43
Appealing to values	5.26	4.77
Exchanging	5.23	4.47
Alliance building	5.03	4.76
Legitimizing	4.65	4.79

► Table 2-2. Global averages for influence effectiveness.

To be more effective at influencing others, you should be aware of the range of possible techniques and how best to use them. Think of these influence techniques as part of your toolbox. To be more effective in more situations, you need to have a full set of tools, know which tool is best for which situation, and have the skills and necessary power sources to use those tools effectively.

KEY CONCEPTS

1. There are three basic influence strategies: explaining or telling (rational approaches), finding common ground (social approaches), and finding inspiration (emotional approaches).

2. The rational approaches to influence include logical persuading, legitimizing (or appealing to authority), exchanging, and stating.

3. The social approaches to influence are consulting, socializing, appealing to relationship, and alliance building.

4. The two emotional approaches to influence are appealing to values and modeling.

5. Influence effectiveness depends on some things influencers can control and some things they cannot. The things an influencer can control are reflected in the TOPS model, where T is the choice of influence technique, O and P are the influencer's organizational and personal power sources, respectively, and S is the skill with which the influencer uses the technique. What the influencer cannot control are the influencee's latitude, interests, and disposition (described more fully in chapter 1).

6. Managers and leaders both use influence to accomplish their goals, but leaders rely on influencing almost entirely as they try to lead other people. There can be no leadership without influence.

7. Around the world, people tend to use five of the influence techniques significantly more often than the other five. These *influence power tools* are logical persuading, socializing, stating, consulting, and appealing to relationship. In nearly every culture, these are the five most frequently used influence techniques. No matter where you live or work, these are the techniques you are likely to encounter most often.

CHALLENGES FOR READERS

1. Reflect on the ten positive or ethical influence techniques. Which of these techniques do you think you use most often? Most effectively? How do you try to influence other people and what works best for you?

2. Think about some recent situations in which others tried to influence you. What were they trying to accomplish and how did they go about it? Were they successful? If so, why were they successful? What was it about the person, your relationship with that person, or the way the person approached you that you found compelling or persuasive? In other words, why did you say yes? If the influence attempt failed, why did you say no?

3. What do you think it takes for an influence attempt to succeed?

4. Do you agree that leaders mainly accomplish their goals through influence rather than authority? Think of some examples. Think of some effective leaders you know. How do they go about getting what they want? How do leaders you know get other people to help them accomplish their goals?

5. Do you see a difference between leadership and management? Try an experiment. Take a piece of paper and make two columns on it. In the left column, list words that describe what managers do or what tools they use. In the right column, list words that describe leaders or what tools they use. How would you define the difference between management and leadership? To what extent does each rely on influence rather than authority?

6. Reexamine tables 2-1 and 2-2 and the analysis of the research findings. What additional conclusions would you draw from the data? What are your conclusions about the ten influence techniques and their use and effectiveness?

PART II

ETHICAL INFLUENCE TECHNIQUES

The second part of this book explores how people influence each other in ethical ways. There are ten ethical influence techniques because none of them alone is the right tool to use every time. Each technique has advantages and disadvantages, and the effectiveness of all of the techniques depends not only on the skill with which you use them but also on how receptive people are to them. To a greater or lesser extent, most people respond to logical persuasion, but in some circumstances logic will not be compelling or persuasive. Furthermore, if you want the people you are trying to influence to become committed to the course of action you are proposing, then logical persuasion probably won't work. When you want commitment, you are better off appealing to the values of the people you want to influence, modeling what you want them to do, or appealing to relationship (if you know the influencees well and they trust you). In other circumstances, you will not succeed unless you use exchanging or alliance building—techniques the research shows are much less common but are the only tools to use in certain situations.

The point is that none of these influence techniques works with everyone all the time. For this reason, the people who are consistently most effective at influencing others have a full toolbox, and they know which tool to use for each circumstance and each person they are trying to influence. Here, then, is a short summary of the ten ethical influence techniques and key facts about them. Part III of this book describes the four influence strategies that belong to the dark side of influence.

RATIONAL APPROACHES

Logical persuading	Using logic to explain what you believe or what you want. This is the number-one influence power tool throughout the world and the most frequently used and effective influence technique in nearly every culture, but it does not work with everyone—and in some circumstances will not work at all.
Legitimizing	Appealing to authority. On average, the least-effective influence technique in the world, but it will work with some people most of the time and most people some of the time and can result in quick compliance.

Exchanging	Negotiating or trading for cooperation. This approach is most effective when it is implicit rather than explicit. It is used less often globally than any other influence technique, but it is sometimes the only way to gain agreement or cooperation.
Stating	Asserting what you believe or want. This influence power tool is most effective when you are self-confident and state ideas with a compelling tone of voice, but it can backfire if overused.

SOCIAL APPROACHES

Socializing	Getting to know the other person; being open and friendly; finding common ground. Complimenting people and making them feel good about themselves is a critical technique in many cultures and situations. This influence power tool is the second most important one in frequency and effectiveness globally.
Appealing to relationship	Gaining agreement or cooperation with people you already know well. This influence power tool leverages the length and strength of your existing relationships, and as a technique it is third highest rated in effectiveness globally.
Consulting	Engaging or stimulating people by asking questions; involving them in the problem or solution. This influence power tool is ranked fourth in frequency and effectiveness globally. This technique works well with smart, self-confident people who have a strong need to contribute ideas.
Alliance building	Finding supporters or building alliances to help influence someone else; using peer or group pressure to gain cooperation or agreement. This technique is not used often and is not always effective, but in the right circumstances it may be the only way to gain consent.

EMOTIONAL APPROACHES

Appealing to values   Making an emotional appeal or an appeal to the heart. Because it is one of the principal ways to influence many people at once and the best technique for building commitment, the emotional appeal is a frequent technique of religious or spiritual leaders, idealists, fund-raisers, and politicians.

Modeling   Behaving in ways you want others to behave; being a role model; teaching, coaching, counseling, and mentoring. It is possible to influence people without being aware that you are influencing. Parents, leaders, managers, and public figures influence others through modeling all the time—positively or negatively—whether they choose to or not. This influence technique ranks fifth globally in effectiveness.

CHAPTER 3

LET ME EXPLAIN

Logical Persuading and Legitimizing

In George Orwell's dystopian novella *Animal Farm*, Old Major, the prize Middle White boar of the Manor Farm, has a disturbing dream one night and decides to share it with the farm's other animals. The next night, as Farmer Jones lies in a drunken stupor, Mrs. Jones snoring soundly beside him, the animals slowly gather in the big barn to hear what Old Major has to say. The prize boar is revered among the farm's animals, and most listen attentively when he begins to speak:

> Comrades, you have heard already about the strange dream that I had last night. But I will come to the dream later. I have something else to say first. I do not think, comrades, that I shall be with you for many months longer, and before I die, I feel it my duty to pass on to you such wisdom as I have acquired. I have had a long life, I have had much time for thought as I lay alone in my stall, and I think I may say that I understand the nature of life on this earth as well as any animal now living. It is about this that I wish to speak to you.[1]

In this confessional preamble, Old Major engages his audience's sympathy while portraying himself as a sage among the animals, a guru who is obligated by his sense of duty to pass on the wisdom he has acquired during a long life. By casting himself as an expert on "the nature of life on this earth," he is positioning what he is about to say as The Truth:

> Now, comrades, what is the nature of this life of ours? Let us face it: our lives are miserable, laborious, and short.[2]

This assertion may resonate with any of the animals who agree with it, but it lacks the proof necessary to persuade the animals who haven't felt this way about their lives. So Old Major offers evidence to back up his assertion:

> We are born, we are given just so much food as will keep the breath in our bodies, and those of us who are capable of it are forced to work to the last atom of our strength; and the very instant that our usefulness has come to an end we are slaughtered with hideous cruelty.[3]

Old Major posits that their lives are miserable, and one element of proof is that they receive only as much food as will keep them alive. While this falls short of starvation, any animal wanting more food than it gets would likely agree that the dearth of food constitutes misery. Furthermore, they are forced to work "to the last atom of our strength," which makes their lives laborious, and they are slaughtered once they are no longer useful. They will know this is true from the fate of animals who have gone missing or been led off to slaughter, so Old Major's arguments will ring true. The old boar summarizes:

> No animal in England knows the meaning of happiness or leisure after he is a year old. No animal in England is free. The life of an animal is misery and slavery: that is the plain truth.[4]

Old Major has not yet arrived at a call to action, but he has been laying the logical foundation for an argument that exposes the agent of their misery and will lead them to conclude that they must revolt. The foundation laid, he now moves to link cause and effect. But first he wants to eliminate a logical alternative to the conclusion he is driving toward:

> But is this simply part of the order of nature? Is it because this land of ours is so poor that it cannot afford a decent life to those who dwell upon it? No, comrades, a thousand times no! The soil of England is fertile, its climate is good, it is capable of affording food in abundance to an enormously greater number of animals than now inhabit it. This single farm of ours would support a dozen horses, twenty cows, hundreds of sheep—and all of them living in a comfort and a dignity that are now almost beyond our imagining.[5]

So, their lives are miserable but not because the land could not provide more. His proof? The soil is fertile. The climate is good. The land could provide much more food, enough for many more animals than now live on Manor Farm. Having ruled out the environment as the cause of the animals' misery, he sets them up to accept his central premise:

> Why then do we continue in this miserable condition? Because nearly the whole of the produce of our labour is stolen from us by human beings. There, comrades, is the answer to all our problems. It is summed up in a single word—Man. Man is the only real enemy we have.[6]

There it is. The effect is misery; the cause is Man, says Old Major. We animals are miserable because human beings steal nearly the whole of the product of our labor, which does not leave enough for us to live in a happier state. Now he concludes with his call to action:

> Remove Man from the scene, and the root cause of hunger and overwork is abolished for ever.[7]

The utopian dream is available to them, he argues, if they get rid of Man. Old Major's speech includes some emotional appeals, but it is essentially a logical argument:

We are miserable.
Man is the cause of our misery.
If we get rid of Man, we will no longer be miserable.

The old boar tries to influence them through logical persuasion, and he succeeds. Emboldened by his vision of utopia, and persuaded that Man is the cause, the animals revolt and evict Farmer Jones. Afterwards, they rename their home "Animal Farm."

One of the most common ways we try to influence others is to make our request or position seem reasonable or justifiable. By explaining logically why we want something or believe something, we assume others will agree or consent—because what we want is reasonable; because it makes sense; because any other rational person would make the same argument, offer the same evidence, and reach the same conclusion. We assume, in other words, that people are logical and rational, and therefore if we make a logical request, then logically, they will consent. When we use a rational approach to influencing we are in essence saying, "I want X because . . . ," or "I think the right answer is X because . . . ," or "I would like you to do X because . . . ". The word because may be stated or implied, but it is always present because a rational approach to influence is either an explanation based on rea-son or a justification based on authority. You should do X "because it is logical to do so," or you should do X "because a legitimate authority says you should do it."

One of the most common ways we try to influence others is to make our request or position seem reasonable or justifiable.

Four of the ten ethical influence techniques are rational approaches to influencing: logical persuading, legitimizing, exchanging, and stat-ing. This chapter discusses logical persuading and legitimizing: how they work, what makes them effective or ineffective in different cir-cumstances, the power sources that are crucial for each technique, the other influence techniques most closely related to them, and the skills required to use them effectively. The rational approaches to influenc-ing—particularly logical persuading and stating—are frequently used in every country in the world; however, they are not always the most effective techniques. Even so, we tend to prefer these rational approaches to influencing because we assume that people are rational and will make rational decisions. But, as we will see, often that's not the case.

LOGICAL PERSUADING

In all but one of the forty-five countries I've studied, logical persuad-ing was the most frequently used influence technique (in chapter 5, I'll tell you which country was the exception). In India, China, Ger-many, America, and many other countries, it is not only used more often than any other influence technique, it is used *significantly* more often than the others, which makes it the default influence approach used throughout most of the world. Why would this be the case? I believe it is largely because of the tradition of reasoned thought handed down to us from Parmenides (fifth century BC), his disciple Zeno of Elea (author of Zeno's paradoxes), and other Greek philosophers who were not content to merely assert what they believed was true. They sought to prove their assertions by constructing irrefutable arguments, and in so doing they invented logic. Logic is essentially the search for objective truth, the kind of truth that can be proven and agreed upon by all rational observers. In contrast, Eastern thought incorporates relational and intuitive ways of understanding experience and arriving at truths that are more subjective (e.g., attaining harmony with nature or with one's ancestors) and not capable of being proven through rational methods.

While both Eastern and Western ways of understanding experience influence how people around the world think and behave, logic holds the strongest appeal. Like a virus, logic spread throughout the ancient world and modified, if you will, the DNA of how people think. It became the intellectual foundation of many fields of study— mathematics, physics, chemistry, biology, engineering, language, law, psychology, sociology, philosophy, and medicine—and underlies our approach to education. What schools teach, beyond skills and facts, is how to think about the world—how to think logically and rationally.

Because of our educational bias toward rationality, we imagine ourselves to be wholly rational beings. We expect ourselves and others to behave rationally and make rational decisions. When two-year-olds ask their parents *why* the sky is blue or *why* they have to go to bed now, they are trying to understand the world, and they expect answers that make sense to them, answers that seem reasonable within the scope of their understanding. We look askance at people who are not rational (we sometimes confine them to mental institutions). So our default mode when we seek to influence others is to offer a logical explanation for what we want. We try to make our requests or positions seem reasonable. Here are some examples of logical persuading:

► "Customers attach value to products in proportion to the perceived ability of those products to help solve their problems. Hence a product has meaning only from the viewpoint of the buyer or the ultimate user. All else is derivative. Only the buyer or user can assign value, because value can reside only in the benefits he wants or perceives."[8] (This is a classic logical argument. If you accept the assertion in the first sentence, then the rest of the argument follows logically.)

► "In today's uncertain market, people have learned that security no longer rests in the corporate nest egg, but in their own skills. For that reason, talented people are drawn to companies that will help them develop new skills, knowledge, and experiences."[9] (The phrase "for that reason" signals the logical connection between the two thoughts.)

► "Dissipative structures demonstrate that *disorder* can be a source of *order,* and that growth is found in disequilibrium, not in balance. The things we fear most in organizations—fluctuations, disturbances, imbalances—need not be signs of an impending disorder that will destroy us. Instead, fluctuations are the primary source of creativity."[10] (The logical argument here is that if the principle of *order from chaos* is true in nature, then it is also true in organizations.)

These examples come from classic business books, but logical persuading is also evident in far more prosaic contexts; for instance:

- ► "Bill, let's go to the Red Sox game on Saturday. Jon Lester is pitching, so it should be a good game." (If Lester pitches, it logically follows that the game will be good.)
- ► "I was going to make a chocolate cake for José's birthday. Then I remembered that he doesn't like chocolate, so I made a carrot cake instead. I hope that's okay with you." (My decision was rational. I didn't make a chocolate cake *because* José doesn't like chocolate.)

Whenever you seek to influence someone by explaining logically what you want or why you want it, you are using logical persuading. This influence technique also occurs when you try to show that your approach or conclusion is the best alternative based on sensible criteria; when you use a proven process to arrive at a decision; when you rely on knowledge or expertise to present factual reasons for your position; and when you try to prove your case by providing charts, graphs, data, statistics, photographs, or other forms of evidence.

Insights on Logical Persuading

I doubt if anyone exemplifies the use of logical persuading more than Albert Einstein. He's been called the father of modern physics as well as the greatest scientist of all time, and he was *Time* magazine's Person of the Century for his extraordinary contributions to twentieth-century science. But Einstein's beginning was anything but auspicious. Born in 1879 in Ulm, Germany, he was an unusual child. His mother thought he might be deformed because his head was too large for his body, and his speech development lagged well behind that of a normal child. He did not begin speaking until after age three, may have been dyslexic during his early school years, and did not begin speaking normally until he was nine. Speech problems did not affect his curiosity, however. When he was five, his father (an engineer) gave him a small compass, and Einstein puzzled over what made the needle

Library of Congress—Oren Jack Turner/
Getty Images

► Albert Einstein was a master of
influencing through logical
persuading.

move. He had a natural affinity for mechanical devices and was eager to understand what made the physical world work.

During his later school years, his genius for mathematics and physics became evident, and in 1900 he graduated from the Federal Polytechnic Institute in Zurich with a teaching diploma. Unable to find a teaching job, he finally accepted a position at the Swiss patent office in Bern, where he evaluated patent applications involving mechanics and electricity. The ensuing years were highly productive for the young scientist. He published a number of papers, including ones on special relativity and the photoelectric effect, and he received a PhD in experimental physics from the University of Zurich. He later left the patent office and worked as a lecturer and professor and, in 1914, as director of the Kaiser Wilhelm Physical Institute in Berlin. In 1921, he was awarded the Nobel Prize in Physics for his work on the photoelectric effect (relativity was still not an accepted concept at the time).

Like all scientists, Einstein sought rational explanations for the phenomena observed in the world. His famous thought experiments led him to challenge the conventional view of the mechanics of the universe and to show, among other things, that mass and energy are equivalent, that the speed of light is a constant, and that gravity and acceleration are indistinguishable. To prove these assertions, he offered logical explanations and mathematical equations. His theories were so radical that many people disputed them until subsequent scientific experiments proved, time after time, that Einstein's revolutionary theory of relativity is correct.

Another scientific revolution occurred with the discovery of quantum mechanics. Whereas Einstein's relativity described the physics of the very large, Werner Heisenberg, Niels Bohr, Wolfgang Pauli, and others sought to describe the physics of the very small. One of the conundrums of physics is that elementary particles like electrons can be proven experimentally to be both particles and waves simultaneously. Exploring this puzzle and others involving elementary particles led Heisenberg to formulate his famous uncertainty principle, which states that although you can know the position or momentum of an electron, you cannot know both at the same time. This nondeterministic view of nature did not sit well with Einstein. It wasn't rational, and he refuted it by saying, "God does not play dice with the universe." Unfortunately, relativity, which works well in describing what happens at the macro level of existence, breaks down when applied to the micro level, while quantum mechanics, which brilliantly describes the subatomic world, breaks down when applied to the macro level. Both theories are right, but they are incompatible. To the end of his days, Einstein sought a unified theory that would reconcile quantum mechanics and relativity, that would unite the physics of the very large with that of the very small, but he did not succeed (and to this day no one else has, either).

People like Albert Einstein who frequently use logical persuading as a means of influencing others have certain characteristics that they share. Many of them have degrees in accounting, business, science, mathematics, or another technical field, or they work in a profession, such as law, that demands rational approaches to problem solving and decision making. They have been taught to be logical, their profession demands it, and they think logically every day. Those who use logical persuading the most tend to use it *significantly* more often than the other influence techniques. They depend on logical persuasion, and if that doesn't work, they often continue using logic as though if they use enough of it, if they pile on enough proof, enough facts, they'll wear down the resistance of those they want to influence. Because they depend so much on logical persuading, they may not be comfortable with other influence techniques or don't think to try them.

Another interesting observation emerged from the research. People who are most effective at influencing through logical persuasion also tend to be proficient at influencing by building alliances of supporters and by asking questions that stimulate people to see and accept the influencer's perspective. I think they are good at alliance building because their persuasive abilities enable them to find and convince potential allies to support them, and their ability to build strong arguments enables them to identify the right questions to ask that will lead others to reach the same conclusions they reached. Finally, people effective at logical persuading also tend to be skillful negotiators. They know how to formulate logical proposals and use facts to support their arguments, and these skills make them better at influencing by negotiating or bartering (an influence technique called exchanging).

In *The Elements of Power,* I identified the power sources that people need to be effective at influence and leadership.[11] (A summary of these power sources also appears in appendix A of this book.) It would seem logical that two of those sources, knowledge and information, would be essential for anyone wanting to be highly effective at logical persuading, and although being knowledgeable and well informed is obviously important, research shows that the most important source of power for logical persuading is expressiveness—the ability to communicate clearly and powerfully. Knowledge and information alone do not make people skilled at using logical persuasion. It is more important that they be skilled at articulating their ideas in ways other people find compelling.

Another key power source for logical persuading is reputation—how well you are regarded in your organization or community. This was an intriguing finding from the research. It indicates that the more highly regarded you are, the more likely people are to accept your logical propositions. However, if you are less well known or not highly regarded, you will be less successful at persuading others, even if your logical reasoning is sound and your facts are correct. This paradox tells us a lot about what influences people and what doesn't.

In a similar vein, character as a power source is highly correlated with the effective use of logical persuasion. So a man whose character is in question is likely to be less effective at logical persuading than another man whose character is unblemished. This is hardly surprising. It reinforces the old admonition that when evaluating the merit of what someone has to say, you must consider the source. Interestingly, the research shows that there is no correlation between the effective use of logical persuasion and a person's role or position in an organization or the person's control of important resources. So when the senior executives of a company try to persuade employees to do something by giving logical reasons for their requests, they are not necessarily more believable because of their rank. Rank may have privileges, but not when it comes to logical persuasion. Likewise, wealthy people or those who control vast resources have no advantages when it comes to using this influence technique.

What skills do people need in order to use logical persuading effectively? The research shows that people who excel at this technique are skilled at logical reasoning (of course), analyzing and displaying data visually, asking insightful questions, finding creative alternatives, and using a compelling tone of voice. These results are not surprising, but others are. It turns out that people who excel at logical persuading are also highly skilled at listening and at building rapport and trust with others. Being listened to is a pleasant experience for anyone. It makes us feel validated and worthwhile, so when a person who is trying to influence us takes the time to listen to what we have to say, it makes us more receptive to his arguments. Moreover, if the influencer takes the time to build rapport and trust with us beforehand, we will be more likely to accept what he has to say. The implications of these results are profound. When you are trying to influence people by using logical persuasion, your ideas will be more believable and compelling if you build rapport and trust with them ahead of time and *actively listen* when they are speaking.

The Limitations of Logical Persuading

Management consulting firms like McKinsey & Company, Bain, Boston Consulting Group, and Accenture pride themselves on their rational approach to problem solving. Their structured data gathering and rigorous analysis of client problems and opportunities are intended to yield the best, most rational solutions and recommendations. Yet by the reckoning of some of their senior partners, clients fully adopt their recommendations less than half the time—after paying millions of dollars for those engagements. Why? If a logical analysis by some of the best minds in the world produces the most rational approach to a business problem, why don't executive teams always fully implement the consultants' recommendations? One answer is that there's more to "best solutions" than logic. Marvin Bauer, the legendary director of McKinsey & Company, said once that people don't make decisions rationally. They make emotional decisions, he said, and then justify them with logic.

From Aristotle and Plato in ancient times to the present day, philosophers, psychologists, and, more recently, neuroscientists have tried to explain the roles of reason and emotion in human decision making and behavior. What distinguishes the human brain from the brains of other primates is the size of our neocortex (the white matter), which permits consciousness, judgment, and rational thought. But our neocortex is built on top of and works in conjunction with the more primitive parts of our brain, including the amygdala, which sits just above the brain stem and is a fundamental part of our emotional circuitry.[12] In the continuous stream of thought that forms our mental life, we evoke both reason *and* passion, cognition *and* emotion. In fact, what makes us human—as every *Star Trek* fan knows—is that we can't separate reason from emotion. So Marvin Bauer's observation appears to be valid. It seems that every decision we make, every conclusion we draw, and every argument we consider is influenced in some way by our emotions, although we may not be consciously aware of it at the time. It seems that we are physiologically incapable of exercising pure reasoning as we evaluate logical propositions, and even the most factual, logically correct argument may fail to influence someone who has an emotional or psychological bias toward doing something else.

In his landmark book on the psychology of influence, Robert B. Cialdini noted, for example, that we are often influenced by our need to reciprocate a favor given to us.[13] If someone has given us something, we feel socially bound to give something back, *even if it's not logical.* We are also influenced by our need to appear consistent, so if we make a commitment to do something we feel obligated to go through with it, *even if it no longer makes sense to do so.* Furthermore, we are influenced by what other people do, *even if what they are doing is illogical.* We tend to believe that higher-priced clothing, jewelry, electronic gadgets, and works of art, among other things, are of higher quality and greater value than lower-priced alternatives, even though there may be no connection between price and quality.

We tend to assume that people who are physically attractive are also smarter, nicer, better behaved, and more likely to succeed than people who are unattractive. It's called the halo effect. Clearly, this is irrational, yet the halo effect has been demonstrated in numerous sociological studies. We are also fooled by the placebo effect. In pharmaceutical studies, half of the patients with some medical condition receive the actual drug being tested; the other half (the control group) unknowingly receive a placebo, an inert pill that should have no effect. Yet in thousands of studies, some patients in the control group also improve. Why the placebo effect works remains a mystery, but it is commonly believed to arise from people's *expectation* that they will benefit from taking the drug.

We are not as rational as we would like to think we are, and our decisions are influenced by many emotional, psychological, and social factors that we may not even be aware of.[14] Some areas of human endeavor are more rational than others. We expect more rationality in areas like science, mathematics, engineering, technology, and business. We expect to apply facts, analyze data, and draw logical conclusions from the outcomes of our problem solving and decision making. We like to think that our strategies and plans are rational—and to some extent this is true. In these areas, logical persuading is an appropriate influence technique to use. But it is nonetheless important to recognize that even in these highly rational areas, logical persuading may fail to influence people, at least some of the time, because nothing human beings do is entirely rational. If you are solving an engineering problem with facts and mathematical formulas, then a rational approach is the right one, but if you are trying to convince others that your solution to a social or family problem is best, then using logical persuading may not be as effective as you'd like because people are not machines and other hidden factors may influence their decision making.

In *John P. Kotter on What Leaders Really Do,* Kotter observes that leaders can't expect people to follow a constant stream of orders just because they come from the boss. Furthermore, "Trying to influence others by means of persuasion alone will not work either. Although it is very powerful and possibly the single most important method of influence, persuasion has some serious drawbacks, too. To make it work requires time (often lots of it), skill, and information on the part of the persuader. And persuasion can fail simply because the other person chooses not to listen or does not listen carefully."[15] This, then, is the limitation of logical persuading. No matter how sound your logic, it may fail to influence others if they are not listening, if they are predisposed toward another solution, if they are biased against you or what you represent, if they are reluctant to support you before knowing where others stand, if they need more time to think about it, or if other hidden factors prevent them from agreeing with you.

When to Use Logical Persuading

Logical persuading is the preferred method of influencing in some situations, but it is likely to result in compliance rather than commitment. Use logical persuading in these situations:

- ► When the person you are trying to influence has already shown that she is responsive to logical persuading. For instance, when someone has just tried to persuade you of something by giving you a logical argument, chances are that person will be responsive to a logical argument in return.
- ► When the people you wish to influence *expect* a logical plan or solu-

tion; for instance, if you are presenting a scientific paper, business proposal, technical plan, financial analysis, or something of that sort. Certain contexts—such as a business meeting to evaluate an acquisition candidate—demand a logical approach, at least initially.

► When you are not in a crisis situation or don't need quick compliance. In a crisis, you need an influence technique that can result in quicker compliance, such as legitimizing. If people have time to reflect and be thoughtful, then logical persuading can be effective.

► When the culture of the country or organization is slanted toward logical persuasion. At technology companies such as Cisco Systems or accounting firms like KPMG, logical persuading is the preferred means of influencing; however, in human services organizations or those engaged in the arts, other methods (e.g., appealing to values, consulting) are often more appropriate.

► When you have knowledge, skills, expertise, experience, or insights that the person you are trying to influence does not have. In these situations, your superior knowledge and information power can be decisive.

► When you are eloquent or highly expressive and can use your verbal gifts to put forth a compelling case. Remember that expressiveness is the most highly correlated power source with the effective use of logical persuading. Conversely, if you are not eloquent or convincingly expressive, then logical persuading may not be an effective technique to use.

► When you have a preponderance of evidence to support your case. If the facts overwhelmingly support your argument, logical persuading can be effective, even in the face of emotional resistance.

► When the influencee is disposed to agree with you. And herein lies the rub. Logical persuading is generally effective only when the people you are trying to influence are already inclined to go along with what you want. If they are not so disposed, they are likely to resist your logic, no matter how sound it may be. You can usually tell when this is the case because someone will disagree with you for reasons that often either don't make sense or are beside the point. When this occurs, you are encountering resistance based on emotional or psychological factors or other barriers that make the influencee unable or unwilling to consent. Giving this person more facts or logical reasons is unlikely to be persuasive, so switch to another influence technique.

► When you need compliance rather than commitment. Logical persuading usually will not gain people's heartfelt commitment to a cause. If you need commitment, use appealing to values or modeling.

How to Use Logical Persuading Effectively

1. Know your audience well. Understand who they are and how they operate. Know what's important to them and what they would expect from you.

2. Use this simple test. Ask, *Why would they say yes and why would they say no?* What would they find convincing and compelling? How might they argue against what you are proposing (and what will you say if they do)? What issues might they raise (and how will you respond to those issues)?

3. Be clear in your own mind about why they *should* agree with what you are proposing. Be able to state, as precisely yet simply as possible, your premise as well as the principal facts and arguments supporting your premise. It's often useful to outline your argument, to ensure that it is logical.

4. Build your case by finding supporting facts and evidence. If appropriate, find ways to present or display that information in a compelling way.

5. Make your influence attempt at the right time—when people are not pressed by other urgent business and when they have time for thoughtful reflection and to fully hear your arguments.

6. Listen carefully to their responses. Remember that listening is one of the skills most closely correlated with logical persuading. Listening, responding thoughtfully, asking questions that engage people in the discussion, and summarizing periodically are techniques that help make logical persuading more effective.

7. Remember that influence is often a process rather than an event. You may need to present your case, understand where the resistance lies if people say no, and then return later with a revised case that addresses their resistance.

LEGITIMIZING

In George Orwell's novella, after the animals have successfully expelled Farmer Jones from the property, two large pigs emerge as the natural leaders of Animal Farm—Snowball and Napoleon. They decide that the animals should govern themselves according to the principles of Animalism, which they reduce to seven commandments. Snowball perches perilously on a ladder (climbing a ladder is difficult when you have hooves) and paints these commandments on the wall of the barn:

THE SEVEN COMMANDMENTS

1. Whatever goes upon two legs is an enemy.
2. Whatever goes upon four legs, or has wings, is a friend.
3. No animal shall wear clothes.
4. No animal shall sleep in a bed.
5. No animal shall drink alcohol.
6. No animal shall kill any other animal.
7. All animals are equal.[16]

These are to be the unalterable laws that govern how the animals will live thereafter. In proclaiming these seven commandments the law of the land, Snowball and Napoleon are attempting to influence the other animals' behavior by establishing and giving legitimacy to the rules they expect all the animals on the farm to follow. Later, Napoleon secretly raises a pack of vicious dogs who are loyal only to him. His dogs drive Snowball from the farm, and Napoleon consolidates his power. One by one, he alters the seven commandments until, when he and his fellow pigs reign supreme, the seven commandments have been reduced to one totalitarian maxim:

All animals are equal. But some animals are more equal than others.[17]

Orwell's novella is a parable about the dangers of totalitarianism, and Napoleon illustrates the perversion of law by a ruthless dictator who rewrites the rules to suit himself and the toadies who keep him in power. However, influencing by appealing to authority is not necessarily done for evil purposes. Indeed, it's a common way people try to get others to do what they want. When people try to influence others by legitimizing, they are trying to invoke authority. They are saying that what they want or what they want the influencee to believe, accept, or comply with is legitimate because someone or something in authority says so. Instead of using a logical argument, which would take longer and may not succeed, they invoke authority as a justification for their request or position, hoping the influencee will accept it without question. Legitimizing is a shortcut, and it usually takes one of the following forms:

You should believe me		*an authoritative source says it's true*
We need to do X	because	*it's traditionally done this way*
Please do it this way		*an authority (e.g., Mom, Dad, a boss, a professor, a judge, a district party chief, a priest, a rabbi, an imam, etc.) said that's how to do it*

Legitimizing works because obeying and respecting authority is one of the behavioral foundations of civilization. Laws, customs, traditions, agreements, standards, rules, precedents, institutions, positions, and titles were created to enable us to live with each other in an orderly way and to define what is and isn't permissible. These instruments of authority amount to a shared agreement among civilized persons about how to behave, and when people violate these social norms they are often ostracized or punished in some way.

Consider the simple stop sign. It is both an instrument of the law and a symbol of civil authority. It permits the orderly and safe flow of traffic and is normally an effective way for society to regulate how people drive vehicles. In other words, stop signs are an influence technique, a way of legitimizing. The badge a police officer wears is another form of legitimizing, as are the robes a judge wears, the robes and caps worn by clerics, and the robes and mortarboards worn by professors at graduation ceremonies. All are symbols of authority, and people who hold these positions wear them as a way of legitimizing what they do, say, and think—and what they want others to do. There are many ways to legitimize an influence attempt by invoking authority, including:

- Displaying or wearing the *symbols* of law or authority (as previously discussed)
- Citing a *person* who is recognized as an authority (as I did earlier in this chapter when I quoted Robert B. Cialdini and John Kotter, among others)
- Citing an *institution* ("The Supreme Court ruled today that . . . ")
- Citing a person's *title, position,* or *rank* ("The archbishop announced that . . ." or "The CEO wants us to move on this project quickly" or "Mom said we're supposed to wait for her")
- Citing a *group* that represents authority ("The Labour Party has decided to . . ." or "Sunni leaders met yesterday to discuss . . . ")
- Citing *accomplishments* or *honors* ("He is a Nobel Prize winner" or "She won the Strega Prize in 2009")
- Citing *laws, regulations,* or generally accepted *standards* ("According to state law, we have no choice but to do this" or "The standard procedure for sterilizing the site is to . . . ")
- Citing a *previous work, precedent,* or *publication* ("I read in the *Journal of the American Medical Association* that . . ." or "This is how we did it before, and it worked well, so . . .")
- Citing *behavioral norms, morals,* or *traditions* ("After you sneeze, you

should say excuse me" or "The Golden Rule says you should treat others the same way you want them to treat you")

► Citing an *agreement* ("This is what we agreed to do. So let's do it that way" or "The agreement between the parties stipulates that . . .")

► Citing *cultural customs* (Age is venerated in Japan, so when you go to a party you should first greet the oldest person there, even though the person may not be the highest ranking.)

Obviously, these types of authority are not equal in force (laws typically carry far more weight than customs, for instance) and they don't command an equivalent amount of respect. In fact, some people don't respect authority at all. In my research on power and influence, I asked respondents to rank, on a 1 to 5 scale, how much they respected authority. Nearly 8 percent of women and just over 13 percent of men said they had little or no respect for authority (conversely, 62 percent of women and 53 percent of men said they had high or very high respect for authority). Some people will respect one form of authority but have little respect for another. And this raises a crucial point about legitimizing: It can be effective only if the influencee respects the type of authority cited in the influence attempt.

Legitimizing is influencing by appealing to or invoking authority. When you use legitimizing, you are justifying your position or request by citing an authority that supports you.

In the 2009 presidential election in Iran, incumbent Mahmoud Ahmadinejad was declared the victor with two-thirds of the votes, but there were widespread allegations of vote fraud inside and outside Iran. When the outcome was announced—only hours after the polls closed following record voter turnout—millions of Iranians rose up in protest. For weeks afterward, protesters filled the streets of Tehran and other major cities, prompting an often-violent crackdown by Iranian police. In an attempt to bring the populace into line, Supreme Leader Ayatollah Ali Khamenei declared that Ahmadinejad's victory was a divine assessment. Claiming that you have talked to God is the ultimate form of legitimizing, and it is a time-honored tradition among religious leaders who want people to quickly comply with their wishes.

However, Khamenei's divine assurances did not satisfy hundreds of thousands of Iranians who continued to risk life, limb, and freedom to express their outrage. What we witnessed here were people who no longer respected the authority Khamenei represented (or misrepresented, as many of them would say), so his attempt to influence them by legitimizing failed. Again, legitimizing works only if those you are attempting to influence respect the authority being invoked.

Influence Effectiveness and Respect for Authority

As my research shows, most people respect some authorities or some sources of authority most of the time. Then there are the born rebels among us who do not respect most authorities or sources of authority most of the time. As an influence technique, legitimizing will obviously be less effective with the rebels. We often celebrate those rebels—just think of James Dean in *Rebel Without a Cause,* or Jean-Paul Sartre and Simone de Beauvoir challenging convention on Paris's Left Bank, Picasso abusing the rules and traditions in painting, David Byrne of Talking Heads defying expectations in pop music, Albert Einstein declaring that the laws of physics don't work the way Isaac Newton thought they did. There's something wonderfully freeing about thumbing your nose at authority, and we expect the finest of our artists and scientists to do that. Intriguingly, however, the research shows that in business and everyday life, people who disrespect authority are considerably less influential than those who respect it.

As we would expect, people who respect authority are much more likely to use legitimizing when they influence others. But they are also considerably more likely to try consulting, appealing to values, logical persuading, exchanging, and socializing as well. In short, they tend to use more of a variety of influence techniques. They are judged to be significantly more effective at influencing others and are considered to be more sensitive to other people's feelings and needs; more genuine in showing interest in others; and better at resolving conflicts, building rapport and trust, and listening. Clearly, they have superior social skills. Interestingly, when it comes to "using authority without appearing heavy-handed," they also receive a significantly higher rating. When people who do not respect authority attempt to invoke it, they often lack the skill to do it with subtlety and finesse, so they tend to bluntly state what they want and come across as more intimidating as a result.

The Limitations of Legitimizing

People use legitimizing because it is an expedient means of influencing others and can result in quick compliance. When a police officer yells, "Stop!" most people comply immediately. However, legitimizing is a little like the sandpaper in a toolbox. You need to use it sparingly and only when it's the right tool for the job because legitimizing is one of the coarser grades of sandpaper, and it will rub people raw if overused. Even people who respect authority will chafe under a constant dose of it, and, as the flawed Iranian election showed, people must respect the authority in order to willingly comply with it.

Another limitation of an appeal to authority is that it can be a logical fallacy. When someone makes an assertion and then legitimizes it by appealing to an authority, people should question whether that authority can be trusted. A well-known actress appearing in an advertisement for mouthwash may be appealing (because she has high attraction power), but she's unlikely to be an authority on mouthwash. Similarly, if I assert that nonviolent protest is preferable to violent protest, and I support my assertion by quoting Gandhi, I am legitimizing. Quoting Gandhi doesn't make my assertion untrue, but it doesn't make it true, either. However, if you revere Gandhi and know his stance on nonviolent protest, then you may agree with my assertion. But if I support my assertion by quoting Chairman Mao, you are likely to question my grasp on history. The point is this: When you use legitimizing, you have to ensure that the authority you cite is a credible and trustworthy source, and that the people you are trying to influence will accept this authority as authentic and convincing.

Insights on Legitimizing

Ruth Bader Ginsburg and her fellow justices of the U.S. Supreme Court offer an excellent example of legitimizing. Bound by their oaths and the rule of law, they both appeal to authority (in citing legal precedents) and represent the authority others appeal to. Judges, lawyers, police officers, administrators, clerks, and others in positions governed by laws, rules, regulations, precedents, and traditions often invoke authority to justify their statements and decisions. Whether or not we accept what they say, they are the voices of authority.

Born in 1933 in Brooklyn, New York, Ginsburg graduated with a bachelor's degree from Cornell University and in 1954 attended Harvard Law School, one of only nine women in a class of more than 500.

Bloomberg via Getty Images

► Ruth Bader Ginsburg and her fellow Supreme Court justices frequently use legitimizing to justify their decisions.

She later transferred to Columbia Law School, where she received her law degree. In a distinguished early career, she became known for her independence as well as her ability to work with people whose political philosophy differed from hers. She was a research director at Columbia, a professor of law at Rutgers and Tulane, a fellow at the Center for Advanced Study in the Behavioral Sciences at Stanford, general counsel for the American Civil Liberties Union, and a judge at the U.S. Court of Appeals in Washington, D.C. President Bill Clinton (a Democrat) nominated her to the Supreme Court with the strong support of U.S. Senator Orrin Hatch (a Republican). On the Court, she normally votes with the liberals, but her closest colleague is conservative Justice Antonin Scalia.

My research on power and influence shows that people like Ruth Ginsburg who frequently use legitimizing to influence others also frequently use alliance building. I define alliance building as finding others who support your views and then using the power of the group to persuade someone else. For instance, if I want to persuade my boss to support adopting a flextime system for our employees, but I don't think he'll agree if I make the proposal by myself, I first talk to the other line managers at my level. They all support the idea, so I ask them to join me in making the proposal to our boss. By going to him as a group, we are using a form of peer pressure as an influence strategy. In effect, we are legitimizing our proposal through the weight of group opinion. So legitimizing and alliance building are related influence techniques, and it makes sense that someone who frequently uses one would also use the other. Naturally, then, Ruth Bader Ginsburg and her fellow justices on the U.S. Supreme Court are as likely to use alliance building as they are legitimizing in their attempts to influence judicial opinions.

The power sources that correlate most strongly with the effective use of legitimizing are *expressiveness* (because a skillful appeal to authority is likely to be more persuasive and appear less heavy-handed), *reputation* (because legitimizing is better received when it comes from someone who is well regarded), *role* (because people expect those in authority to use their authority now and then), and *network* (because well-networked influencers are better able to invoke the authority of the group as a form of legitimizing and are better connected through their network to other people they can cite as authorities). This is virtually a portrait of Ruth Bader Ginsburg. She is a gifted communicator, has a sound reputation, occupies one of the most powerful positions in the country, and has built an extensive network throughout her career. She is also very knowledgeable in her domain and has access to an extraordinary amount of information. Not surprisingly, *knowledge and information,* as sources of power, are also strongly correlated with the effective use of legitimizing. To legitimize effectively, you have to know which sources of authority will be most compelling and persuasive. So the more you know, the greater your ability to use this technique skillfully.

As we might expect, the power source attraction is negatively correlated with the frequent use of legitimizing. Attraction is the capacity to attract others or cause them to like you. The research showed that people who used legitimizing frequently were judged to be less attractive than those who legitimized infrequently. As I noted earlier, legitimizing is like rubbing coarse sandpaper on someone's skin. If you do it too much, you will rub them raw. Clearly, an adverse reaction to legitimizing is far less likely to occur in the U.S. Supreme Court (as well as other venues where people expect authority to be invoked). In these cases, legitimizing is not only acceptable, it may actually be preferred.

However, in business as well as everyday life, a little legitimizing goes a long way, and you risk alienating people if you overdo it, and the research bears this out. The people who were rated most effective in using legitimizing did not use the technique very often. The reverse was also true. Those who used the technique most frequently were rated lowest on using it effectively. The two skills most strongly correlated with the effective use of legitimizing are, as one would expect, behaving authoritatively and using authority without appearing heavy-handed. However, influencers who use legitimizing very effectively also excel at building consensus, resolving conflicts, and bargaining or negotiating. In short, they are good at facilitating agreement when they can cite the right authority at the right time to bring people closer together.

When you use legitimizing, ensure that the authority you cite is credible and trustworthy and that the influencees will accept this authority as authentic and compelling.

When to Use Legitimizing

In normal business and life circumstances, legitimizing is intended to produce quick compliance or agreement, and it has the power of authority behind it. Use it in these circumstances:

- ► When all you want is compliance, and you don't have time to present a logical argument, negotiate for agreement, or use other influence techniques that take more time.
- ► When what you want is consistent with policies, procedures, regulations, laws, customs, or traditions, and the influencee either is not aware of it or needs to be reminded of it.
- ► When the situation demands unquestioned compliance—for instance, when a law, regulation, contract, or other agreement must absolutely be followed; when safety or something else important is at stake; or when the consequences for the influencee would be significant if he doesn't do what you want. ("Your mother said not to run with scissors, so don't do it.")
- ► When someone in authority is compelling you to influence others and you can legitimize your demands by appealing to their authority. ("The boss says this is how we have to do it.")
- ► When referring to a legitimate authority would add gravitas, credibility, or trusted elaboration to your statements (e.g., quoting from a credible source).
- ► When you are operating in a culture or an organization that is more formal or bureaucratic and following rules and respecting authority are the social norms. In these situations, legitimizing may not only have greater acceptance, it may be expected.

► When your organization is in crisis and the situation is broadly acknowledged and understood. People tend to obey authority more readily in a crisis.

► When the influencee respects authority and is unlikely to comply with what you want unless you invoke authority.

How to Use Legitimizing Effectively

1. Know your audience well. Only cite authorities they will find credible and respect.

2. Refer to policies, procedures, standard practices, rules, regulations, or traditions as the basis for your decision. ("According to department procedures, all engineering drawings should be submitted to . . . ," "The policy manual says we are supposed to . . . ," "Traditionally, the company has handled these situations by . . . ," or "We promise in our promotional literature to . . . ")

3. Cite higher authority in making your request or statement. ("I have authorization from the group vice president to implement this plan, and I need your assistance in . . ." or "The director of manufacturing asked me to look into our use of polyvinyl. . . .")

4. In writing or speaking, use quotations from respected authorities to substantiate or reinforce the points you are making.

5. Where applicable, cite precedents that support your decisions or proposals. ("An earlier 2008 study by the Environmental Protection Agency supports these findings. . . .")

6. Don't overuse this technique or use it in a blunt or heavy-handed fashion. Gauge the influencee's reactions, and if you sense resistance or skepticism, consider using a different influence technique. Across the globe, legitimizing is the least-used of all the influence techniques because, by and large, people don't like to be told what to do, so they may bridle under what they perceive as the heavy hand of authority. Use this technique only when you need to.

KEY CONCEPTS

1. The four rational approaches to influencing are logical persuading, legitimizing, exchanging, and stating.

2. One of the most common ways in which we try to influence others is to make our request or position seem reasonable or justifiable.

3. Logical persuading is the most frequently used influence technique around the world. However, it is often not as persuasive as we would like. A growing body of evidence indicates that we are consistently and often subconsciously influenced by a variety of emotional and psychological factors that make us anything but rational. So people often make emotional decisions and then justify them with logic.

4. Legitimizing is influencing by appealing to or invoking authority. When you use legitimizing, you are justifying your position or request by citing an authority that supports you.

5. When you use legitimizing, you have to ensure that the authority you cite is a credible and trustworthy source, and that the people you are trying to influence will accept this authority as authentic and compelling.

CHALLENGES FOR READERS

1. Of the two rational approaches to influencing discussed in this chapter—logical persuading and legitimizing—which do you use most often?

2. Which of these techniques are you most and least skilled at?

3. What kinds of logical arguments do you find most persuasive? If someone is trying to influence you by logical persuading, what must that person do to be compelling?

4. Think of an important situation where you are going to need to influence someone in the future. Assume that you have to use logical persuading. What will your argument be? What evidence can you present? Why would this person say yes? And why might the person say no?

5. How much respect do you have for authority? Which kinds of authority do you tend to respect more and which ones do you respect less?

6. Imagine the same scenario as in question 4. This time you have to use legitimizing. What authorities would you appeal to? How would you justify what you want by legitimizing? Would the person you are trying to influence respect those authorities? Could you make a compelling case?

CHAPTER 4

BELIEVE ME

Exchanging and Stating

One of the most amusing examples of influence in American literature occurs in Mark Twain's *The Adventures of Tom Sawyer*. It's a beautiful Saturday morning, and Tom had many other plans for the day, but his Aunt Polly is making him whitewash a board fence thirty yards long and nine feet high. He thinks of all the fun he'll be missing and the other boys who'll make fun of him because he has to work. He contemplates paying others to do the work for him, but he has few worldly possessions to bribe them with. Then he has an inspiration. When the first of his friends comes along and begins to taunt him, Tom pretends to enjoy what he's doing: "Does a boy get a chance to whitewash a fence every day?" This intrigues the friend. Presently, he asks if he can take a turn whitewashing the fence, but Tom is reluctant to let anyone else do it until the boy offers him part of an apple in return. It goes on like this, with other boys coming along and offering Tom something in exchange for the joy of painting the fence. Twain writes:

> And when the middle of the afternoon came, from being a poor poverty-stricken boy in the morning, Tom was literally rolling in wealth. He had, besides the things before mentioned, twelve marbles, part of a jew's-harp, a piece of blue bottle glass to look through, a spool cannon, a key that wouldn't unlock anything, a fragment of chalk, a glass stopper of a decanter, a tin soldier, a couple of tadpoles, a kitten with only one eye, a brass doorknob, a dog collar— but no dog—the handle of a knife, four pieces of orange peel, and a dilapidated old window sash. He had had a nice, good, idle time all

the while—plenty of company—and the fence had three coats of whitewash on it! If he hadn't run out of whitewash, he would have bankrupted every boy in the village.[1]

When people have something you want, an often effective way to influence them to give it to you is to offer them something you have in exchange for it. This is a rational form of influencing because it invokes a calculation in the influencee's mind: "Do I want to give up what I have in exchange for something else? Would this be a fair trade?" This calculating may not be conscious, but it is impossible to be presented with a proposal to trade things of value without weighing the pros and cons of the exchange, just as it's impossible to consider a retail purchase without implicitly assessing whether the item is worth the amount shown on the price tag.

Another rational form of influencing that invokes a calculation is stating. In the underrated 2009 satire *The Men Who Stare at Goats,* Ewan McGregor plays Bob Wilton, an investigative reporter who meets a character named Lyn Cassady (played by George Clooney) who says he is a former member of a secret U.S. Army group called the New Earth Army. Members of this unit were trained to use psychic powers to resolve conflicts and defeat their enemies. Although skeptical, Wilton is intrigued and follows Cassady to Iraq to learn more. During the time they spend together, Cassady makes some outlandish assertions about his psychic abilities, which include enhanced intuition, remote viewing, invisibility, cloud bursting, walking through walls, and a form of telekinesis (he stopped a goat's heart by staring intently at it). Wilton doesn't believe all these claims at first, but Cassady makes them with such lunatic conviction that Wilton begins to see Cassady as a shaman and comes to believe that some of his claims are true. Such is the power of stating.

When people try to influence you by stating, they simply assert a viewpoint or position. You have to determine whether to believe what they are saying. You have to calculate, in other words, whether their position seems reasonable, whether it's acceptable to you, or whether you want to challenge it. The more confidently and boldly they state their assertions, the more likely you are to accept them—unless the assertions are outlandish, offensive, threatening, or in some other way unsatisfactory to you. This chapter explores both of these rational means of influencing in more depth.

EXCHANGING

Exchanging goes by many names: bartering, bargaining, negotiating, horse trading, haggling, dickering, trading, and swapping. It's used by people in flea markets, garage sales, marketplaces, swap meets, classified ads, auctions, eBay, Craigslist, and stock exchanges, to name just a few places. Bargaining is deeply embedded in the human psyche and extends back through prehistory to the point where our earliest ancestors learned the survival value of cooperation. Influencing others by offering them something you have for something you want is among the oldest ethical influence techniques we know.

It may seem odd to think of the buying and selling of goods and services as a form of influencing, but make no mistake about it, that's exactly what it is. When you go to the market to buy bread, you are offering money in exchange for the product. And as formulaic as that exchange is, we are acting in a way that attempts to change another person's behavior. Sometimes, we dicker on the price. Sometimes, the seller gives us something at a discount, which is an attempt not only to entice us to buy the product but also to influence us to think favorably of him and come back to buy more or else tell our friends to. The whole process of buying and selling is an exercise in influence, and everyone engaged in the process is trying to influence everyone else.

Influencing by exchanging is often very transparent. Imagine you are trying to buy a rug from a merchant in Tashkent. He tells you of its high quality; he tells you how it was made (he may even show you the people making these fine rugs), how durable it is, how beautiful it will look in your house, how discriminating you are to be talking to him. You love the rug but act as though you are indifferent about it. It may not be the right color, you say, or it may not fit in your living room, or you may find a better bargain elsewhere (he assures you that you won't), and so on. In the end, you buy the rug for a price the merchant says will make his mother weep, and it was more than you wanted to pay, but both of you leave feeling satisfied with the deal you've struck. This whole little drama is an exercise in influencing by exchanging.

Transparent or explicit exchanging also occurs routinely in the halls of Congress and in legislative and governing bodies in every town, city, county, state, territory, tribe, and nation in the world. Whenever rulers or representatives gather to make laws and act in the interests of the people they represent, they haggle, debate, and negotiate compromises in which nothing can be gained unless one is willing to give something up. The art of political compromise is to give what you must in order to get what you can, and virtually nothing gets done in the halls of Congress without an explicit exchange. Representatives and senators (and the lobbyists who try to influence them) would be impotent without the ability to influence others by exchanging. When you are trying to forge an agreement among competing interests, virtually the only influence technique that is viable is exchanging.

In his book *On Leadership,* John W. Gardner wrote, "It is possible to think of the exercise of power as a kind of exchange. You want something from me and you have the power to produce in return certain outcomes that I want—or want to avoid. You can give me an A or flunk me. You can promote me to supervisor or reduce me to clerk. You can raise my salary or lower it. You can give or withhold love."[2] Gardner is referring to an exchange based on the role power leaders and managers possess. However, his concept applies more broadly to everyone because we all have power bases that enable us to influence others by offering to exchange something we have for something we want. Exchanging is influencing through implicit or explicit bartering or give-and-take. In some cultures, this is a highly accepted practice (e.g., Pakistan, China, India, Hong Kong, Taiwan, the United States, and Canada); in others, it is less common to see individuals explicitly exchanging (France, Sweden, Denmark, Poland, the Netherlands), although the kind of exchanging that occurs in marketplaces, stock exchanges, auctions, and legislative bodies is not only acceptable even in these cultures but essential.

When you are trying to forge an agreement among competing interests, virtually the only influence technique that is viable is exchanging.

Some people don't like exchanging as an influence technique because it seems transactional and even seedy, particularly in an interpersonal or workplace context. They may think it's akin to someone saying, "If you look the other way while I pad my expense accounts, I'll recommend you for promotion to supervisor." Occasionally, this kind of manipulative behavior does occur, and it's unethical, but it's not what I'm referring to when I talk about exchanging. The acceptable and commonplace form of exchanging occurs when we barter in good faith, when we ask for our coworkers' help on a project in exchange for some assistance they need, or when we ask for and receive something and then feel an obligation to return the favor later. Here are some examples of influencing by exchanging:

- ► A parent says to her child, "If you clean up your room before dinner you can have dessert." (This explicit exchange is one most parents are familiar with, and it teaches children not only about bartering but also about cooperation and responsibility.)
- ► An employee says to the boss, "The assignment you want me to take is not one I'll enjoy. But I'll do it if you would agree to reassign me to the special investigations unit one year from now." (This is an exchange I actually made when I was in the U.S. Army. My commander agreed to it. I kept my part of the bargain, and he kept his.)
- ► Exchanges between suppliers and customer representatives occur millions of times a day in organizations around the world. In this kind of give-and-take, each person is influencing the other as they reach an agreement or solution that works for both parties:

    SUPPLIER: Joan, I'd like to present our proposed solution to the whole committee.

    JOAN: That would be difficult. Given everyone's hectic schedule, I don't think we could get more than thirty minutes of everyone's time—and probably not until next week.

    SUPPLIER: How about if we give a thirty-minute live overview, and I give them links to a webcast they could view later that would provide the details?

    JOAN: Can you do the overview in fifteen minutes and leave time for questions?

    SUPPLIER: Yes, we'll just hit the high points and then answer questions.

    JOAN: Okay, I'll check people's calendars and let you know when we can do it. But you'll need to be flexible on the time and date.

    SUPPLIER: No problem. Thanks.

- ► A worker, John, says to his colleague, Beth, "Would you mind looking over my outage report? Let me know if you think it's okay. I appreciate it. Thanks." (What's the exchange here? John is asking Beth a favor.

When Beth later needs something from John, she can reasonably expect him to reciprocate. Exchanging is often implicit rather than explicit. Exchanging favors is a large part of how colleagues, friends, neighbors, classmates, teammates, and family members cooperate with one another.)

As this last example illustrates, exchanging is often based on the obligation we feel to return a favor someone has granted to us. In his book on the psychology of influence, Robert Cialdini writes convincingly about the power of reciprocation, which is the obligation we feel to repay debts, favors, gifts, invitations, and kindnesses. He notes that what makes us human is this "web of indebtedness" or "network of obligation" that has enabled us to cooperate with each other and build interdependent societies that bind people together based on sharing, cooperation, and reciprocation.[3] If it weren't for our long-established agreement to cooperate with each other and to reciprocate when someone does something for us, we would not have been able to live in groups or develop a civilization. What this means is that exchanging is deeply ingrained in all of us. Even something as simple as returning a smile when someone else smiles at us is an act of exchanging. We operate, usually at a subconscious level, with the understanding that when we do something for other people, they will feel an obligation to return the favor, and vice versa.

Exchanging is influencing through implicit or explicit bartering or give-and-take. The psychological principle that drives exchanging is reciprocation, which is the obligation people feel to repay debts, favors, gifts, invitations, and kindnesses.

In my experience, exchanging isn't explicit, as a rule, unless you are in a marketplace or in the political arena. In personal relationships, people don't usually try to influence others by making the exchange obvious. You probably wouldn't say to a friend, "I'd really like to go to an Italian restaurant tonight, but I know you'd prefer to eat Japanese food. How about this? If you agree to go to an Italian restaurant tonight, then I'll agree to go to a Japanese restaurant next time we go out." John didn't say to his coworker Beth, "If you will review my out-

age report today, then I'll review something of yours another time."
This is too blatantly transactional for most people, so you are more
likely to say, "I'd like to go to an Italian restaurant tonight. Is that okay
with you?" and "I'd really appreciate it if you would review my outage
report."

As these examples show, most personal exchanges are implicit,
although every now and then the exchange is explicit and amounts to
a negotiation. In either case, this is a rational approach to influencing
because people are, in effect, bartering for cooperation. When someone asks us for something, we place a value on what they are asking
for versus the value of what we can expect in return. For people to feel
okay about an exchange, the value of what is given has to be roughly
equivalent to the value of what is received. If my friend agrees to go to
an Italian restaurant this evening but wants us to go only to Japanese
restaurants for the next year, I will balk because it's not a fair exchange.
If my colleague agrees to review my ten-page outage report now but
later wants me to edit her 5,000-page water table study and ghostwrite
the executive summary for her, then I'll feel that she's trying to take
advantage of the favor I owe her—and I'll decline. This point is an
obvious one but needs to be stated: Exchanging works as an influence
technique only if the parties reciprocate and only if the perceived
value of the exchange is roughly equivalent. You can't ask for more
than you are willing to give in return.

The Limitations of Exchanging

Exchanging is part of the fabric of human life, but it works only when
we can trust that the other party will reciprocate in kind. Consequently, implicit exchanges are more likely to take place among
friends, colleagues, family members, and business associates in the
same culture than they are between buyers and sellers, strangers, people from different cultures, and people representing organizations that
don't trust each other (e.g., between city health inspectors and restaurants that have had safety violations in the past). The four power
sources most closely correlated with the frequent use of exchanging
are character, history, attraction, and reputation. So, in effect, when
someone tries to influence me by exchanging, I will ask myself, in
effect, do I trust this person? How well do I know him? How much do
I like him? And does he have a good reputation? Before granting him
a favor, I need to trust that it is a fair exchange and that he will reciprocate when I need something from him.

In situations of low trust, such as when a stranger tries to influence me by exchanging, I am likely to want the exchange to be explicit and more transactional. I want to know what I'm getting in return for my cooperation. I want that spelled out and maybe written down. Now the exchange is more transparent, which gives me more confidence that I will get what I want in exchange for what I'm giving.

One of the potential limitations of exchanging is lack of trust. Where high trust exists, exchanges are usually implicit and unstated; where there is low trust, exchanges are typically explicit and more transactional. In the marketplace, exchanges between buyers and sellers who don't know one another are formalized, so each party knows the "rules" about how the exchange should occur. If one party actively distrusts the other one, then an exchange may not be possible. In peace talks between warring countries, for instance, the distrust is palpable and exchanges are difficult to achieve. In the end, if there is to be peace, the parties must agree to an often mutually distasteful exchange.

Finally, as mentioned earlier, the value of what is exchanged should be roughly equivalent. Sometimes, however, one person has such a great need that she is willing to give more than she is getting in return. She agrees to host a birthday party for her cousin if her cousin will loan her a dress for a gallery opening she wants to attend. The opening is the next day, and the dress is perfect. Later, the birthday party turns out to be a much, much bigger affair than she'd imagined, and she resents her cousin for "forcing" her into a deal that no longer seems fair. People's perception of the value of what's being exchanged may change afterward, especially when those values are unstated up front, and perceived inequities can later damage the relationship and even cause one party to renege on a stated or implied promise. For exchanging to be an effective influence technique in the long term, the exchange of value must be perceived as fair by both sides, and the level of trust between them must be maintained.

Insights on Exchanging

Kenneth R. Feinberg is perhaps the most skillful mediator since King Solomon. After graduating from New York University's law school, he clerked in the New York State Court of Appeals for several years and then became a prosecutor in the U.S. attorney's office in Manhattan, where he worked alongside future New York Mayor Rudolph Giuliani.

Mark Wilson/Getty Images

► Mediator Kenneth Feinberg is
a master at influencing
through exchanging.

Years later, while working for a law firm in Washington, D.C., he took over a class-action lawsuit filed by Vietnam veterans against the manufacturer of Agent Orange, a defoliant the veterans argued had caused severe health problems for veterans exposed to the chemical during the Vietnam War. The lawsuit had been stalled for eight years as the opposing sides haggled, neither willing to budge from the entrenched positions they had taken. But in just six weeks, Feinberg was able to move them to a compromise that neither side would have preferred but nonetheless found acceptable. Since then, he was asked to help arbitrate the fair market value of the Zapruder film of the Kennedy assassination, to help determine a fair allocation of legal fees in a Holocaust slave labor case, to administer funds to victims and families of victims in the Virginia Tech massacre in 2007, and to determine the compensation of the top executives of companies that had received federal bailout monies after the financial meltdown in 2008–9.

However, he is most famous as the administrator of the September 11 victim compensation fund, a monumental task that he undertook pro bono and completed in thirty-three months. It was the most challenging mediation of his professional life. In the course of it, he was vilified by some family members and praised by others, but he emerged from that experience with the reputation as a master mediator. Most recently, he's been asked by President Obama to administer the $20 billion fund to cover claims arising from BP's Deepwater Horizon oil spill in the Gulf of Mexico. Without question, Ken Feinberg is extraordinarily skillful at influencing people through the technique of exchanging.

Among the more intriguing insights to emerge from the research on power and influence is that there is a strong correlation between the frequent use of exchanging and the frequent use of appealing to relationship, which is discussed in depth in the next chapter. Briefly, when you ask friends or acquaintances for a favor, you are attempting to influence them (to say yes) by appealing to the existing relationship you have with those people. When you have high trust with someone, this technique is very similar to an implicit exchange, hence the strong parallels between the two techniques.

Mediators like Feinberg who often influence others by exchanging also frequently use logical persuading and consulting. They offer logical arguments for why they think a particular exchange has merit or else they engage others by involving them in the problem solving. Feinberg says that he learned to become a much better listener through his mediation experiences. He frequently works by asking questions (to elicit the perspectives of the various parties) and by using logical statements (to point out the efficacy of alternatives to an intransigent position taken by one or more of the parties).

The primary power sources for exchanging are character, history, attraction, and reputation. Character matters because people are more willing to negotiate or exchange with someone they trust. History is important because familiarity facilitates implicit exchanges. People are more willing to make deals with a person they like, which speaks to the power of attraction. People are also more willing to offer and accept concessions when they hold the other person in high regard, which is why a good reputation is important. Negotiators and mediators like Ken Feinberg who are also knowledgeable and highly expressive also tend to excel at exchanging. Knowledge gives them greater capacity to formulate exchanges that are likely to be acceptable to the other party, and expressiveness enables them to articulate the exchange in a more compelling way.

Curiously, the research shows that the power source that is least important in the effective use of exchanging is resource power. It may seem logical that controlling resources others want or need would give the influencer something of value to exchange, yet character, history, attraction, and reputation are considerably more important. These four primary power sources are the foundations of trust, and a key insight into negotiating or exchanging is that trust building is substantially more important than the power derived from wealth or control of resources.

The skills needed for effective exchanging are ones that we see in skilled negotiators and mediators: listening, building rapport and trust, supporting and encouraging others, having insight into what others value, speaking conversationally, finding creative alternatives, showing genuine interest in others, and displaying sensitivity to other people's feelings and needs. Note that most of these are interpersonal skills and involve a deep level of understanding of other people. Exchanging is an effective technique when influencers understand what other people value and are sensitive to their feelings and needs. Influencers who are highly effective at exchanging are good listeners, and they are creative, which helps them find options that others will accept in exchange. And they excel at building rapport and trust. Conversely, if we examine the people who are lowest-rated in effectiveness at exchanging, we see that their highest-rated skills are persisting, asserting, behaving self-confidently, using assertive nonverbals, and behaving authoritatively. In other words, they come on strong and don't know when to quit. They are the proverbial bulls in the china shop, which is why they are less effective when using exchanging as an influence technique.

When to Use Exchanging

As any experienced mediator would acknowledge, the process is more likely to result in compliance rather than commitment. You may achieve an acceptable outcome, but none of the parties are likely to have received everything they wanted. However, in normal circumstances, exchanging can result in outcomes acceptable to everyone involved. Use exchanging in these circumstances:

- ► When you have a trust-based relationship with people and they would be open to granting a favor or request. (It's imperative that you be willing to reciprocate later.)
- ► When the influencee needs or would value something you have to offer in exchange.
- ► When you have a collegial or collaborative relationship with the influencee and cooperation between you is typical. In collaborative work teams, for example, exchanging is the standard modus operandi. People are expected to give and take continually in order to accomplish the team's tasks. The collaboration need not be explicit; however, failure to collaborate will be noticed and is usually punished.
- ► When you have little role authority and need to barter for cooperation. Exchanging is often the influence technique of last resort for people who have little power. Street beggars learn, for instance, to present themselves in a way that makes anyone who gives them money feel better about themselves for helping the downtrodden. In effect, what

the beggar has to exchange is the capacity to make donors feel better about themselves.

► When you are trying to influence strangers or people with whom you do not have a trust-based relationship. In these cases, explicit bargaining is actually more comfortable for both sides.

► When the influencees are looking for a favorable exchange and what you have to offer would be compelling to them.

► When people would otherwise have little reason or incentive for cooperating with you.

► When exchanging is the only way you will reach an agreement or compromise with the other party (which is common in political exchanges).

When Not to Use Exchanging

► When you don't trust the influencee or when he doesn't trust you.

► When the influencee might take advantage of you later and ask or demand more from you than you received. Be careful who you are indebted to.

► When too much explicit exchanging could create a relationship that is entirely transactional. This occurs when parents "bribe" their children by offering rewards for anything they want the children to do. After a while, the children won't do anything without receiving a reward for it. Purely transactional relationships inevitably fail because the price for cooperation keeps rising. In families, the respect children should have for their parents will disappear if every interaction with their parents becomes a transaction.

How to Use Exchanging Effectively

1. Know your audience well. Know what they value and why they would or wouldn't cooperate with you. Use this simple test. Ask, *Why would they say yes and why would they say no?* What would they find valuable or compelling in exchange for their cooperation or agreement?

2. Before you even reach the point of trying to influence by exchanging, try to build good rapport and trust with the people you want to influence. Having a trust-based relationship makes exchanging much easier and more effective.

3. As you are exchanging, listen carefully and be responsive. Look for creative alternatives if people don't accept your initial proposal.

Determine what would work for you and them by seeking an accept-able middle ground. If necessary, be willing to offer more than you had initially proposed.

4. Take the initiative to do unconditional favors for others. Don't attach any strings or explicitly seek anything in return. This way people will more naturally feel indebted to you and will be more likely to grant your requests later. As John Kotter observed, "Successful managers often go out of the way to do favors for people who they expect will feel an obligation to return those favors."[4]

5. Avoid creating transactional relationships based entirely on incentives unless you are exchanging in a marketplace or compromising to achieve political objectives and you don't care if the relationships are transactional.

6. Be creative in thinking about what you have to exchange. Sometimes, what you have to offer may be nothing more than your time, your attention, your friendship or admiration, or your willingness to listen to others when they need to talk. Remember that much of what people exchange in personal and collegial relationships is intangible.

7. Be willing to reciprocate. You must follow through on your promises, and you must be there when they need you.

8. In explicit exchanges, clarify what's being exchanged and why. The more transparent the exchange, the more trust and confidence each side will have in the outcome and the reasons for doing the exchange.

9. When you can, do more for people than they expect. Treat them well, and they will remember it—and reciprocate.

10. Be sure that any exchanges you make will stand up to public scrutiny. This is more of an issue in the political and executive arena, where deals may be struck that are compromising or embarrassing when they come to light. You should never agree to an exchange that you would not want to see printed on the front page of a newspaper or shown on YouTube.

STATING

In the comedy *Mrs. Doubtfire*, Robin Williams plays Daniel Hillard, an out-of-work actor who loses custody of his three children after a bitter divorce and is distraught at the prospect of seeing them only once a week. When he learns that his ex-wife is trying to hire a housekeeper, he disguises himself as an elderly Scottish woman and applies for the job. Wearing makeup, a wig, and a dowdy dress, he arrives at his ex-wife's house and rings the doorbell. When she answers, he introduces himself as Euphegenia Doubtfire. The ruse works, and he gets the job. His disguise and Scottish accent help persuade his ex-wife that he is an elderly housekeeper, but he also influences her with his self-confident assertion that he *is* Mrs. Doubtfire. Although it's a fictional film, it is surprising how often people are successful by simply asserting something they want someone to believe or accept.

The simplest and most direct way to try to influence people is to state or assert your views or positions. In effect, you are making an assertion based on your own authority and self-confidence. This influence technique is the opposite of consulting (which I discuss in chapter 6). Stating is *telling* whereas consulting is *asking*. Here are some examples of stating:

- ► The captain of a ship in distress tells his crew, "This is how it is. . . ." (The crew gets a strong, direct statement from the commander. He is firm, and no one argues with him. Orders and directions from bosses sometimes come in the form of direct statements.)
- ► A manager says to a direct report, "Mark, I need you to do this for me." (The phrase "I need you" makes this form of stating a bit softer, but it's still a direct statement intended to influence Mark to comply.)
- ► A teenager says to her mother, "I don't care if that's what you want. I'm not going to do it." (Stating in this case is an assertion based on one's own authority as a human being. The person hearing this message can choose whether to accept it—that is, be influenced by it—or not. Teenage rebelliousness is often expressed through stating.)
- ► John Gardner, writing about leadership, states that "one of the most important prerequisites for trust in a leader is steadiness. The need for reliability is not only ethically desirable, it is generally a practical necessity."[5] (Gardner wants readers to accept the truth of his assertion but offers no proof other than his bold assertion. His credibility comes from his wisdom, experience, and reputation, but his influencing technique here is stating.)
- ► An upwardly mobile professional is meeting with her manager and says, "I think I am the right person for that position." (When people express their beliefs, they usually use stating.)
- ► In a business partnership, one partner says to another, "We could not have done this without you." (The person hearing this direct assertion may or may not believe it—that is, be influenced by the claim—but that's the partner's intent.)

Hundreds, maybe thousands, of times a day we hear people asserting their thoughts, beliefs, and perspectives with direct statements. If we accept what they assert, they have successfully influenced us.

Stating works for several reasons. First, unless we know someone is a chronic liar or what they assert seems exaggerated or fabricated, we tend to believe what people tell us. Conversely, what's funny about tall tales is that we know they are untrue ("Believe me, I caught a fish THIS big!"), but there's humor in the extent of the exaggeration. Most of the time, with most people (except stand-up comedians), we tend to believe that if someone introduces herself as Mrs. Doubtfire, then she must be Mrs. Doubtfire. Second, to dispute someone's direct statement is to invite conflict, and most people prefer to avoid conflict. So unless the statement is provocative, contentious, disturbing, or fantastic—or listeners have their own agenda and need to dispute what's been said—most people are fairly accepting of another person's reasonable assertions. There are, of course, people who feel the need to dispute virtually everything anyone else says—and they often do it by asserting their own opinions (even louder). Much of the time, however, when people make an assertion, we simply accept it as either factual or an accurate representation of their point of view.

The simplest and most direct way to try to influence people is to state or assert your views or positions. In effect, you are making an assertion based on your own authority and self-confidence.

Finally, people are more likely to be influenced by stating if the influencer is bold, assertive, and self-confident. Self-confidence alone can be incredibly persuasive. I found in my research that people who behave authoritatively are more than twice as influential as those who don't. People who speak with a compelling tone of voice are also more than twice as influential as those who are soft-spoken. Assertive people are more than three times more influential than unassertive people, and people who behave self-confidently are more than four times more influential than people who lack self-confidence. The evidence is bold and clear: If you state your views assertively and self-confidently, you will be substantially more likely to persuade people to believe what you say—provided that your assertions make sense and do not impinge upon or violate the other person's self-interests.

The Limitations of Stating

Stating can be an expedient means of influencing others that brings about quick compliance, especially when the person doing the stating is recognized as an expert or occupies a position of authority. However, when this is the only influence technique the person uses, he can quickly come across as pompous, overbearing, arrogant, bombastic, or self-centered. Stating is a commonly used influence technique around the world. Nonetheless, if it is overused the influencer can come across as intimidating or threatening and can engender noncompliance or resistance.

In some contexts, too much stating can make the influencer appear uncooperative and unwilling to listen to other points of view. In scientific inquiries, collaborative teams, brainstorming sessions, and open dialogues, stating has its place, but influencers should balance it with consulting (asking questions to engage others), logical persuading (introducing logical arguments and evidence), socializing (finding common ground), and other, more engaging influence techniques. Stating is telling, and too much telling from one person for too long can cause a negative reaction—unless the situation calls for it and the influencees expect it, as we will discuss in the next section.

Insights on Stating

Stating would not have worked for Kenneth Feinberg when he was administering the September 11 compensation fund for victims and their families. Stating a position to grieving families, especially a position they did not agree with, would have backfired badly for the mediator. Even as capable as Feinberg was, he still had some lessons to learn. At one point, he said to one family member, "I know how you feel," and the family member bluntly replied, "You have no idea how I feel." (Both Feinberg and the family member tried to influence the other using stating, and in this case, Feinberg learned an important lesson and never made that statement again. So, in terms of influence, the family member was successful.)

However, there are certain situations in which we not only accept stating, we expect it. On sports teams, for example, we expect coaches to be direct and even blunt as they coach players: "Braddock! Keep your eye on the ball!" Teachers in driver's education programs have the same leeway: "Before changing lanes, always check to be sure the lane is clear and then signal your turn." We expect directness from advisers of various kinds, too: "Before making a cold call, do some research on the company and know what is happening in its business. Tailor your pitch to what it needs or is trying to accomplish, and always highlight how our products can help it."

One of the most famous American coaches of all time is Vince Lombardi, legendary coach of the Green Bay Packers in the National Football League. Lombardi was a strong disciplinarian and could be tough on players who weren't pushing themselves as hard as he knew they could be pushed. But he also taught them, encouraged them, and led them to victories in the first two Super Bowls, which Green Bay won by wide margins.

After college graduation, Lombardi had a number of assistant coaching and head coaching positions, most notably at the United States Military Academy at West Point, where he was the offensive line coach under legendary head coach Red Blaik. In 1954, he became part of the New York Giants coaching staff and, in 1959, took over a Packers team that had lost all but two games the year before. In just one year, by demanding that his players be physically and mentally tough and that they devote themselves wholeheartedly to the team, he led them to the league championship game, and the rest, as they say, is history. Lombardi became renowned not only for his coaching but also for his ideas about leadership. He said, for instance, that winning is a habit, but unfortunately so is losing. Speaking about failure, he said that there is no shame in getting knocked down; there is only

► Legendary football coach Vince Lombardi frequently influenced others through bold statements of opinion.

shame in not getting back up. When a notable person like Lombardi expresses a belief in a simple statement, people can accept it or not, but given his stature and the wisdom of his remarks, most people will be inclined to agree with him, and some will find his remarks uplifting and inspirational.

The research shows that people who frequently use stating tend to use it significantly more often than any other influence technique. For them, the default influence technique is not logical persuading, as it is for most people in the world. For them, influencing others does not mean persuasion; it means asserting their will. The downside of this strategy is that stating won't always work, but people who have only one dominant influence technique tend to use it even when it is not working. As the saying goes, if the only tool you have is a hammer, you will treat every problem as though it is a nail.

The research also shows that people who use stating most often typically underuse exchanging, alliance building, appealing to relationship, and socializing. In short, they make relatively little use of the social approaches to influence, and they don't want to bargain. Moreover, while their highest-rated skills are behaving self-confidently, persisting, and asserting, their lowest-rated skills are showing sensitivity to others, resolving conflicts, having insight into what others value, building consensus, building close relationships, and listening. This truly is the portrait of a bull in a china shop. People who use stating least often have nearly the opposite profile—they rank high in social and interpersonal skills and lower in asserting.

The power sources most closely correlated with the effective use of stating are character (people are more likely to accept an assertion from someone of high character), history (similarly, people are more likely to accept assertions from influencers they know well), expressiveness, reputation, knowledge, network, and attraction. In short, people are more likely to be effective using stating as an influence technique if they are known and trusted by other people. Interestingly, the two power sources least closely correlated with effective stating are role and resources. Being the boss doesn't necessarily make someone more effective at stating. Finally, the research shows that people use stating more than they realize. According to self-ratings in the Survey of Influence Effectiveness 360-degree assessment, 48 percent of the people studied said they use stating frequently or very frequently; however, 65 percent of the other people who rated them said they use stating very frequently. (See appendix B for more on the Survey of Influence Effectiveness.) Most people experience themselves as less assertive than they appear to others.

The research shows that if you state your views assertively and self-confidently, you will be substantially more likely to convince people to believe what you say.

When to Use Stating

Like legitimizing and exchanging, which are also rational approaches, stating is likely to result in compliance rather than commitment. Use it in these circumstances:

- ► When you have the authority to be assertive and need quick compliance.
- ► When you are exercising leadership or management and need to be direct.
- ► When you don't want to invite a debate or discussion or don't have time for it.
- ► When you feel strongly about what you want or believe.
- ► When you are with someone who expects you to be straightforward.
- ► When you have been asked for your opinion or perspective; when people are expecting you to be assertive.
- ► When you are joining a team or project and need to establish your voice and personal authority (just don't overdo it).
- ► When someone is dominating the discussion or being overly assertive and you need to ensure that this person is not the only voice being heard.
- ► When you are in a team meeting, know the right answer, have an important contribution, or otherwise need to speak up to keep the group on track.

How to Use Stating Effectively

1. Act with confidence. For some people, this is easier said than done, but there is no substitute for clearly knowing what you want or believe and clearly stating it.
2. Avoid being aggressive, loud, or overbearing. Stating is not bullying; being assertive is different from being aggressive. You are not trying

to beat people into submission. You are just trying to express your opinion in a clear and self-confident way.

3. Don't undermine your position by expressing uncertainties or doubts or offering excuses for having a perspective. Women tend to do this more than men, and it makes them less effective at influencing others. In our research, women were more likely to be advised to be more logical, use their authority more, and do more to show the value of their ideas. Men were more likely to be advised to listen more, be more sensitive to others, and ask for other people's opinions more often.

4. Try to use a compelling tone of voice. Again, it's easier said than done. Some people are born with deeper, stronger, or more resonant voices, and they have a natural advantage. But what contributes to a compelling tone is attitude and confidence. If you have a clear perspective and feel strongly about it, your voice is likely to convey your conviction.

5. Use assertive nonverbals to emphasize your points. Maintain eye contact, stand with your shoulders squared (don't slouch), lean slightly toward the influencee, use broad and expansive gestures, and stress key points by raising your voice. Essentially, it's about conveying energy and enthusiasm. However, what is appropriate varies considerably by culture. What would be emphatic in one culture could be way over the top in another. Know the cultural preferences, and use physically emphatic displays that will gain you respect.

6. If you encounter too much resistance and aren't influencing with direct statements, then use other influence techniques. In business and professional situations, logical persuading and consulting are often the best alternatives.

KEY CONCEPTS

1. The four rational approaches to influencing are logical persuading, legitimizing, exchanging, and stating.

2. Exchanging is influencing through implicit or explicit bartering or give-and-take. The psychological principle that drives exchanging is reciprocation, which is the obligation people feel to repay debts, favors, gifts, invitations, and kindnesses.

3. When you are trying to forge an agreement among competing inter-

ests, virtually the only influence technique that is viable is exchanging.

4. The simplest and most direct way to try to influence people is to state or assert your views or positions. In effect, you are making an assertion based on your own authority and self-confidence.

5. The research shows that if you state your views assertively and self-confidently, you will be substantially more likely to convince people to believe what you say.

CHALLENGES FOR READERS

1. Of the four rational approaches to influencing—logical persuading, legitimizing, exchanging, and stating—which do you think you use most often? Why?

2. Which of these four techniques are you most and least skilled at—and why?

3. In your organization or national culture, which of these approaches is more appropriate? Which do you observe most often in other people? Least often? Why do you think that is?

4. Reflect on the most influential people you know. Which of these rational approaches do they use most often? What makes them so effective?

5. How comfortable are you with exchanging? If you are not comfortable with it, what would make it more comfortable for you? What would have to be true for you to enjoy and be highly successful at exchanging?

6. Think of the people you know who are highly skilled at exchanging. How do they do it? What makes them so skillful at this technique?

7. Think of an important situation where you'll need to influence someone in the future. Assume that you have to use exchanging. What could you offer in exchange for the other person's agreement or cooperation? Walk through the dialogue in your mind. How would it go? What would make it successful?

8. Stating is a direct assertion of your position or need. How comfortable are you asserting yourself? How self-confident are you?

9. Do you know people who are too assertive and who state too often? Are they successful much of the time? Do they turn people off? What effect do they have on others?

10. Imagine the same scenario as in question 7. This time, you have to use nothing but stating as your influence technique. Walk through this interaction in your mind. How would it go? What would you do if the other person disagreed or argued with you or did not accept your assertions? How would you respond to that situation?

CHAPTER 5

FINDING COMMON GROUND

Socializing and Appealing to Relationship

It would be difficult to write about influence without mentioning Dale Carnegie's *How to Win Friends and Influence People*, which first appeared in 1936 and is still being published. In this book, Carnegie identified thirty principles for handling people, being a leader, making people like you, and persuading them to think as you do. Among his principles are "give honest and sincere appreciation," "be a good listener," "let the other person save face," and "make the other person feel important."[1] Although there is more to influence than being friendly and making others feel important, it is hard to argue with Carnegie's advice. What he advocates amounts to exercising good interpersonal skill, and his principles reflect commonsense best practices in the social approaches to influence.

Because we are social creatures, we are more likely to say yes to people like us and people we like. Our relationships matter to us, so we are influenced by what other people think and how they feel about us, especially those closest to us. We are also influenced by the social norms of our society and the groups we belong to. Our thoughts, feelings, and behavior are shaped by the norms and values we learned as we were growing up, the communities in which we live, and the era in which we are living. Finally, we are influenced by how other people behave, which is a deeply rooted impulse. Babies in nurseries often cry if another baby is crying (an indication that empathy is hardwired). Children learn to conform to how other children behave (or they risk being ostracized). Even as adults, we look for social confirmation in the attitudes, values, beliefs, and behaviors of the people we live and work with. This is not to suggest that we blindly follow everything others do, but the social conditioning we experience throughout our lives has a profound impact on us. However we think of ourselves, we have a strong need to be accepted by the people we most closely identify with, so some of the most powerful influences in our lives derive from our relationships with other people, individually and collectively.

There are four social approaches to influencing: socializing and appealing to relationship (which are discussed in this chapter) and consulting and alliance building (which are discussed in chapter 6). These approaches to influencing are essentially about finding common ground with people. By this, I mean that one way we can try to influence others is by invoking the psychological principles of similarity and liking. We try to make connections with people, to close the distance between us and them, to find or build upon the similarities between us. Or we try to make people like us more, to overcome indifference and create empathy.

If we already have a relationship with the people we want to influence, then we might rely on our history power with that person and appeal to the relationship. (Appendix A has an explanation of history power and other power sources.) This isn't so much about finding common ground as using the common ground that already exists. Appealing to the relationship may be as simple as asking a colleague for help on a project, asking a family member for a favor, asking friends to donate to a charitable cause, or presenting an investment proposal to a group of longtime business associates. In each case, the influencees will be predisposed to say yes because of their existing relationship with the influencer. Of course, they might still say no for a variety of reasons, but their inclination will be more positive than negative because they know and presumably like and trust the person doing the asking. This is partly how Bernard Madoff perpetrated his massive Ponzi scheme—he preyed upon many people with whom he had a close relationship (more about him in chapter 10).

The intent of genuine socializing is to relate to people on a human level, to learn more about them and share experiences with them, and to develop mutual understanding and empathy over time and without hidden motives. When Dale Carnegie advises readers to be genuinely interested in other people, to remember their names and be friendly to them, he is talking about socializing as I define the term. This is one of the most commonly used influence techniques in the world, but in some cultures (e.g., Japan, China, Australia, and New Zealand) it is a particularly important influence technique—so much so that you may fail to be influential in those cultures unless you know how to socialize effectively in each of them.

Socializing and appealing to relationship are important influencing techniques. Socializing is the second most frequently used influencing technique in the world (logical persuading is first). Appealing to relationship is among the top five. In terms of effectiveness, my research shows that socializing and appealing to relationship rank second and third in overall effectiveness globally. There is no question that these social approaches to influencing are among the most used and most effective influence techniques everywhere in the world. If you want to influence others effectively, you need to understand what these techniques are, when to use them, and how to use them well.

SOCIALIZING

Appealing to relationship works when you already have a good relationship with someone else. But how do you influence someone you have just met? If you don't already have a history with someone, how do you do it? The answer is an influence technique I call *socializing,* which includes establishing a connection with other people; being open, friendly, and genuine; finding similarities through conversation and shared experiences; and building rapport and trust through interpersonal interactions. In our research, socializing was rated one of the most effective influence techniques in the world (slightly lower than logical persuading and just higher than appealing to relationship). In the forty-five countries I studied, logical persuading was the most frequently used influence technique, except in New Zealand, where socializing ranks number one. New Zealanders are a very social group of people.

Some writers on power and influence have referred to this influence technique as ingratiation. In his classic book on leadership, for instance, Gary Yukl said, "Ingratiation is an attempt to make the target person [influencee] feel better about the agent [influencer]. Examples include giving compliments, doing unsolicited favors, acting deferential and respectful, and acting especially friendly."[2] Still, the term *ingratiation* carries some negative connotations. Some writers have associated it mainly with flattery and have observed that flattery works only when it is perceived to be genuine. However, Ronald Deluga, writing in *Business Forum,* said, "Within organizations, ingratiation is defined as illicit attempts by subordinates to increase their interpersonal attractiveness in the eyes of their manager."[3] The terms often used to describe this kind of manipulation include *sucking up, brown nosing, schmoozing, apple polishing, boot licking,* and being a *yes-man.* We've all known people who behave like this, and whatever words are used to describe their behavior, it is clearly an obsequious attempt to manipulate people (see chapter 10 for a fuller discussion of manipulative attempts to influence others). Largely for this reason, I think the best word to describe this influence technique is socializing.

Socializing includes connecting with other people; being open, friendly, and genuine; finding similarities through conversation and shared experiences; and building rapport and trust through interpersonal interactions.

Socializing operates on the psychological principles of similarity and liking. People are more likely to say yes to someone they know than someone they don't, so socializing is an attempt to get to know the person you are trying to influence and, more important, get that person to know you. It's an attempt to find out what you have in common, such as working for the same company, living in the same or a similar neighborhood, hailing from the same or a similar part of the world, having the same interests or values, belonging to the same clubs or groups, liking the same books or films, having the same perspectives, and so on. In fact, the points of similarity can involve virtually anything. Of course, when we meet and get to know people, we may also discover important differences (e.g., liberal versus conservative outlooks), and the differences may outweigh the similarities. Nonetheless, when we socialize we are attempting to discover similarities.

We are also trying to increase liking. As we get to know people, we generally find some people we really like, and who like us in return. Not only do we share similarities with them, but we may enjoy spending time with them and value their friendship. As the relationship grows, our empathy for these people grows. We understand them better. We care what happens to them. We become invested in maintaining or furthering the relationship. And when we share enough experiences with them, our mutual history power grows, and we can begin influencing by appealing to the relationship. But even before we reach this point, we become more influential with the people we meet by socializing with them. Here are a few of the behaviors typically associated with socializing:

- ► Being friendly and approachable
- ► Introducing yourself in a warm and inviting way
- ► Taking the time to get to know someone at the beginning of a meeting (instead of rushing into the business content)
- ► Listening well; being at least as interested in the person's agenda as you are in your own; being responsive and forthcoming
- ► Being respectful, courteous, and kind
- ► Being genuinely interested in people; asking questions about them; remembering the facts about their lives and interests
- ► Revealing appropriate information about yourself, and being willing to disclose it
- ► Respecting personal boundaries (which often vary by culture)
- ► Being inclusive; inviting others to join you
- ► Showing genuine appreciation; complimenting others without having a hidden agenda
- ► Extending a hand; helping someone when you have no obligation to do so
- ► Showing empathy toward others; being understanding and sympathetic when the situation calls for it
- ► Being trustworthy and manifesting high integrity

Obviously, these are all good interpersonal skills, and that's what socializing amounts to. People with high attraction power are often adept at these skills, as are many extroverts. Dale Carnegie's tips for winning friends and influencing people include many of these skills, and they are often listed as the behaviors of people who have high emotional intelligence. Socializing works because we are more inclined to say yes to people we know and like. However, it's important that the socializing be genuine. Many psychopaths are also adept at socializing, not because they care about other people (they don't) but because they are clever enough to mimic what other people do to gain someone's goodwill. Fortunately, most people have "crap detectors" that signal when a person with disguised intention is playing nice to get something he wants—and then the effect is repulsion rather than attraction. Only when socializing is used genuinely and skillfully is it highly effective at building similarity and liking and creating a favorable disposition in the people you are trying to influence.

Insights on Socializing

The research shows that people who use socializing frequently and effectively also tend to make frequent and effective use of consulting and appealing to values. These three influence techniques are similar in that all involve engaging other people. People who excel at engaging others appear to be comfortable using all three techniques and probably move fluidly between them, depending on the circumstances. They are much less likely to use the more forceful techniques of stating or legitimizing (appealing to authority). It would be fair to say that if they are more comfortable using a softer approach, they will resort to more forceful techniques only when necessary.

Effective socializing depends mostly on likability. However, people who score low on socializing effectiveness also receive low ratings on character. It could be that their attempts to socialize are perceived as "kissing up." Whatever the case may be, these findings support the idea that effective socializing must be—and must *appear* to be—genuine rather than self-serving.

Naturally enough, the skills most closely correlated with effective socializing are interpersonal: speaking conversationally, building rapport and trust, showing genuine interest in others, listening, displaying sensitivity to others' feelings and needs, being friendly and sociable with strangers, and building close relationships. However, two other key skills are rated in the top ten for socializing: conveying energy and enthusiasm and behaving self-confidently. People who excel at socializing are more outgoing and enthusiastic, optimistic, and self-confident. These attributes increase their attraction power and make others more receptive to their attempts to connect.

The Limitations of Socializing

Socializing is one of the most common and effective influence techniques around the world. However, it does have some limitations. First, it usually takes time to build the interpersonal goodwill necessary for someone you haven't met before to warm up to you, although this is not always the case. Some years ago, I was standing in line at the airport, waiting to speak to an agent after the flight I booked was canceled. The man ahead of me was furious about the flight cancellation and was belligerent with the agent. She checked and rechecked the options but said she could do no better than to rebook him on a flight the following morning. He steamed off, threatening to get her fired. When I stepped up, I said, "It looks like you're having a bad day." She nodded and said, "Some people always take it out on us." I said, "I know. Sorry about that." Then I handed her my ticket and said I would appreciate whatever she could do for me—and she booked me on the next flight out.

Sometimes, just commiserating with someone—just being friendly and kind instead of being a jerk—is enough to influence people to treat you better than they treated someone else. That's socializing in action. Generally speaking, however, if you don't have time to build a relationship, socializing is not the best technique (instead, consider legitimizing or stating as influence techniques). Although it normally takes time to build a relationship with someone you don't know, socializing is always an effective "accelerant" of influence. When you are open, outgoing, and engaging with other people, whatever other influence techniques you use are likely to be more effective.

Another limitation of socializing is that its effects are not always predictable. You can do excellent socializing with people and still not build enough goodwill to influence them in a particular way. It could be that no matter how connected they feel to you, they don't have the latitude to say yes or are disinclined to do so for some other reason. Legions of salespeople have been taught to socialize with their customers, and that kind of schmoozing can be effective at creating a favorable disposition toward a particular salesperson and his products—but not always. Experienced customers know what's going on when they are invited to dinner or a sports event with a salesperson, and they know not to allow that socializing to cloud their professional judgment when it comes to purchasing products or services. Does this mean you shouldn't socialize with customers? No. It just means that socializing is often a necessary but insufficient condition for influencing customers and closing sales. Interestingly, because socializing is such a powerful influence technique, some companies prohibit their buyers from socializing with salespeople or accepting gifts from vendors.

Finally, some people are not naturally sociable, so their attempts to socialize can seem contrived and awkward. The solution, candidly, is for them to develop their social skills because there is no substitute for being able to bridge the gap with other people and establish a relationship. Moreover, as I noted previously, if you are not authentic when you socialize—or are *perceived* to be inauthentic—the technique can backfire and create skepticism or resistance, which will make you less influential.

When to Use Socializing

Socializing is a powerful influence technique because when you connect with other people and start building commonality and empathy with them, you increase your effectiveness at influencing them with every other influence technique. So it is an appropriate technique to use all the time, even in potentially adversarial situations such as negotiations between unions and management and between peace negotiators for warring countries. Establishing a human connection softens people's positions and adversarial stances toward one another and makes it easier to find pathways to compromise and agreement. That said, socializing is particularly relevant to use in these situations:

- ► When you have just met someone you need to influence or may need to influence in the future.
- ► When you are new to a group; when you do not have existing relationships with the people you need to influence.
- ► When you are in an unfamiliar situation, don't know the existing relationships between the other people, aren't sure of the politics, or don't know the rules of interaction.
- ► When you lack role authority and need to influence laterally or upward.
- ► When the influencees are receptive to socializing and are warm and open with you first. Then you should reciprocate.
- ► When the influencee invites socializing in some way. Imagine you are on a sales call to a new customer and the person you are meeting has a number of family and vacation photos in his office. People who display personal items in their offices are, in effect, inviting people to socialize.
- ► When you have time for social conversation before getting down to business.

How to Use Socializing Effectively

1. Set aside time for socializing so that it doesn't appear contrived or rushed. Be sensitive to signals from the other person about the appro-

priate amount of socializing. In meetings, when people have reached their "socializing quota," they will typically give some signal that they are ready to discuss business.

2. Take a genuine interest in getting to know the other person and connecting with him on a human level. If it doesn't feel genuine to you, then don't do it.

3. If you don't know the person, break the ice by introducing yourself, exchanging pleasantries, and asking nonthreatening social questions such as, "How are you?" If you're traveling on business, you can ask, "Where's a good place to eat around here?" or "How long have you been here?" Most people are happy to talk about themselves, so another good way to initiate socializing is to ask questions about them: "Where are you from?" or "Where'd you go to school?" If you see photos of children on someone's desk, that's a giveaway, and you can try to get the person talking by asking, "Do you have children?" or "How old are they?" And so on. If the person seems open and engaged, then consider asking more insight-provoking questions (using the consulting technique, which is discussed in chapter 6).

4. Be willing to self-disclose to approximately the same degree the other person is disclosing information about herself.

5. Be present and listen carefully.

6. Listen for and comment on similarities between you and the other person. ("I loved that movie, too. I especially enjoyed the scene where . . .")

7. Smile and be friendly. These simple behaviors go a long way.

8. Focus more on the other person than on yourself. If the person asks a question about you, respond and then ask him a similar question about himself. Don't allow the conversation to be just about you.

9. Try to be as warm and accepting as possible given the circumstances. Of course, this doesn't mean agreeing with everything you hear. The key to effective socializing is authenticity—and accepting that you aren't going to connect with everyone you meet, especially those whose behavior, beliefs, or values are antithetical to yours.

The key is finding similarities that enable you to connect with the other person. Last year, I bought some model trains and accessories for my grandchildren to play with when they come to our house. More recently, I was out of town and traveling by taxi, and the cab driver mentioned that he was a model train hobbyist. His face lit up when I told him about my trains, and we had a nice conversation about our mutual interest. He gave me a business card for the best model train store in his city and asked me to call him when I was back in town so that we could visit the store together and talk trains. I may never need to ask him for a favor, but if I do, he will be more disposed to grant it because we made this connection. Generally speaking, it is better to make connections with more people rather than fewer. So, when you meet people, try establishing some mutual goodwill by socializing. You never know when you might need to ask for a favor or make a request or otherwise call upon someone you've met.

APPEALING TO RELATIONSHIP

In James Taylor's classic song "You've Got a Friend," he wrote that when you're down and need a helping hand, you can just call his name and he'll come running. This is history power in action. It's the power of existing connections with other people: People may feel strong ties to one another (family, clan, or tribal members); they may have many positive, shared experiences (friends, classmates, close colleagues); and there may be a strong degree of liking between them (best friends, lovers, spouses, close family members). When you need immediate assistance, when you need to influence people to drop what they're doing and come help you, it's best to appeal to someone with whom you have a close existing relationship. Whoever these people are in your life, they will nearly always come through for you, and that's why appealing to relationship is among the most frequently used and most effective influence techniques in the world.

Like socializing, appealing to relationship is based on liking and the feelings of similarity we have with other people—but it also invokes the psychological principle of reciprocation. When you do a favor for a friend or close colleague or when you allow that person to influence you, you have a reasonable expectation that he will return the favor at some later time and be open to being influenced by you. Mutual respect, trust, and cooperation depend on a reasonable degree of equity in the give-and-take that constitutes the relationship. Without reciprocation, the relationship would eventually fail. So appealing to relationship goes both ways. It can be a conscious request, where you reach out and ask a colleague or friend for assistance, as illustrated by these examples:

► "Michel, would it be possible for you to trade shifts with me on Thursday? I have a dental appointment that would be difficult to reschedule." (Assuming that Michel and the influencer have a good collegial relationship, Michel is likely to say yes if he has the latitude to make the change. Collegial relationships often involve an exchange of favors and courtesies. Personal favors like this one are the grease that makes the gears of collaboration run smoothly.)

► "Charlie, I have a big favor to ask of you." (This is a pretty direct appeal to the relationship. A close friend is likely to say yes, as long as the influencer isn't asking Charlie to do something he wouldn't feel comfortable doing and provided he has the latitude to do it.)

► "Bonnie, I'm in trouble, and I don't know whom else to call." (An emotional appeal is based on a close relationship. The friend will likely feel guilty if she isn't able to help. Because close relationships are emotional connections, appeals like this one are not unusual, but they can strain the relationship if they are made too often. People who are exceptionally needy may use friendships as a crutch and become a burden to their friends, which ultimately may destroy the relationship. Nonetheless, the temptation to use friends is powerful because appealing to relationship is the influence technique most likely to succeed *if* you have a good existing relationship with the influencee.)

► "I love you." (When one spouse says this to the other, or when a parent says this to a child, it reinforces the emotional bond; in good relationships, the other person will reciprocate the feeling.)

Most of the time, however, appealing to relationship is unconscious. There is no direct appeal or request, but there may be a suggestion, a question, or an opinion. People simply exert influence with close colleagues, friends, associates, or family members through the normal course of their social and professional interactions. For example:

► "You want to go to the movies this weekend?" (If you have the latitude to say yes and enjoy the influencer's company, you will be inclined to say yes. One of the pleasures of close relationships is spending time together.)

► "What do you think about the new leave policy?" (People with good existing relationships often ask for or share opinions as a way of socializing and validating their ideas. Because close friends and colleagues tend to think and act alike, this kind of socializing of ideas is a common method of influencing them—and opening oneself up to being influenced by how they think.)

► "I don't really feel like going out tonight." (Perhaps this is how you respond to a suggestion from the person you are closest to. In good spousal relationships, the partners engage in continuous mutual influencing. I've tried to analyze how my wife and I influence one another every day, but it's impossible to keep track. The flow of influencing back and forth is evident, however. Next time you are in a conversation with your spouse, simultaneously keep track of who is influencing whom moment by moment. Try it.)

We know how appealing to relationship works because most of us have friends, colleagues, or others with whom we have strong relationships—the people you would do anything for and who would do anything for you. The bonds of loyalty between people who share a close relationship can be extraordinarily strong. In fact, the inclination to say yes is so powerful that it can sometimes overwhelm common sense and good judgment. Such was the case with Kevin Foster and his followers in a teenage gang that called themselves the Lords of Chaos. Foster was a charismatic young man who knew how to pervert the power of friendship to satisfy his psychopathic needs. In Fort Myers, Florida, in 1996, the gang embarked on a crime spree that began with vandalism and ended with arson, armed robbery, carjacking, and the murder of a high school teacher. One of the boys, Derek Shields, was a good student and member of the high school band. The others may not have had Shields's prospects but were not bad kids. However, they felt alienated from their mainstream classmates and lacked the courage to stand up to Foster (who called himself God) even when they knew what they were doing was wrong and events spiraled out of control. Today, all are serving life sentences except for Foster, who was sentenced to death.

Because of the human need for acceptance and belonging, we are susceptible to powerful influence from the people with whom we have existing relationships, especially close ones (just as they are susceptible to considerable influence from us). That power derives from our mutual affinity, trust, and liking. It's like a physical force that has tremendous power but limited reach. Appealing to relationship is the most powerful form of influence we have, but it is limited to the people with whom we have the strongest existing relationships.

Insights on Appealing to Relationship

Appealing to relationship is the fifth most frequently used influence technique in the world (it ranks below logical persuading, socializing, stating, and consulting). It is used significantly less often than logical persuading and socializing—but significantly more often than legitimizing, appealing to values, modeling, alliance building, and exchanging. The people who are most effective at appealing to relationship do not use this technique very frequently because (as noted) its use is limited only to those with whom the influencers have a close, existing relationship. The influence techniques they use most frequently are consulting, modeling, socializing, and appealing to values—which suggests that people who excel at building close relationships prefer the social and inspirational approaches to influence and use the rational approaches only when necessary.

As we would expect, the power sources most closely correlated with the effective use of appealing to relationship are character, attraction, history, and reputation. Appealing to relationship is a manifestation of history power, so that power source should be strong. The other power sources are closely correlated because of the effects of liking and similarity. People in close relationships with others are likely to perceive that the other person has integrity, is attractive or likable, and is well regarded in the community. No doubt this is in part a self-confirming projection of attributes people believe they manifest themselves.

Not surprisingly, the skills most closely correlated with the effective use of appealing to relationship are showing genuine interest in others, having a willingness to do favors for others, building close relationships, displaying sensitivity to others' feelings and needs, supporting and encouraging others, building rapport and trust, and being friendly and sociable with strangers. Especially noteworthy in this list is willingness to do favors for others. Appealing to relationship is the only influence technique closely correlated with high ratings for this skill, which suggests that to be highly effective at appealing to relationship you must demonstrate your willingness to do favors for others.

The Limitations of Appealing to Relationship

As noted already, this influence technique only works with people you already have close personal and professional relationships with. And these same people may have expectations about the kind of influencing that is acceptable within the boundaries of the relationship. For instance, you normally could not ask friends or close colleagues to pay your debts, buy your old car for more than it's worth, or do anything else they would consider taking advantage of the relationship. People have a sense of what's acceptable and what isn't in every kind of relationship they have with others. If you violate or even appear to violate those boundaries with people, you may lose power and influence with them. So, although this is a powerful influence technique to use if you have enough history with people, it comes with some important restrictions on how it is used.

When to Use Appealing to Relationship

Appealing to relationship is the preferred influence technique to use:

- ► When the person you want to influence is a friend, close colleague, close family member, or someone else with whom you have a good existing relationship.
- ► When you and the influencee have a natural affinity for one another, even if you haven't known the person that long. Appealing to relationship may work if the influencee likes you or feels a connection to you in some way.
- ► When what you are asking for is within the bounds of the relationship and the influencee would not feel taken advantage of.
- ► When you would like the person to be committed to your ideas or to helping you. Appealing to relationship can result in commitment (instead of mere compliance) if your relationship has a solid base of mutual trust, loyalty, and liking.
- ► When the influencee owes you a favor.
- ► When you won't be compromised by the obligation to reciprocate.

How to Use Appealing to Relationship Effectively

1. Ensure that what you are asking is within the ethical bounds of the relationship. Don't take advantage of the relationship.
2. Be forthcoming yourself. If you do favors for the people closest to you without expecting anything in return (in other words, without exchanging), you will create an urge in them to reciprocate when you need something. However, be careful about making your appeals too transactional. In the best relationships, people are genuinely helpful to one another and no one is keeping score.

3. If someone does you a favor or extends a courtesy, show appreciation for it and reciprocate when you can. The practice of sending "thank you" cards originated because people recognized the value of appreciation and goodwill in sustaining relationships of mutual trust, caring, and cooperation.

4. Be thoughtful about the people with whom you develop good relationships. According to John Kotter, "Recognizing that most people believe that friendship carries with it certain obligations ('A friend in need . . .'), successful managers often try to develop true friendships with those on whom they are dependent."[4]

Influencing by appealing to an existing relationship is a very powerful form of influence, so it makes sense to build close relationships with others, especially those people whose approval, support, cooperation, or assistance you may need in the future. If you are a house painter, for instance, you should build good relationships with contractors and home builders, as well as with previous customers. Those relationships—and doing excellent work—are the keys to keeping yourself employed. If you are a sculptor, then it makes sense to build good relationships with gallery owners, patrons of the arts, and art critics. If you are a staff manager in a corporation, it makes sense to build good relationships with the line managers your function serves, as well as other staff managers, and so on.

My research on power and influence shows, incidentally, that people who excel at building close relationships are significantly more effective at influencing others compared to people who are less skilled at building close relationships. The former are two to three times more effective at using nearly every influence technique, and their skill ratings are substantially higher on all of the twenty-eight skills measured in the Survey of Influence Effectiveness. Without question, your ability to build close relationships is a critical factor in your capacity to influence others.

KEY CONCEPTS

1. Two important social approaches to influencing are socializing and appealing to relationship.

2. Socializing is influencing by establishing a connection with other people. It includes being open, friendly, and genuine; finding simi-

larities through conversation and shared experiences; and building rapport and trust through interpersonal interactions.

3. Socializing is one of the most frequently used and most effective influence techniques around the world.

4. Appealing to relationship is influencing by asking for assistance or support from people with whom you already have a good relationship. This is history power in action, and it's based on the psychological principles of liking, similarity, and reciprocity.

CHALLENGES FOR READERS

1. Socializing is easier for people who are naturally outgoing and connect easily with strangers. How comfortable are you socializing, especially with people you have just met?

2. How skillful are you at socializing? At building rapport and trust? At making interesting conversation? At establishing connections with people you don't know or don't know well? Review this chapter's list of suggestions under "How to Use Socializing Effectively." Which of these skills are you good at and which ones are difficult for you? What can you do to build your socializing skills?

3. Think of an important situation where you are going to need to influence someone in the future. Assume that you have never met the person you need to influence and must use socializing. Imagine that meeting. How could you use socializing to establish a connection and make that person favorably disposed toward you and what you want? How would the meeting go? What would make it successful?

4. Think about the people with whom you have the best relationships. It may be difficult to discern how often and how much you influence each other, but try it. How much do you influence each other's thinking? Plans? Attitudes? Values? What would you be willing to do for these people? What would they be willing to do for you?

5. How comfortable are you doing favors for people you know, especially those you know well? How comfortable are you asking for favors? If you are not comfortable asking for favors, why?

6. Imagine the same scenario as in question 3 only this time the person you need to influence is someone you already know well enough to make an appeal to the relationship. How would you try to influence this person? How easy or difficult would it be?

CHAPTER 6

WHAT DO YOU THINK?

Consulting and Alliance Building

The social approaches to influencing are essentially about finding common ground with people. We try to make connections with people, to close the distance between us and them, to find or build upon the similarities between us. Or we try to make people like us more, to overcome indifference and create empathy. So, we engage other people by asking questions, by involving them in the problem-solving process, by asking for their ideas—by *consulting* with them. The fact that we are asking for their opinions or ideas shows that we are interested in what they think. People thrive on that. They like feeling noticed, appreciated, engaged, and listened to. They like feeling that their ideas matter. The dialogue stimulated by our questions puts us on common ground: We are discussing ideas together and solving problems, and if we jointly come up with a solution, the people we are trying to influence are more likely to support the solution because they helped create it. In effect, they now have some ownership of it. The research shows that consulting is one of the most widely used influence techniques around the world—and one of the most effective.

The final social approach to influencing is alliance building. When we use this technique we are trying to influence through the power of social norms or peer pressure. We may point out to the person we are trying to influence that many other people are already doing what we are proposing, or we may build support for our ideas among our colleagues before approaching our boss. When advertisers say, "Four out of five doctors recommend our product," they are using alliance building. They are also legitimizing by appealing to medical authority, and in fact a strong correlation exists between legitimizing and alliance building (which could be described as appealing to *social* authority). When we build an alliance, we are trying to bring the influencee onto the common ground already shared by the people who constitute our alliance or the common ground defined by the social norms of our company, team, clan, tribe, or society. Alliance building is not used as frequently as the other social approaches to influencing, but it can be powerful in the right situation with the right person. This chapter focuses on consulting and alliance building—two powerful influence techniques in the right circumstances.

CONSULTING

As simple as it may sound, you can sometimes influence someone profoundly just by asking the right question. In a previous book, I observed that "a good question can open a closed door. It can stir people's memories; stimulate them to think about things in ways they've never thought about before; and provoke insight and change by causing them to examine their aspirations, motivations, choices, assumptions, priorities, and behavior."[1] You influence others when you ask questions that cause them to explore and challenge their thinking. Great leaders, teachers, coaches, and therapists use questioning to guide (i.e., influence) others by stimulating their minds and helping them do the change work themselves. Research shows that people retain only about 10 percent of what they learn through classroom instruction by listening to lectures and memorizing facts. However, they retain about 70 percent of what they learn through experience and self-discovery. So a more effective influence technique than telling people something you want them to know is to ask them questions that enable them to arrive at the answers themselves. Here are examples of questions that may provoke insight:

MOTIVATION QUESTIONS (TO PROBE DECISION PROCESSES, PRIORITIES, AND UNDERLYING MOTIVATIONS)

- ► What led you to do that? *or* Why do you suppose they did it that way?
- ► What were the factors in your decision? Which factors were most important? If you had it to do over again, what else would you consider?
- ► What is most important to you? *or* What do you think is most important to them?

CHALLENGING QUESTIONS (TO TAKE PEOPLE OUT OF THEIR COMFORT ZONE OR CHALLENGE ASSUMPTIONS)

- ► I know it's always been done that way, but why? Why can't it be done differently?
- ► What are the underlying assumptions here? What are people assuming to be true that might not be?
- ► I'm not sure that's as big a roadblock as you think. What's really keeping you from moving ahead?
- ► Okay, so it could fail. So what? What's the worst that could happen if it did fail?
- ► All I'm hearing are downsides. What are the upsides to this course of action?

IDEAL OUTCOME QUESTIONS (TO EXPLORE GOALS, DREAMS, AND VISIONS OF THE FUTURE)

- ► What are you trying to achieve? Are you aiming high enough? Under ideal circumstances, what more would be possible?
- ► What is the best outcome? What would you ideally like to see?
- ► If there were no constraints, what would be possible?
- ► What would it take to get there?

HYPOTHETICAL QUESTIONS ("WHAT IFS" TO CHALLENGE SOMEONE'S THINKING OR CHANGE THE PARADIGM)

- ► I know you think the board isn't open to it, but what if it was? How could you make your case so compelling that it would support you?
- ► What if the goal were $40 million? What would it take to get there?
- ► Suppose we didn't go. What else could we do?
- ► I'm as frustrated by this process as all of you are. What if we stopped having these meetings altogether? How else could we syndicate what everyone is doing and engage in productive, joint problem solving?

IMPLICATION QUESTIONS (TO EXPLORE THE POTENTIAL CONSEQUENCES OF ACTIONS OR EVENTS)

- ► What could happen if this event or action occurred?
- ► If you do or don't do [this action], what could happen? What are the consequences of either acting or failing to act?
- ► What would be the impact of doing one thing or another?
- ► How bad could it get? *or* How good could it be?

"COLUMBO" QUESTIONS (PLAYING DUMB, LIKE TELEVISION'S LIEUTENANT COLUMBO, TO GET SOMEONE TO REVEAL INFORMATION)

- ► How does that work again? I don't get it.
- ► What I don't understand is why? Help me out with that. . . .
- ► I'm really curious about why people turned you down. Do you think they understood you? Did they get it? If they didn't, why not?

"WHAT ELSE?" QUESTIONS (TO COUNTER COMPLACENCY OR PUSH SOMEONE'S THINKING)

- ► Okay, that's one reason. What else?
- ► I understand what you're saying, as far as it goes. But what else is going on? Are any other factors important in their decision?
- ► I don't know. Are you sure that's all there is to it? Maybe there's more.

TURNING STATEMENTS INTO QUESTIONS (SO THAT YOU ARE ASKING INSTEAD OF TELLING)

- ► What do you think of Jack Welch's view that Six Sigma projects should be focused on making your customers more competitive? (You are asking instead of just stating what Welch said.)
- ► It seems like you have only two choices, neither of which is very attractive. Do you see any other options? (Instead of saying, "You have only two choices.")

These kinds of questions stimulate people to think more deeply about a subject than they may have previously. However, one insight-provoking question is often not sufficient. You may have to follow it up with another question, and another. If you can do that without the influencee feeling interrogated, you can often help people achieve breakthrough revelations, although you may not know in advance what those revelations will be or which direction the influencee will go—and that's partly the point. As an influence technique, consulting is not about asking questions that lead people to one conclusion (the one you already knew). It's more about guiding them through a process of discovery, and you probably won't know where that process will take them. Still, someone who excels at consulting knows how to ask the right sequence of questions to enable people to have insights they would not have had if the questions had not been asked.

In *What People Want*, I wrote that one of the secrets to managing people effectively is to have a deeper level of curiosity about them.[2]

You can lead people superficially, never getting to know them as human beings, but if you do, your influence over them will be limited to the authority you exercise through your role. On the other hand, you can make a genuine human connection with other people and not only develop your potential as an inspirational leader, but also invoke the key social influence techniques. When you have one deeper level of curiosity, you go below the surface of whatever people tell you, especially about themselves. If an employee says, "I really enjoyed working on that project," you could say, "Great. I'm glad to hear it," which tells the employee nothing. Or you could say, "What did you enjoy about it most?" The employee's response will tell you what she thinks and what's important to her—and the employee may learn something about herself as well. When you show this kind of curiosity about people, you convey that you care about them and what makes them tick. You are interested. You took time to probe deeper. You listened. People will like you more for it, and your capacity to influence them will grow.

Consulting is influencing by asking questions that stimulate and engage others in ways that give them some ownership of the solution.

Once again, the art of consulting as an influence technique is to use questions to guide others without manipulating them. If you already know the answer and you are just asking questions as a means of driving people to that answer, then you are being manipulative. If they recognize what you're doing, they will feel manipulated, may despise you for it, and will certainly learn to distrust you. The ethical way to ask insightful questions is not to presume a particular outcome but to use good, probing questions as a way to stimulate people to think more deeply and discover the right answers for themselves— whatever those answers may be. The finest questions are ones that lead to transformations in the person's awareness, attitudes, or perspectives. As writer Ingrid Bengis said, "The real questions are the ones that obtrude upon your consciousness whether you like it or not, the ones that make your mind start vibrating like a jackhammer, the ones that you 'come to terms with' only to discover that they are still there.

The real questions refuse to be placated. They barge into your life at the times when it seems most important for them to stay away. They are the questions asked most frequently and answered most inadequately, the ones that reveal their true natures slowly, reluctantly, most often against your will."[3]

> *"My greatest strength as a consultant is to be ignorant and ask a few questions."* —PETER DRUCKER

The Socratic Method

A particular application of consulting as an influence technique is the Socratic method, which is used in education as a pedagogical device for teaching students to think more critically about the issues being discussed. In this method, which is used widely in law and business schools, the teacher asks a question and calls on a student to answer it. Based on the student's response, the teacher typically asks further questions to clarify the student's thinking, solicit greater specificity, or challenge the student's assumptions. The teacher may also pose a hypothetical situation and then use the Socratic method to challenge students to see a situation from various perspectives. In the 1973 film *The Paper Chase,* Professor Kingsfield explains this method to his students:

> We use the Socratic method here. I call on you, ask you a question, and you answer it. Why don't I just give you a lecture? Because through my questions you learn to teach yourselves. Through this method of questioning, answering, questioning, answering, we seek to develop in you the ability to analyze that vast complex of facts that constitute the relationships of members within a given society. Questioning and answering. . . . You teach yourselves the law, but I train your mind. You come in here with a skull full of mush, and you leave thinking like a lawyer.[4]

The Socratic method has come under some criticism, in part because, in the wrong hands, it "resembles a game of 'hide the ball' in which the professor asks questions that he knows the answers to while his students do not. The object of the game is to produce the answer that the professor thinks is correct. If the student fails to answer correctly, personal humiliation follows in various forms."[5] Manipulative questioning is a real issue, of course. If the purpose of your questioning is to lead someone to discern what's in your mind, then it is a game. However, if the questions are intended to teach students the kinds of questions that are useful in the process of discovery and critical examination, then it is an effective form of influence, and I have seen many business leaders use questions in this way. When he was teaching at GE's Crotonville, New York, campus, Jack Welch was famous for asking tough questions of GE managers that forced them to examine their assumptions and priorities. He taught several generations of GE leaders how to think about business and management. That is effective influencing using the consulting technique.

Building Ownership Through Questioning

Another application of consulting is to engage influencees in the problem-solving process so they codevelop the solution and thus have some ownership of it. People are more willing to support a solution that they have helped create. So you can influence others, for instance, by asking for their reaction to a proposal you plan to make and then incorporating some or all of what they advise as you revise your proposal. When you show them your revised proposal, which now includes their ideas, and then ask for their support, they are more likely to say yes, in part because they feel some ownership in the final product and in part because they will want to appear consistent (and, of course, they had already blessed the parts of your proposal that they had no comments on earlier). People like being asked for their input; it validates them when you improve your proposal by incorporating their ideas. This kind of influencing occurs regularly in meetings where one attendee presents an idea and asks for reactions, or when a leader says, "Let's brainstorm some creative ways we could approach our markets." When people are asked to engage in problem solving or idea generation, they are more likely to support the outcome for the simple reason that participation tends to increase commitment. If people see some of their ideas in the solution, and if they concur with the final outcome, they will be even more strongly committed to the solution.

So, a powerful way to influence people is to present an idea, a hypothesis, a plan, or a proposal to the people you want to influence and then ask for their advice, suggestions, or feedback. In effect, you turn them into consultants to you. Clearly, you should use this technique only if you are open to what the influencees have to say. Furthermore, if you can incorporate some of their ideas without compromising the integrity of the final product, then you should do so. In essence, consulting is influencing through collaboration. In our research, consulting ranks fourth in frequency of use and effectiveness among the ten positive influence techniques, and it is especially prominent in the United States, which ranks first in the world in the use of consulting.

Insights on Consulting

One of the masters of influencing through the consulting method was Peter Drucker, the legendary teacher, coach, and consultant to such renowned CEOs as Alfred Sloan Jr. at General Motors, Jack Welch at General Electric, and Andy Grove at Intel. Drucker was born in Vienna in 1909 to a respected family. His mother had studied medicine, and his father was an attorney and senior civil servant in the Austro-Hungarian Empire. During his childhood years, intellectuals, scientists, artists, and high-ranking government officials met regularly in his family's home for wide-ranging discussions, and the young Drucker sat spellbound as luminaries like Sigmund Freud (a family friend) expressed their views and debated them vigorously over schnapps and cigars. From that rich intellectual foundation, Drucker developed his interests in business, economics, and law. He graduated from the University of Frankfurt with a doctorate in international and public law in 1931, but he soon found that the practices of economics and law were less interesting to him than organizational behavior and the practice of management, to which he devoted the rest of his life.

In 1933, as Adolf Hitler and the Nazis gained power, Drucker left Germany for England and later settled in the United States. He taught business and related subjects at Bennington College in the 1940s; at New York University in the 1950s and 1960s; and then at Claremont Graduate University, where he developed the country's first Executive MBA program. Throughout his long teaching career, he also served as a consultant to numerous executives and corporations—and he published nearly forty books, which have been translated into more than thirty languages. But much of Drucker's influence on management and business stemmed from the revolutionary ideas he either introduced or promoted, including decentralizing, treating employees as assets, viewing corporations as communities, and believing that businesses exist to serve customers (rather than existing to earn profits). Drucker was among the first business thinkers to elevate the importance of marketing and customer service and to consider professional managers more important to organizations than charismatic leaders.

George Rose/Getty Images

► Management guru
Peter Drucker did
some of his best
consulting simply by
asking questions.

Finally, he anticipated the paradigm shift in the workforce by recognizing the rise of knowledge workers and the importance of building and retaining talent as a business strategy.

Despite his extraordinary contributions to business and management practice, Drucker had many critics. In his lectures, he sometimes made factual errors, which tarnished his image and caused some people to dismiss him, and throughout his life some academics criticized him because they felt his work and ideas were not sufficiently grounded in research. These issues notwithstanding, Drucker had a remarkable amount of influence on business practice as it evolved during the twentieth century. After his death in 2005, Jack Welch said, "The world knows he was the greatest management thinker of the last century."[6] Like all good consultants, Peter Drucker was an expert at asking questions. According to *Businessweek*, "It was never [Drucker's] style to bring CEOs clear, concise answers to their problems but rather to frame the questions that could uncover the larger issues standing in the way of performance. 'My job,' he once lectured a consulting client, 'is to ask questions. It's your job to provide answers.'"[7] In this approach, Drucker exemplifies influencing by asking questions.

This influence technique is the fourth most frequently used influence technique in the world (after logical persuading, socializing, and stating). It also ranks fourth in effectiveness globally (after logical persuading, socializing, and appealing to relationship). That's why I also consider consulting one of the five influence power tools.

One of the most interesting findings from the research is that the effective use of consulting is most closely correlated with the power sources character and attraction. This indicates that people who excel at collaborating with others and engaging them by asking questions are perceived to have high character and be very likable, which may be true because influencees are projecting these qualities on the influencers because of the positive feelings they experience at being asked for advice. So if you are adept at influencing by consulting, you are likely to be perceived as having higher character and attraction power. Why is this important? Because it has the halo effect of increasing other power sources and making you more influential overall.

People who frequently use consulting often also frequently use socializing, appealing to values (an inspirational approach to influencing), and exchanging. Socializing and exchanging both involve a high degree of social interaction, so these correlations make sense. However, the correlation with appealing to values is interesting. It suggests that people who excel at consulting and use it frequently are perceived to be more inspirational than influencers who are more apt to use stating, which is a telling strategy. There is a strong correlation between the effective use of consulting and the effective use of logical persuading. It seems likely that the most effective influencers don't use one or the other technique exclusively. They probably blend telling and asking, logic and consulting. Furthermore, asking the kinds of questions that provoke insight is not an easy skill to acquire. It takes both cognitive and emotional intelligence to ask skillful questions at the right time, and in fact there is a close correlation between the effective use of consulting and the skill of logical reasoning.

The skills most closely correlated with the effective use of consulting are listening, having a genuine interest in others, building rapport and trust, supporting and encouraging others, speaking conversationally, asking probing questions, and logical reasoning. This finding supports my argument that people who use consulting well are not manipulative. They have a genuine interest in other people. They are exceptional listeners. They build trust and are perceived as being supportive and encouraging.

The Limitations of Consulting

Consulting has two key limitations as an influence technique: It takes longer than some other techniques, and you can't control or predict the outcome. Engaging others by asking questions and inviting a discussion is obviously more time-consuming than stating or legitimizing. However, if you have time and the influencee's commitment to the course of action is important to you, few influence techniques are better than consulting.

The bigger issue, for some people, is the control they relinquish when they invite others to contribute ideas and open up the discussion to alternative answers. If you are a professor of mathematics, for instance, and there is only one right answer to a particular problem, then the Socratic method is probably not the best pedagogical technique to use (a lecture followed by an application or simulation would be better). In business, if you have a well-developed proposal with little margin for change, then using consulting to gain someone's buy-in may not be the best technique (instead, you might use logical persuading or legitimizing). Consulting is a collaborative technique. Its power comes from engaging people in the subject matter. If you are comfortable doing that and you have time, then consulting is an effective strategy.

When to Use Consulting

Consulting is an excellent technique to use in these circumstances:

- ► When you are trying to build an alliance. Our research shows that people who are most adept at alliance building use consulting, modeling, and logical persuading as their three primary techniques for building their alliance. Then they use the social authority of the alliance to try to influence others.
- ► When you are teaching or coaching. The Socratic method or variations of it are excellent ways to guide others in discovery and learning in most subjects.
- ► When you want to stimulate people to challenge their assumptions and develop new insights or perspectives. Questioning of this kind requires some skill, but it is highly effective when done well.
- ► When your purpose is to engage others in a thoughtful dialogue and you can use questions to stimulate the discussion and lead by asking insightful questions. Consulting is a very useful tool for team leaders and managers who need to raise the performance of their teams or groups.
- ► When you want or need to gain the influencee's commitment to a course of action or plan. Consulting, modeling, and appealing to values are the three influence techniques most likely to result in commitment or, beyond that, leadership. When you are trying to inspire

others, a combination of appealing to values and consulting can be very powerful.

- ► When the quality of the solution would be enhanced by incorporating multiple points of view.
- ► When you are trying to influence many people at once. Posing the right question to a large audience can influence many people simultaneously.
- ► When the people you want to influence might be antagonistic toward you, and asking questions would engage them and help them see that you are open to their ideas and feelings. Trying to use logical persuading or stating to a hostile audience nearly always fails. However, a softer approach, like asking thoughtful questions, can gain converts and change people's opinions of you. Asking is better than telling if you are trying to win people over.

How to Use Consulting Effectively

1. Listen. The interpersonal skill most closely correlated with the effective use of consulting is listening.
2. Don't ask leading questions or questions designed to direct people to a particular right answer. In short, don't be manipulative. Consulting works best when there are many right answers and when your purpose is to solicit and use ideas from others.
3. Ask insightful questions that provoke thought. Review the examples of motivation questions, what-if questions, "what else?" questions, and the others that were listed previously in this chapter. Before you engage with influencees, it is often useful to brainstorm a list of insightful questions you might ask them. Have a repertoire of questions in mind as you begin the dialogue, but also be open to new questions that arise based on what they tell you (remember, you've got to listen to them first). The finest consulting dialogues don't sound like an interrogation or an interview; they sound like naturally flowing conversations where the questioner is keenly interested in what the influencees are saying.
4. Probe more deeply than you normally would. Remember the axiom about having one deeper level of curiosity about the people you are talking to.
5. Be open to what the influencees are telling you. Weave them into your plan or solution if you can do so without compromising quality or integrity.

6. When you use people's ideas, find a way to credit them for their ideas whenever possible. Even a simple "Thanks for your feedback" shows appreciation for what they contributed and will help reinforce their "ownership" and implicit approval of the outcome.

ALLIANCE BUILDING

Numerous research studies have shown that we are influenced not only by the psychological forces of liking and seeing similarity with other people, but also by social proof. That is, people have a tendency, especially in ambiguous or uncertain situations, to want to see what others are doing before deciding how to behave. As the authors of one book on persuasion noted, "When people are uncertain about a course of action, they tend to look outside themselves and to other people around them to guide their decisions and actions."[8] Imagine that you are at a chamber music concert. The musicians finish their first piece. It's a virtuoso performance, and you are inclined to rise and give them a standing ovation, but no one else stands. So you stay seated, thinking that if you stand and no one else does, you'll look foolish. The musicians perform another piece, and it's another outstanding performance. You stay seated, applauding, but then two people in front of you stand, and then others follow. So now you rise, joining the crowd of people now applauding on their feet. This is social proof in action.

The use of canned laughter on television situation comedies is another manifestation of social proof. Even though viewers know the laughter is fake, research shows that viewers find such programs funnier with canned laughter than without. Like it or not, our behavior is influenced by the herd, even if the herd is electronic! We want to fit in. We fear being ostracized. We care what other people think. When we aren't sure about something, we ask others or observe what they are doing before we act. Of course, I'm generalizing here. There are many cases where we don't care what others think, where we want to be alone or are confident in our beliefs and don't need social validation. Be that as it may, it would be foolish to dismiss the power or pervasiveness of social proof. It influences more of our thinking than we realize.

Alliance building is the attempt to influence others by invoking social proof. Here are some examples of alliance building:

► Several students are talking about what they are going to do after school. Tommy wants to play soccer but the rest want to play baseball.

Tommy keeps arguing for soccer. Then one of the boys says, "Come on, Tommy. Everybody else wants to play baseball." (Peer pressure is one way influencers use social proof to gain agreement. The alliance consists of the students who want to play baseball.)

► During the first meeting of a new task force, the woman leading the team says, "I think we should set some ground rules about how we want to work together. You were selected for this task force because you've all been key members of high-performing teams. From your perspective, what made those teams work so well? What ground rules would you suggest?" (By asking them to generate the ground rules, the leader is making every member of the team part of her alliance. The ground rules amount to social norms she can later use if individual members become uncooperative, because she can then say, "As you recall, we all agreed . . . " This is a clever use of alliance building because the influencees themselves created the social proof the leader can later use to influence their behavior.)

► An instructor is conducting a seminar on workforce planning and is demonstrating a technology application for scenario modeling. One participant strongly asserts that they'll never use this software and should move on, but the instructor believes it's important to understand how these kinds of programs work. Rather than force the issue with the vocal participant, the instructor turns to the group and asks if they'd like to continue with the demonstration or move on. The overwhelming majority say they'd prefer to see the rest of the demonstration, so the instructor continues.

► A research scientist at a laboratory writes a technical paper and asks a number of colleagues to review and comment on it. He revises the paper based on their feedback and then submits it to the publications committee, noting that he has completed an extensive peer review inside the lab. (By incorporating his peers' feedback in the revised paper, he has in effect made them allies in his effort to persuade the publications committee to accept his paper.)

► Several employees would like to work on a flextime schedule, something their company currently does not permit. They don't think their boss will agree and know it would represent a major change in company policy. So they decide to investigate the pros and cons of flextime and research how it's been used in other companies. Once they've gathered their information, they poll other employees to find out how widespread interest in flextime might be and learn that about one-third of employees would be interested in it. So they approach both their manager and the director of human resources with the information they've compiled. Their manager is skeptical but agrees that the HR director should explore the costs and benefits of this policy change. After his review, the HR director concludes that the policy change would be beneficial and recommends it, with the manager's blessing, to the executive committee.

This final scenario is a classic example of alliance building as an influence technique in the workplace. Believing that their boss won't support the policy change if they go to her directly, the employees find the evidence they need to support their case, build a larger alliance by identifying and engaging other employees who would like to have a flexible work schedule, and then approach their boss and the HR director together. After reviewing their proposal, the HR director decides to support it and becomes a key member of their alliance as the proposal goes to the executive team. When you don't have the power to influence someone any other way, building an alliance of supporters is often not only the *most effective* influence technique you have, it may also be the *only* one you have. Another key lesson is that building an alliance requires other influence techniques. The employees in this scenario surveyed other employees (consulting) and researched how other companies used flextime. Then they presented their proposal (logical persuading) to the two managers. However compelling their case might have been, the added weight of the alliance they'd built was social proof of the merit of the proposal and helped persuade the managers to accept it.

Alliance building is the attempt to influence others by invoking social proof. When used in the right situations, it can be very powerful.

Alliance building is a staple of influencing in politics and government, but it also frequently occurs in business and other organizations whenever someone builds support among others for a plan, a pro-posal, or an initiative before taking it to the authorities who can approve it. It is also a useful technique whenever a group of people agree on ground rules, operating principles, codes of conduct, or bylaws and then require anyone else joining their group to abide by those agreements. The latter is an example of *social norming*. In every group, norms that determine which behaviors are acceptable and which aren't either are selected (e.g., by setting ground rules) or emerge. For individuals to remain members in good standing, they must adhere to the group's norms. If someone violates those norms, the group leader or other members will likely remind the errant person what they had agreed to. In cases of serious violations, the miscreant may be punished or ostracized. So we can think of a group, especially one that has completed the norming process, as a type of alliance. Someone joining the group has to be socialized by learning the group's norms, and existing members are resocialized every time someone or something reminds them of the rules they agreed to follow. People influence by alliance building whenever they reinforce the social norms of the group. This type of influencing is similar to legitimizing because it amounts to an appeal to (social) authority.

Insights on Alliance Building

A remarkable example of alliance building as an influence technique occurred in 1990 after Iraq invaded Kuwait. Very soon after the Iraqi invasion, the U.N. Security Council passed a resolution condemning the invasion. The Arab League passed a similar resolution but demanded that the solution come from within the Arab League and warned about external forces becoming involved in the conflict. Several days later, the U.N. Security Council voted to impose economic sanctions against Iraq and authorized a naval blockade. Posturing and negotiating ensued on all sides of the conflict, but Iraq refused to withdraw its forces unless acceptable concessions were made by others. Then the U.N. Security Council passed a resolution calling for the immediate withdrawal of Iraqi forces by mid-January 1991, which Saddam Hussein rejected.

When it became increasingly clear that diplomatic solutions to the crisis would not succeed, the George H. W. Bush administration began creating a coalition to oppose and forcibly remove the Iraqis from Kuwait. Eventually, this coalition included Argentina, Australia, Bahrain, Bangladesh, Belgium, Canada, the Czech Republic, Denmark,

Egypt, France, Greece, Honduras, Hungary, Italy, Malaysia, Morocco, the Netherlands, New Zealand, Niger, Norway, Oman, Pakistan, the Philippines, Poland, Portugal, Qatar, Saudi Arabia, Senegal, Sierra Leone, Singapore, South Korea, Spain, Sweden, Syria, Turkey, the United Arab Emirates, and the United Kingdom. Germany and Japan contributed funding but no troops.

A remarkable number of Arab and Middle Eastern countries joined the coalition, which added to the Bush administration's global credibility and support for military intervention. After the coalition liberated Kuwait and entered Iraq, Saddam Hussein attempted to fracture the alliance by firing SCUD missiles into Israel. Had the Israelis responded with force, Arab members of the coalition would likely have withdrawn their support for the coalition, but the Bush administration wisely counseled Israel to exercise restraint, and the Israelis complied. The members of the alliance had differing reasons for joining. Some opposed Iraq's aggression. Some feared that Iraq would push on and occupy the oil fields in Saudi Arabia. Some joined because of offers to receive economic aid or have debts forgiven, and some may have been responding to the need to maintain good diplomatic relations with important allies or world powers. Whatever their reasons for joining, the Bush administration and its close allies drove the formation of the alliance and used various influence techniques to create a strong, global coalition to oppose Iraqi aggression.

Alliances of this magnitude are rare, but on a lesser scale they occur periodically in business as companies form alliances with suppliers, create partnerships with key customers, or even join with competitors occasionally to jointly bid on significant projects that neither might be able to win on their own. Alliance building is most useful when individual influencers are not powerful enough by themselves to accomplish their influence goals. The research shows that alliance

► President George H. W. Bush, Secretary of Defense Dick Cheney (left), and Chairman of the Joint Chiefs of Staff Colin Powell (right) were among the principal architects of the Desert Storm alliance.

Jerome Delay/AFP/Getty Images

building as a deliberate influence technique does not occur as frequently as the other influence techniques. Globally it ranks ninth (just ahead of exchanging). Interestingly, the people who are rated highest in effectiveness at alliance building use it less often than any other influence technique, which supports the conclusion that alliance building is a technique to be used only in special circumstances.

The research also shows that people with high role power are rated the least effective at using alliance building, which suggests that if they have considerable role authority, they don't need to build alliances. A comparison of the people who are least and most effective at alliance building reveals that the most closely correlated power sources for those who are highly effective are reputation, expressiveness, attraction, knowledge, and network. Clearly, having a good reputation and being well connected can help you build an alliance. Being expressive, likable, and knowledgeable will also attract people to an alliance or make it more palatable to influencees when you invoke social proof. The people who are best at alliance building have superior skills in these areas: building consensus, resolving conflicts and disagreements among others, building rapport and trust, taking the initiative to show others how to do things, convincing people to help them influence others, using authority, and having insight into what others value. They also excel at bargaining or negotiating.

The Limitations of Alliance Building

The limitations of alliance building are similar to those of legitimizing. Unless it's done with finesse, alliance building can seem heavy-handed. The target of the alliance-building strategy might feel like people are "ganging up" on him and pressuring him to do something he doesn't want to do. Moreover, some people resist adhering to group norms just for the sake of getting along with others. They may not like conforming or "going along with the crowd." Some people may resist alliance building simply because it feels like they're being pressured.

Applying social pressure can also lead to "group think," the phenomenon where people in groups tend to think alike because no one wants to challenge what appears to be the prevailing line of thought. For this reason, you should be cautious about using alliance building to influence a decision unless you are certain that the relevant information is available, the right people have been consulted, and the ideas have been carefully examined and challenged.

When to Use Alliance Building

Alliance building can be an effective influence technique to use:

- ► When norms, customs, traditions, or agreements exist that the influencee(s) are likely to respect.
- ► When you can identify potential allies who would share and support your vision, goals, perspectives, or initiatives.
- ► When you don't have a strong enough power base to persuade the influencee using other influence techniques and you need other people's support, expertise, or encouragement.
- ► When the influencee would require or respect evidence of broader support for an idea or a proposal and won't be moved unless you already have a consensus. Some leaders/managers operate this way. They are participative by nature and expect you to discuss ideas with others and present the team's view.
- ► When your organizational culture favors participative management or collaboration.
- ► When the person you want to influence has already shown that he is influenced by public or group opinion.
- ► When applying social pressure will not result in a suboptimal solution.

How to Use Alliance Building Effectively

1. Before "ganging up" on someone, try other, less threatening influence techniques. An alliance built to influence a single, more powerful individual (such as your boss) can appear mutinous.
2. Consider whether other people are likely to support you and whether the influencee is likely to respond favorably to an alliance or group perspective.
3. Identify likely allies and think about why they would or would not support you. Then approach them using other influence techniques to try to gain their support. At a minimum, they should agree with your purpose. Ideally, they would also have something to gain by helping you achieve your purpose.
4. Try to get some powerful people on board first. Ideally, they should be well networked, have an excellent reputation, be credible, and be visible in the organization. If you have them as allies, it will be easier to enlist the support of other people.
5. If any of your allies are opinion leaders in your organization, consult with them on the best way to accomplish the goal and try to persuade

them to help you influence others. Getting their active involvement will increase the momentum. If they are well connected, see if they can reach out through their network of contacts for additional support.

6. Consider establishing a team, a task force, an ad hoc committee, an advisory group, or a technical panel to explore and advance the ideas. If these kinds of groups are relevant, they may add visibility, credibility, and prestige to your effort.

7. Actively maintain the alliance. Don't assume that once on board, always on board. If your influence attempt will unfold over time, you may need to work at sustaining alliance members and their commitment and active support.

KEY CONCEPTS

1. Two important social approaches to influencing are consulting and alliance building.

2. You can sometimes influence someone profoundly just by asking the right question. Consulting is influencing by asking questions that stimulate and engage others in ways that give them some ownership of the solution.

3. The kinds of questions that may provoke insight include motivation questions, challenging questions, ideal outcome questions, hypothetical (what-if) questions, implication questions, "Columbo" questions, and "what else?" questions.

4. One powerful way to influence people is to present an idea, a hypothesis, a plan, or a proposal and then ask for their advice, suggestions, or feedback. In effect, you turn people into consultants to you. By using some of their input, you make them co-owners of the outcome so that they are more likely to support it.

5. Alliance building is the attempt to influence others by invoking social proof. The people who use alliance building most effectively do not use it very often. When used in the right situation, however, alliance building can be very powerful.

CHALLENGES FOR READERS

1. Consulting is a powerful influence technique, especially if you can provoke insight in others by asking the right questions. How would

you rate your ability to ask insight-provoking questions? Return to the list of sample questions (presented previously in this chapter) and identify the ones that you don't normally use. Find some situations where you can ask these questions and practice using them. It may feel awkward at first, but over time you will master them.

2. Think of an important situation in which you will need to influence someone in the future. Assume that you have to use consulting. How will you engage this person? What questions will you ask? Brainstorm a list of the most compelling questions you could ask. Then go do it.

3. The challenge with consulting is to incorporate some of what other people tell you so that they feel some ownership of the solution and are more likely to support it. How will you do that? One hint: You have to be open to a solution that is not entirely your own.

4. How effective are you at building alliances when you need to use social proof to influence someone? What do you do well in alliance building? What could you improve?

5. Think about the people you know who use this technique well. What do they do? Why are they effective?

6. Imagine the same scenario as in question 2. This time, you probably won't succeed in influencing the person unless you build an alliance. Who would you try to bring on board? How would you persuade them to support you? Play out the whole scenario. What would you do to build your alliance?

CHAPTER 7

FINDING INSPIRATION

Appealing to Values and Modeling

In the third summer of the American Civil War, Jefferson Davis, president of the Confederacy, and Robert E. Lee, commanding general of the Army of Northern Virginia, hatched a bold plan they hoped would force an end to the war. Months earlier, the South had won the Battle of Chancellorsville and the Union Army, commanded by Joseph Hooker, was retreating. Fledgling peace movements were gaining ground in the North as politicians despaired over a series of military defeats, and the will to continue the struggle wavered. Lee reasoned that if he attacked north through Pennsylvania and swung east to threaten Philadelphia, Baltimore, and Washington, morale in the Union states would plummet and those clamoring for peace would demand that President Abraham Lincoln negotiate an end to the war.

As Lee led his army of 72,000 men north through the Shenandoah Valley and into Pennsylvania, the reorganized Army of the Potomac, now led by General George Meade, raced north to confront them. The two sides met in the small town of Gettysburg on July 1, 1863. The initial skirmish on low ridges northwest of the town ended with Union troops fleeing back into Gettysburg, but they gained the time needed for the main body of the Union Army to reach the battlefield. By July 2, the two armies faced each other south of the town along parallel ridges running from north to south. Lee saw that the weakest part of the Union defenses lay at the southern end of the Union lines along Cemetery Ridge, which was anchored by two hills named Big and Little Round Top, and he ordered a massive assault on that part of the Union line.

As the attack on Cemetery Ridge began, Union Brigadier General Gouverneur K. Warren climbed to the top of Little Round Top and discovered that the hill was undefended—but the glint of sunlight on rifles revealed that Confederate troops had occupied Big Round Top and were massing for an imminent attack on the summit where he now stood. The Union was in grave peril, as historian Robert Cowley explains: "Little Round Top, then a bare, boulder-choked eminence about 200 feet high, gave the side that held it a virtually unobstructed view of the entire battlefield and controlled Cemetery Ridge to the North, where the Union Army was arrayed. If Confederate batteries had been established on its summit, they could have enfiladed the Union line, forcing a retirement and handing the victory to Lee."[1] General Warren sent an urgent order for a Union brigade to occupy Little Round Top. The staff officer carrying that order came upon twenty-six-year-old Colonel Strong Vincent in a nearby wheat field, and Vincent took it upon himself to move his brigade into position. He positioned one of his regiments, the 20th Maine, on the far south side of Little Round Top—literally at the end of a Union line stretched for miles.

The 20th Maine was commanded by Colonel Joshua Lawrence Chamberlain, a thirty-four-year-old professor of rhetoric and modern languages at Bowdoin College who had no military training but felt a patriotic duty to serve his country. Before marching his regiment to Gettysburg, Chamberlain had faced one of his most daunting leadership challenges. When the 20th Maine was formed, it had more than 1,000 men. After a year of fighting, there were fewer than 300 left, and Chamberlain was asked to accept 120 men from the recently dissolved 2nd Maine regiment into his unit. He needed the firepower, but there was a problem. These men were refusing to serve. They had enlisted in the 2nd Maine and did not want to serve in another unit. Moreover, they had signed three-year enlistments—a year longer than their fellow 2nd Mainers, who had already been discharged—and they were war weary and demoralized. If they deserted, Chamberlain had the authority to shoot them, something he refused to do, but he couldn't afford the manpower to keep them under guard, either. He needed the fighting strength they would give him—if they chose to fight.

So Chamberlain met with the men to hear their grievances and petition them to join the 20th Maine. What he said to them that day was not recorded, but author Michael Shaara reconstructed the speech based on soldiers' letters and memoirs in his Pulitzer Prize–winning novel *The Killer Angels*. In Shaara's account, Chamberlain treats them like soldiers instead of criminals. We won't shoot them, he says, because they are fellow Maine men. And he needs them. The coming battle is critical. If they lose this fight they may lose the war. He argues that their cause is noble and just, that unlike any other army in history their purpose is to set other men free. They are not fighting for a king or for loot or land. "It isn't the land—there's always more land. It's the idea that we all have value, you and me, we're worth something more than the dirt. I never saw dirt I'd die for, but I'm not asking you to come join us and fight for dirt. What we're fighting for, in the end, is each other."[2] Whatever Chamberlain actually said, his appeal succeeded. All but six of the mutineers agreed to join the 20th Maine.

They formed their line on Little Round Top just ten minutes before 700 battle-hardened veterans of the 15th Alabama Regiment charged up the hill toward the 20th Maine's hastily formed defenses. They repulsed the first wave, but the Alabamans reformed and charged again. The losses were staggering on both sides, but when the fighting began the Confederates had outnumbered the 20th Maine two to one. The commander of the 15th Alabama kept shifting his men farther to the right, trying to find the end of the Union line and circle behind it. Chamberlain responded by shifting his men to the left and then bending back the left side of his line. After two brutal hours and five uphill charges by the Confederates, the Union line was stretched thin and the men who could still fight were running low on ammunition. They had been issued only sixty cartridges per man. Now some had only a few cartridges left; two-thirds of them had none. Below, Chamberlain could see the Alabamans reforming for another charge.

After ordering the 20th Maine into this position, Colonel Vincent had reminded Chamberlain that the 20th Maine was the extreme left of the Union line. "You cannot withdraw," Vincent said. "Under any conditions. If you go, the line is flanked. If you go, they'll go right up the hilltop and take us in the rear. You must defend this place to the last."[3] As he watched his foe prepare for another assault, Chamberlain made a desperate decision. He knew his men could no longer defend this position. One of his lieutenants wanted to advance to a rock formation below their lines where some wounded men lay. Chamberlain told him to return to his position and then ordered his men to fix bayonets. As the Alabamans roared up the hill, Chamberlain commanded his men to sweep down the hill in a counterattack. Stunned by the unexpected bayonet charge, the Alabamans wavered and then broke in confusion, hundreds scurrying out of harm's way. Their commander later admitted, "We ran like a herd of wild cattle." Those who didn't run were captured by the exhausted soldiers of the 20th Maine, many of whom had no cartridges in their rifles. The battle for control of Little Round Top was over. The following day, Lee ordered a ruinous frontal assault (known as Pickett's Charge) on the center of the Union line, and the Confederates were soundly defeated. On July 4th, America's Independence Day, they began a long retreat back to Virginia.

Many historians consider the Battle of Gettysburg the turning point in the war. For his leadership in the defense of Little Round Top, Chamberlain was later awarded the Congressional Medal of Honor, the highest award for valor given to members of the American military. It is impossible to know how the Battle of Gettysburg would have ended had the 20th Maine been overrun and Confederate artillery been able to rake the Union lines up Cemetery Ridge, but it seems clear that had Chamberlain not been able to persuade the majority of the soldiers from the 2nd Maine to join them in the fight, he would have been woefully short of the resources he needed to turn back successive frontal assaults by a determined foe. Consequently, one of the first keys to victory on Little Round Top was Chamberlain's ability to influence those mutineers to fight with the 20th Maine. That single act of leadership and influence may well have determined the course of the war and America's history since.

Chamberlain was skilled in the art of rhetoric. He knew that rational and social approaches to persuasion would fail. In that critical situation, when men's emotions were running high, the only thing he could do was to inspire them to join the 20th Maine by appealing to their values. *Appealing to values* is one of the two influence techniques people commonly use to inspire others by engaging their emotions. The other technique is *modeling,* which is acting as a role model whom others may be inspired to emulate or influencing people through active teaching, coaching, or counseling. The inspirational approaches to influence are most likely to result in commitment or leadership, but their success depends on congruence between the influencer's values and the influencee's. Imagine that instead of giving an inspiring speech to the mutineers Chamberlain had said, "I hear you have complaints. Well, get over it. Everybody has complaints, and nobody gives a damn, least of all me. You signed your enlistment papers, so you are obliged to join the 20th Maine whether you like it or not. We're moving out in twenty minutes, and I expect every one of you to get off your lazy behinds and march with us. So who's with me? Let me see a show of hands." It's doubtful that any of them would have willingly joined

Chamberlain had that been his approach. Nor would he have been an inspiring role model for the men to follow.

The inspirational approaches to influence are most likely to result in commitment or leadership, but their success depends on congruence between the influencer's values and the influencee's.

The inspirational approaches to influence are unique in that they have the capacity to inspire many people at once, even millions of people, including (obviously) many people the influencer does not know and has never seen. Consequently, these are the favored influence techniques of political and religious leaders. Those seeking to influence people en masse are likely to appeal to their values or model the way they want others to think or behave. Both appealing to values and modeling are potentially very powerful techniques. In fact, my research shows that people who excel at appealing to values are more than three times more influential than people who are not inspirational. Similarly, people who are viewed as excellent role models are nearly three times more influential. These techniques are not used as often as the five influence power tools (logical persuading, socializing, consulting, appealing to relationship, and stating), but they can be extraordinarily powerful when they are done well, and they are virtually the only techniques to use when you want to influence many people at once.

APPEALING TO VALUES

Appealing to values is the opposite of logical persuading. The former is an appeal to the heart; the latter, an appeal to the head. As noted in chapter 3, we are partly rational creatures and partly emotional. But no one would doubt that the emotional side is the more powerful. How else could you explain love? Or religious devotion? Or patriotic fervor? When we become emotionally committed to a cause, an ideal, a philosophy, a movement, or a leader, we will do things that may otherwise make no sense whatsoever. That which we love or admire, on the one hand, or hate, on the other, has the power to influence our behavior in ways no rational argument can. Except in the sciences, no great movement has ever occurred that wasn't led by someone who either appealed to people's values or was an exemplary role model.

Appealing to values succeeds because it connects with something deep inside people, something they feel but may not be able to articulate. It inspires them because it connects with what they hold dear, with what gives their lives meaning and stirs their souls. It connects with what drives them; what they hunger for; what they need most to feel worthwhile, fulfilled, or justified. And these values need not be universal or even positive. Adolf Hitler was a master at appealing to values—but his appeals succeeded only because they came at a time and place where a particular people were hungry to embrace them. He appealed to a populace that felt weakened and humiliated by the outcome of the First World War, to people whose self-respect had to be rebuilt through fear of a common enemy, who needed to feel superior to those they believed had victimized them. Hitler's appeal did not inspire all Germans in the 1930s, of course. Some were either indifferent to his message or alarmed by it. To accomplish his goals, Hitler also had to resort to intimidation, manipulation, threats, and violence. But there is no question that his appeals did inspire many followers because he said what they wanted to hear.

Appealing to values succeeds when it connects with something deep inside people, something they feel but may not be able to articulate. It inspires them because it connects with what they hold dear, with what gives their lives meaning and stirs their souls.

Appealing to values and modeling are related but distinct. When influencers appeal to values, they do it by communicating a value-laden message. With modeling, they may simply behave in a way that others find inspirational or worth emulating (or worth rebelling against if they abhor what the person is doing or stands for). Here are some examples of how people appeal to values in business:

► A company CEO speaks to a group of employees during a town hall meeting about the company's operating principles. She gives examples of how customers' experience of the company and its services improve when employees apply those principles.

► During a strategy meeting, a company executive argues that the company has an ethical obligation to ensure that its offshore suppliers do not use child labor.

► During a performance review, a manager challenges an employee to make a greater contribution. He says, "Linda, you're doing good work but not inspired work. I think you are capable of much more and you'd feel better about the job if you had a more challenging assignment." She agrees. He mentions several possibilities and asks her to consider which one would be the most challenging and fulfilling, which would excite her more.

► A retired venture capitalist becomes alarmed about the amount of waste generated every year around the world. He creates a presentation that dramatically illustrates the problem and delivers it whenever he can to civic groups and schools.

Appealing to values is powerful when the message is aligned with the influencees' key values or beliefs and is stirring enough to spur them to action, but even the most effective influencer will not succeed with everyone all the time. The Reverend Billy Graham was one of the most well-known and effective Christian evangelists in the twentieth century. He led many well-organized and well-publicized crusades to bring the unconverted into the church and inspire current believers to greater devotion, but many people (perhaps most) who heard his inspiring messages remained unmoved and unconverted or lost their enthusiasm once the hubbub subsided. I noted earlier in this book that Barack Obama is an inspirational speaker. His speeches frequently include "value" messages, and he was a far more effective speaker during the 2008 American presidential election than his opponent, John McCain. Still, Obama's appeal to values did not influence everyone because not everyone shared his values. He won with just 53 percent of the popular vote. Nonetheless—and this is an important point—appealing to values doesn't have to influence everyone. It only has to influence enough of them for the influencer to accomplish his goals.

What people find inspiring is often so memorable that they record it, copy it, and pass it on to others. Here are a few of the memorable quotations (with emphasis added) that appealed to other people's values:

"The difference between a *successful* person and others is not a lack of *strength,* not a lack of *knowledge,* but rather a lack of *will.*"
—VINCE LOMBARDI

"Associate yourself with men of *good quality* if you *esteem* your own *reputation.* It is better to be *alone* than in *bad company.*"
—GEORGE WASHINGTON

"*Cautious, careful* people, always casting about to *preserve* their *reputation* and *social standing, never can bring about a reform.* Those who are really in *earnest* must be *willing* to *be anything or nothing* in the world's estimation, and publicly and privately, in season and out, *avow their sympathy* with *despised* and *persecuted ideas* and their *advocates,* and bear the consequences."—SUSAN B. ANTHONY

"*Control your own destiny* or someone else will."—JACK WELCH

"*Celebrate* what you've *accomplished,* but *raise the bar* a little higher each time you *succeed.*" —MIA HAMM (AMERICAN SOCCER STAR)

The popularity of these kinds of inspirational sayings is evident in the countless books, articles, posters, calendars, and bumper stickers that bear them. Why are they so popular? Because they represent a higher state of being or behavior that many people aspire to. Aspiration gives us both hope and direction. It means we don't have to remain the imperfect people we are today because we have room to grow, and the inspirational thought tells us how.

Here's how it might work: Let's say I've been doing good work but not great. I'm feeling stuck and unmotivated. I'm in a rut. Then I have a chance to hear Mia Hamm speak at our company's sales convention. I've admired her since the American women's soccer team won the gold medal in the 2004 Olympics. She talks about how you have to celebrate what you've done but can't be satisfied with it. You have to raise the bar a little each time. Okay, sure, this is obvious. Nothing new here, but it strikes me at the core because I realize I haven't been pushing myself. I gave up because I tried to do too much too quickly and failed. Then I got discouraged. "From now on," I tell myself, "I'll celebrate each win and then try for just a bit more next time."

When people successfully appeal to our values, I believe an interior monologue like this one occurs. We may share it with a friend or colleague, but often we do not articulate it and may not even be consciously aware of it. However it happens, an appeal to our values stirs

► Mia Hamm is an inspiration to thousands of girls who aspire to be like her. In her public appearances, Hamm frequently uses appealing to values to influence others.

in us an awareness or a realization that may lead to a change in our commitments, beliefs, or behaviors—and that is influence.

Insights on Appealing to Values

Among the ten positive influence techniques, appealing to values ranks seventh in frequency globally. Thankfully, it does not occur more often. Appealing to emotions too often would be tiresome. This technique has power when it is used infrequently—but at just the right moment. The people who are rated highest in effectiveness at appealing to values are also highly effective at socializing, modeling, consulting, and exchanging. The first three make sense—all are relational or inspirational influence techniques—but the correlation with exchanging is surprising. It may be that people who excel at appealing to values are better negotiators precisely because they can successfully appeal to the other side's values and emotions. Certainly, they would have a good understanding of what other people value and could use this knowledge as they exchange.

When we compare people with the highest and lowest ratings on effectiveness, we find that the greatest difference is expressiveness. The power of expression is what really makes the difference between those who are merely good at appealing to values and those who are great. The skills most closely correlated with the effective use of appealing to values are conveying energy and enthusiasm, building rapport and trust, speaking conversationally, listening, supporting and encouraging others, showing genuine interest in others, having a compelling tone of voice, acting self-confidently, and having insight into what others value. However, when you compare people who excel at appealing to values and those who don't, the biggest skill gaps are in their insights into what others value, their ability to convey energy and enthusiasm, and their listening skills. The people who are most effective at this technique have skill ratings more than three times higher than the skill ratings of their less effective counterparts. This astonishing difference highlights what it takes to truly master this influence technique. Most important is having insight into what others value, which is a critical component of emotional intelligence. People with this degree of interpersonal insight can empathize accurately, which enhances the emotional connections between them and others.

Conveying energy and enthusiasm is also critically important because you cannot inspire people if your effort is flat. Dull, lethargic speakers leave people unengaged and unconvinced. To light a fire, you need some spark. It's extraordinary that listening makes such a difference, too. No doubt, effective listening is how masters of inspirational appeals develop their insight into what others value, and knowing what others value enables them to appeal to the right ones. That listening is so important to effective appealing to values is a very key learning from the research. The most inspirational leaders among us are not merely great speakers; they are also greater listeners.

The Limitations of Appealing to Values

I received a call recently from a friend and former colleague who was raising money for a nonprofit. She did a nice job at appealing to values, but her cause is not one that excites me. I don't care about it enough to contribute, so I turned her down. This is the principal limitation of appealing to values. It works only when the influencee has an emotional connection and response to the values or the cause you are espousing. Either you have to know what your influencees value or you have to cast a wide enough net, making an appeal that resonates with as many people as possible while not expecting it to resonate with everyone.

Another limitation is that the technique can backfire if misused. Making emotional appeals too often or too stridently can create antagonism or weariness instead of commitment. Furthermore, your appeals must be genuine. If influencees sense that you are being either melodramatic or disingenuous, you may lose credibility and, with it, the power to influence them.

When to Use Appealing to Values

Appealing to values is an excellent technique to use in these circumstances:

► When you feel passionate yourself about the subject matter and when the values you are expressing flow authentically from within.

► When your goals and values are congruent with the goals and values of the people you wish to influence.

► When you want to influence many people at once, including people you may not know. (Martin Luther King Jr.'s "I Have a Dream" speech is an example.)

► When you need commitment or even leadership, because mere compliance will not suffice.

► When you need people to do something extraordinary and you must inspire them beyond the normal course of action. (In his speech about landing a man on the moon, President John F. Kennedy needed to stir belief and passionate commitment to the outcome.)

► When you need people to undertake something difficult or unpleasant. (This was the situation Colonel Chamberlain faced at Gettysburg's Little Round Top.)

► When your organization faces difficulties or is in peril and you need to rally people, focus their efforts, and give them hope.

► When rational and social approaches are not likely to succeed.

► When other people find you inspiring; when you are an effective leader and are seen as a role model and have the skills and power base to successfully appeal to people's values.

How to Use Appealing to Values Effectively

1. There is a direct correlation between the effectiveness of this influence technique and the degree to which people value what you are appealing to. If you are making a religious appeal to people who are agnostic, you are unlikely to succeed; if they are halfhearted believers, you may or may not succeed; but if they are zealots and your appeal is congruent with what they already hold dear, then you are

likely to gain not only their commitment but perhaps their leadership. Consequently, to use this technique effectively, you need to know what people value, especially what they value *most*. Influencers with a high degree of empathy generally have more insight into other people's values because they sense people's emotions and understand their feelings. If you aren't naturally gifted with a high degree of empathy, then you need to study people carefully. Observe. Listen. Learn what's important to them.

2. It is possible to say the right words without believing them. Psychopaths are often able to mimic what they see other people doing and articulate the ideas they think other people value, but this is a pathological charade. People who excel at appealing to values speak from an authentic voice. As Kevin Cashman says, "Integrity goes far beyond telling the truth. Integrity means total congruence between who we are and what we do. . . . Expressing yourself authentically is sharing your real thoughts and feelings in a manner that opens up possibilities."[4] Most people have good enough instincts and "crap detectors" to know when people are faking sincerity or expressing values they don't truly believe. If you act insincerely and are detected, you will lose all credibility and trust. So speak from an authentic voice. The values you appeal to should be ones you also hold dear.

3. To be effective at using this influence technique, you must also walk the talk. What you say and do must be aligned or you will again lose credibility.

4. Your articulation of values must make "value sense," which means that the values you express must be congruent not only with each other but also with the universal values and beliefs most cultures subscribe to. If you were to base your appeal to values on the precepts that "greed is good" and "the end justifies the means," you would likely fail because most people would consider those values abhorrent. If your precepts are that "responsibility is good" and "education is the foundation of democracy," people might agree with you but fail to see the connection. However, the following appeal to values would probably resonate with most people because the ideas are congruent with each other and make good value sense:

> Responsibility is good. Carelessness is bad/harmful.
> The earth is our home. It is all we have.
> We are responsible for the earth and must protect it.
> Waste is bad/harmful/irresponsible.
> Waste is harmful to the earth.

We are responsible for cleaning up or eliminating waste. Green is good.

This may read like a logical argument, but the operative words denote values: *good, bad, home, responsible, harmful, protect.* To use appealing to values effectively, you have to ensure that the values you appeal to are congruent with each other and reflect universally held values.

5. The people who are most effective at appealing to values are highly expressive and skilled at articulating their ideas with energy and enthusiasm. To be effective at conveying your engagement and commitment to the ideas, you need to use your whole instrument—your voice, your body, and your facial expressions. In effect, they are the expressive correlates of the words you speak. Can you be effective without conveying a lot of energy and enthusiasm? Perhaps, but using expressive nonverbals and having a compelling tone of voice are force multipliers that make your message that much more powerful and persuasive. Just don't overdo it. You don't need to shout and pound on a podium to show enthusiasm. A firm hand, raised and moving slightly forward, is a good way to emphasize a point, and an unhesitant voice expresses confidence and commitment. Good role models for making compelling speeches are Winston Churchill, Franklin Roosevelt, John F. Kennedy, Martin Luther King Jr., and Barack Obama.

MODELING

Here's an interesting experiment. Ask people who influenced them most as they were growing up. Who were their role models? Whom did they most want to be like? Their answers may give you great insight into who they are as people and what their dreams and aspirations are, and may also illuminate one of the most fascinating of the ten positive influence techniques—modeling. With this technique, you influence other people either by acting as a role model they seek to emulate or by actively teaching, coaching, or counseling them. When you model, you manifest a behavior, a way of thinking, or a way of being that others pattern themselves after. It should be apparent that modeling can be an extremely powerful form of influencing. It reflects the old master-apprentice approach to learning and development and is deeply embedded in the human psyche. As babies, we survive and grow largely through the role modeling and teaching of our parents and, later in life, a series of teachers whose purpose is to transform us into fully functioning adults.

Modeling is influencing either by acting as a role model whom people seek to emulate or by actively teaching, coaching, or counseling them. When you model, you manifest a behavior, a way of thinking, or a way of being that others pattern themselves after.

What is fascinating about modeling as an influence technique is that you cannot avoid it. Whether you like it or not, whether you intend it or not, if you are in a position of responsibility and visibility, you are a role model. Parents are role models for their children. Leaders and managers are role models for their followers and direct reports. Public officials are role models for all citizens, which raises an important point about modeling: Not all role models are worth emulating. People like Charles Manson, Bernard Madoff, and Andrew Fastow are examples of people most others would not want to emulate. They are negative role models, object lessons in what not to do, what not to become. A child growing up with an alcoholic parent is so disturbed by the experience that he becomes determined not to become an alcoholic himself. A young woman working for a dishonest boss makes integrity one of the defining values of the company she founds. Sometimes, people use negative role models to define what they don't want rather than what they do. In any case, people often influence us to change our thoughts, beliefs, or behaviors simply on the basis of who they are and how they act.

Role Modeling

One of my role models was George Allen Bacon, my paternal grandfather. He was a simple man—a farmer in southern Missouri and later a laborer at a grain mill (where he lost a finger). By today's standards he was not sophisticated or ambitious. He was well liked but not well traveled. He had few possessions and was not widely read or particularly interested in events outside of his small corner of the world. But he was one of the kindest and gentlest human beings I've ever known.

All that is good about humanity shone in his eyes and was conveyed in his loving touch. Much of what I learned about being a good man I learned from him.

My other principal role model was a man I'd never met: Nobel Prize–winning physicist Richard Feynman. What I found compelling about Feynman was his curiosity and absolute love of life. His life was something large made of something small (his beginnings were modest, too). He showed me that drive is as important as talent and that people can't pigeonhole you if you don't allow them to do it. And he taught me that boldness with respect is a powerful combination. I suspect that many people would list him among their most important influences. And so it is with role models. They are sometimes the people closest to you and sometimes people you've only read about or seen but never met. What they represent is an ideal, a direction, an indication of what's possible, an aspiration—and their influence on you can be extraordinary.

Oftentimes, role models exert profound influence through their works or style as well as through their teaching. Johann Christian Bach was such a role model. He was the eleventh and youngest son of classical composer Johann Sebastian Bach. The younger Bach studied music with his father and, after his father's death, with an older brother. Born in Leipzig, Germany, he lived for many years in Milan and later in London, where he became the music master to Queen Charlotte, who was the wife of King George III, the British ruler during the American Revolution. In 1764, while Bach was composing and performing in London, he was visited by an eight-year-old musical prodigy named Wolfgang Amadeus Mozart. Music historians have noted that "Bach . . . had an important and lasting influence on the boy. Bach enriched his keyboard and symphonic works with features from Italian opera: songful themes, tasteful appoggiaturas and triplets, and harmonic ambiguities. These traits, together with Bach's consistent use of contrasting themes in concerto and sonata-form movements, appealed to Mozart and became permanent marks of his writing. In 1772, Mozart arranged three of Bach's sonatas as piano concertos."[5]

Similarly, Picasso was a decisive influence in the art world in the twentieth century. Prior to Picasso, paintings were meant to represent the three dimensions of the natural world (an artistic tradition since the Renaissance). Picasso's groundbreaking change was to break from the illusion of three-dimensional depth and compose in flat planes. He was a significant influence on Spanish artist Juan Gris (José Victoriano González-Pérez), who lived and worked principally in Paris and considered Picasso a teacher. Gris was one of the central Cubist painters of the era, although he adopted the brighter colors of his friend Henri Matisse rather than the monochromatic hues of Picasso. Also influenced by Picasso was Piet Mondrian, a Dutch painter whose earliest work was impressionistic and naturalistic. In his evolution as an artist, he initially embraced Picasso and Cubism and then rejected this form for an even more radical departure from Renaissance traditions—abstractionism. Subsequently, Mondrian became an inspiration and an influence for abstract artists in Europe and America. And so it goes—one school or tradition in music and art influencing succeeding generations, initially by teaching what is possible and then providing the platform from which to depart into new and different forms.

In business, too, people like Henry Ford, Andrew Carnegie, Sam Walton, Walt Disney, J. P. Morgan, Alfred Sloan, Jack Welch, Ray Kroc, John D. Rockefeller, Thomas Watson, Estée Lauder, Steven Jobs, Bill Gates, Michael Dell, George Eastman, J. Willard Marriott, Warren Buffett, and Coco Chanel pioneered new ways of thinking about business and became role models for hosts of entrepreneurs and business leaders who followed them. In sports, Lance Armstrong, Michael Jordan, Jackie Robinson, Billie Jean King, Babe Didrikson, and Wayne Gretzky redefined their games while inspiring many of us to raise the bar and push ourselves harder than we might otherwise have tried. Isaac Newton, Albert Einstein, Niels Bohr, Werner Heisenberg, Charles Darwin, Louis Pasteur, Galileo Galilei, Marie Curie, Sigmund Freud, Antoine Laurent Lavoisier, and Nicolaus Copernicus revolutionized how we think about the world and became exemplars in the advancement of scientific thought. In every field of human endeavor, role models have shaped the behavior and elevated the aspirations of millions of other people who aspire to be like them. They are powerful and profound examples of influence.

Modeling Through Teaching, Coaching, and Counseling

Leaders can influence others through their self-sacrifices, or through their towering ambition or perseverance in the face of adversity, or through their erudition and penetrating analyses of the issues. They can influence through their creative genius, their insights into the behavior of markets, or their grasp of team dynamics and ability to pull thousands of people together in the pursuit of a lofty goal. Susan B. Anthony successfully led a revolution based on her single-minded devotion to the cause of women's suffrage. Eleanor Roosevelt inspired the United Nations by her selfless commitment to human rights. Katharine Graham transformed an industry through her inspired leadership of the *Washington Post* and stalwart defense of journalistic freedom and integrity. Invariably, these kinds of role models are also teachers and coaches. They lead by doing but also by educating.

> *In every field of human endeavor, role models have shaped the behavior and elevated the aspirations of millions of other people who aspire to be like them. They are powerful and profound examples of influence.*

Vince Lombardi was one of the finest sports coaches of all time. He believed that to coach a great team you had to be a good teacher. "They call it coaching," he said, "but it is teaching. You do not just tell them it is so, but you show them the reasons why it is so and you repeat and repeat until they are convinced, until they know."[6] Lombardi, who coached the Green Bay Packers from 1959 to 1967, transformed a team of losers into perennial winners. Under his leadership, the Packers won National Football League titles in 1961, 1962, and 1965 and Super Bowl I and II in 1966 and 1967. Lombardi not only influenced others through strong statements of opinion (as I wrote in chapter 4 on stating as an influence technique), but he believed that great coaches must live what they teach (in other words, they must model the attitudes and behaviors they want to see). "Coaching is selling," he said. "Selling is teaching. My customers are not so much the fans, but rather the players. I have to first sell them on themselves, and then on the small hurts, because the small hurts are not only a part of football, but also a part of life. And then I must sell them on this team, on this season, on this game, and each individual play as the most important thing in their lives."[7]

Lombardi was a teacher before he became a coach, so teaching was second nature to him. But many executives lack the teaching gene and don't view teaching or coaching as part of their role. That's unfortunate because it's one of the most powerful ways leaders can influence a host of people in positive and productive ways. In his book *The Leadership Engine,* Noel Tichy, a professor at the University of Michigan

Business School, argues that "teaching is at the heart of leading. In fact, it is through teaching that leaders lead others. . . . Teaching is how ideas and values get transmitted. Therefore, in order to be a leader at any level of an organization, a person must be a teacher. Simply put, if you aren't teaching, you aren't leading."[8] Moreover, Tichy believes that leaders must have a teachable point of view, which includes clear ideas and values and the ability to teach them to others: "To influence and lead, one needs teachable points of view not only in the form of teachable ideas and values themselves, but also about how to nurture and develop good ideas and strong values in others."[9]

At one time, leadership may have been about commanding and controlling others, but that is no longer true. Leaders don't accomplish their goals by directing others to perform tasks, and they don't inspire engagement and commitment by using the heavy hammer of power. Instead, they articulate values and vision, appeal to those values in their communications, model the behaviors they want others to embody, and teach others how to accomplish the goals. As an influence technique, modeling is acting either as a role model or as a teacher, coach, or counselor, and the technique applies in the family room as well as in the boardroom. Here are some examples of this technique:

- ► Two parents take their children to a local soup kitchen to help prepare and serve lunch for those less fortunate. Afterward, they have a family discussion about the importance of volunteering and helping others.
- ► The managing director of a professional services firm welcomes each new group of associates by discussing the firm's history, operating principles, and commitment to exemplary client service.
- ► The CEO of a manufacturing company frequently eats lunch in the company cafeteria with groups of frontline employees. She asks for their thoughts and suggestions on the business and shares her views, which she has carefully thought through and communicates in simple, clear messages. One of the company's values is open communication, and she strives to model this value at every opportunity.
- ► Nearing retirement, the chief scientist for a medical devices firm writes a lengthy report discussing his challenges, successes, and key learnings during his thirty years at the laboratory. He holds a number of patents and contributed to or led the teams responsible for the development of some of the firm's leading products. (He may not intend his report as a teaching vehicle, but these types of memoirs often enlighten and inspire younger colleagues.)

► The chairman emeritus of a large corporation volunteers to mentor several high-potential leaders who are candidates for more-senior roles.

► The CEO of a large diversified corporation regularly appears at the campus of the corporate university to hold question-and-answer sessions with the managers attending leadership programs.

► A woman renowned in her field meets a much younger woman at a social event and advises her to be her own best friend. That advice profoundly influences the younger woman.

Something like this last example happened to Ashley Olsen (of Olsen twins and fashion fame). The renowned woman in her case was Diane von Furstenberg, and Ashley writes about it in the book *Influence* (coauthored with her sister Mary-Kate). The book is a series of interviews with famous people who have influenced Ashley Olsen throughout her young life. Although some readers might find it a self-indulgent portrait of the rich and famous, the book is actually an insightful exploration of how role models can shape us and how they help us define who we are and what we both believe and aspire to. In the introduction, Ashley writes, "Whether it's my family, my friends, a novel I've read a hundred times over, or my favorite painting, I'm really just the sum of many different parts. Ultimately, that's what this book is all about. I've been inspired, surprised, supported, and, yes, influenced by every person I've talked about in this book. Their stories, bodies of work, and lives are like open vaults of creativity for me."[10]

The idea that we are the sum of many different parts is not far-fetched. No matter who you are, you are influenced by hundreds of

► Ashley Olsen with Tommy Hilfiger, one of the role models who influenced her.

Jamie McCarthy/Getty Images

people. Each of us is influenced through other people's lives, feats, beliefs, attitudes, teachings, advice, support, encouragement, coaching, and treatment of us and others. In all the ways they enlighten you, challenge you, or captivate you, they influence who you are and what you become. In turn, you influence countless other people through your life, feats, beliefs, and so on. Modeling is a pervasive and powerful form of influence.

Insights on Modeling

The people who are most effective at modeling are perceived by others to use it more frequently than any other influence technique. When we see someone as a role model, we see them that way all the time. The executives at GE who considered Jack Welch a role model saw Welch being himself in his role as CEO. If they encountered him at Crotonville, GE's leadership and learning center, they also saw him as a teacher and mentor. Welch never had to do anything differently to model the type of leader he was, and that's the point. By simply being himself, he was modeling the kind of executive that more-junior leaders at GE aspired to become.

The research on power and influence shows that people who excel at modeling are significantly more effective at using every other influence technique compared to people who are less effective at modeling. They are more than twice as effective at alliance building, socializing, consulting, exchanging, and appealing to values. What makes them good role models is that they are so competent in so many ways.

The power sources most closely correlated with high effectiveness at modeling are character, history, attraction, reputation, knowledge, and expressiveness. It makes sense that effective role models and teachers/coaches would have character and reputation as strong power sources—and that they would have high attraction power. The high ranking for knowledge is noteworthy, however. It suggests that part of what makes someone an attractive role model or teacher/coach is how knowledgeable the person is. Most intriguing, however, is the close correlation between effective modeling and history power. This suggests that most role models are people we already know and have a relationship with. As I reflect on my own experience, it is not surprising that my paternal grandfather would have become a strong role model for me. I knew him and interacted with him frequently enough to admire and respect the person he was. I read once that most people who die in automobile accidents die within thirty miles of their home.

This seems startling until you realize that the vast majority of the driving that people do is within thirty miles of their home. So it is with modeling. We find most of our role models close to where we live, study, or work, but occasionally our role models may be people we haven't known and have only read about or seen in a documentary.

The skills most closely correlated with effective modeling reinforce the importance of teaching and coaching: supporting and encouraging others, taking the initiative to show others how to do things, building rapport and trust, speaking conversationally, showing genuine interest in others, logical reasoning, behaving self-confidently, and listening. To be effective at modeling, you must be oriented toward developing and encouraging other people, and you need to take the initiative to teach, coach, or counsel them.

The Dark Side of Modeling

As I noted earlier, not all role modeling is positive. People frequently do not set good examples: An abusive parent teaches that it's okay to abuse those in your trust; a tyrannical boss conveys the idea that might makes right and those in power can exercise it with impunity; a sales manager who promises customers more than he knows his company can deliver teaches his direct reports that it's okay to cut ethical corners. In chapter 5 (on appealing to relationship), I told the story of Kevin Foster, leader of a teenage gang called the Lords of Chaos. Foster was older than the boys he led, and to them he exemplified the self-righteous rage they all felt as outcasts. He taught them how to build their self-esteem through defiance of society and its rules. Foster was the wrong role model for those boys, but at that time in their lives he was all they thought they had. The lesson here is that you have to be careful who you admire. When you feel yourself being drawn toward someone, it is wise to step back and try to appreciate why you find this person admirable and whether that direction is best for you in the long run.

The Limitations of Modeling

Modeling can be a high-impact influence technique. Effective modeling can influence people to become passionately committed to a cause or direction and even take a leadership role in it. However, modeling takes time. Whether you are teaching, coaching, counseling, or simply acting as a role model, it takes time to build trust, respect, and admiration—which are the foundations of a modeling relationship. The other limitation is that you have to behave consistently. People who are role models and have any visibility are "on stage" all the time. They are constantly being observed. It's like parenting. When you are a parent, you are a role model 24/7/365. Whenever your children are with you, they are watching, listening, and learning. So it is at work. If you manage or lead others, or are a person whom others admire for whatever reason, you act as a role model in every interaction with them. If you behave inconsistently, people may cease to admire you or call into question your credibility or character.

When to Use Modeling

The key issue with modeling is not *when* to use it, but when to use it *deliberately*. If others view you as a role model, you are using modeling when and whether you like it or not.

- ► Use modeling whenever you are responsible for or are leading other people. You can't escape modeling, so use it to your advantage. Know how you want others to think and act—and model those behaviors. If you want your staff to be outstanding at customer service, then you should show them what that means. If you want the people on your team to treat each other with respect, then you should treat them with respect. If you want your employees to take your operating principles seriously and embody those principles, then you must take the lead on living the principles. Although this is common sense, it is more difficult to do than most people realize.

- ► Use modeling when you need to develop people. Teach when you have the opportunity. Establish a coaching or mentoring relationship with the people you want to develop. Or find appropriate times to counsel them.

- ► Use modeling whenever you are in the spotlight, because that's when the most people are going to be looking to you as a role model. Be cognizant of your words and actions and try to model what you want others to do.

How to Use Modeling Effectively

1. Walk the talk. Consistently.
2. Be aware that others are observing you and learning from your exam-

ple, so strive to behave in ways that reflect positive attitudes, beliefs, and behaviors.

3. Read a good book on coaching. Of course, I am partial to *Adaptive Coaching* (Davies-Black Publishing, 2003) because I am one of the authors, but there are any number of resources on how to be a good coach. If you are in a company, your human resources group is likely to have some guidance on coaching or access to coaching programs.

4. Know whether and how people look up to you. Know what it means to be an exemplar in that area and strive to emulate those qualities.

5. If your organization has a mentoring program, sign up for it. Acting as a mentor is a fine way to influence others through modeling.

6. Likewise, if you have the opportunity to teach others, take it. Some of the finest executives have taught in their corporate universities or leadership programs (e.g., Jack Welch at GE, Roger Enrico at PepsiCo, and Andy Grove at Intel). Whether or not you actually teach, develop a teachable point of view and share it with people at the appropriate times.

KEY CONCEPTS

1. The two emotional approaches to influencing are appealing to values and modeling. These inspirational approaches to influence are the ones most likely to result in commitment or leadership, but their success depends on congruence between the influencer's values and the influencee's.

2. Appealing to values and modeling can influence many people at once, so they are the favored techniques of politicians and religious leaders.

3. Appealing to values is the opposite of logical persuading. The former is an appeal to the heart; the latter, an appeal to the head.

4. Appealing to values succeeds when it connects with something deep inside people, something they feel but may not be able to articulate. It inspires them because it connects with what they hold dear and those things that give their lives meaning and stir their souls.

5. Modeling is influencing either by acting as a role model whom people seek to emulate or by actively teaching, coaching, or counseling them. When you model, you manifest a behavior, a way of thinking, or a way of being that others pattern themselves after.

6. What is fascinating about modeling as an influence technique is that you cannot avoid it. Whether you like it or not, whether you intend it or not, if you are in a position of responsibility and visibility, you are a role model.

7. Leaders can influence others through their self-sacrifices, through their towering ambition or perseverance in the face of adversity, or through their erudition and penetrating analyses of the issues. They can influence through their creative genius, their insights into the behavior of markets, or their grasp of team dynamics and ability to pull thousands of people together in the pursuit of a lofty goal.

CHALLENGES FOR READERS

1. Who inspires you? Think about the people who have inspired you the most. What did you find inspirational about them?

2. Whom do you inspire? Who looks up to you or finds you admirable? What is it about you that they find inspiring?

3. What values are most important to you? If someone were to try to influence you by appealing to your values, what appeals would have the most impact? What would you respond best to? What values would you not respond to? What would cause you to react negatively?

4. Think of someone who works with you or for you. What are that person's key values? What does that person respond to best?

5. Think of an important situation where you are going to need to influence someone in the future. Assume that you have to use appealing to values. What values would you appeal to? How would you do it? What would make your influence attempt successful?

6. Who influenced you most as you were growing up? Who were your role models? Who did you most want to be like? What was it about these people that you found admirable or compelling?

7. Who considers you a role model? Why? What is it about you that another person would like to emulate?

8. Are you a good role model? Why or why not? Do you consistently walk the talk? What would you need to do differently to be a more effective role model?

9. Are you an effective teacher, coach, and/or counselor? How much time do you devote to developing other people through these methods?

10. Do you have a teachable point of view? If so, what is it? Can you articulate it in simple, concise terms? What's the core message? How can you best convey that message to other people?

11. Imagine the same scenario as in question 5. This time you have to influence the person through modeling. How would you do it? What would you need to do to make modeling successful?

12. Now consider the two scenarios you rehearsed in your hypothetical influencing situation. Which of the two inspirational approaches would work best for you? Why?

CHAPTER 8

INCREASING YOUR IMPACT

How to Become More Influential

If you are reading this book, then presumably your goal is to become more influential. Specifically, you may want to be more persuasive with your boss, more effective managing your direct reports (without resorting to authority), or more influential with your peers or your customers. Or you might work for a nonprofit and want to be better at persuading donors to give money; or perhaps you are being assigned to an overseas branch of your company and want to learn how to influence effectively in that culture; or maybe all you want is to get a child to do what you ask. In any case, this chapter is for you. What's come before this chapter has been foundational. Now I want to summarize what actions you can take and what skills you can develop to increase your ability to influence others—around the corner or around the world.

Bear in mind what I said at the outset of this book: You will not be able to influence everyone to do what you want all the time. Even the most powerful people in the world do not succeed at every influence attempt. Nonetheless, you can increase your capacity to influence others within and outside your organization, and you can learn to become more effective at using the positive influence techniques I've described in this second part of the book. This final chapter in part II discusses the eight levers you can use to increase your influence effectiveness and have more impact: (1) building your power base, (2) improving your relationships and position, (3) choosing the right influence techniques, (4) developing your influence skills, (5) leveraging other people's decision-making biases, (6) adapting your approach to people's operating styles, (7) adapting to cultural differences, and (8) preparing thoughtfully for important influence challenges.

The chapter ends with an influence effectiveness self-assessment designed to help you identify how effectively you use the ten positive influence techniques described in this book.

BUILDING YOUR POWER BASE

In chapter 2, I introduced the TOPS formula, which says that your effectiveness at influencing others depends on the strength of your organizational and personal power sources and the skill with which you use the influence techniques you've chosen. So one of the biggest levers you have for increasing your influence is to build your power base (appendix A describes the power sources). Table 8-1 summarizes what the research reveals about the difficulty of building these sources of power and the amount of impact each power source potentially has on influence effectiveness.

POWER SOURCE	TYPE	DIFFICULTY	POTENTIAL IMPACT
Network	Organizational	High	Very high
Knowledge	Personal	Moderate	Very high
Reputation	Organizational	Moderate	Very high
Character	Personal	Low	Very high
Expressiveness	Personal	Low	Very high
Role	Organizational	High	High
Information	Organizational	High	High
Attraction	Personal	Moderate	Moderate
Resources	Organizational	Very high	Low
History	Personal	Low	Low

► Table 8-1. Power source difficulty and potential impact.

In this table, the column labeled "Difficulty" indicates how hard it is to build each source of power. My data are based on surveys of 64,000 subjects and more than 300,000 respondents, and the results reflect the averages of that database. So while the research shows that resource power is the most difficult power source to build, a particular individual may have found it easy to develop substantial resource power. The "Potential Impact" column indicates how much each power source can potentially contribute to one's ability to influence others. Again, these results show average outcomes. Nonetheless, there are some important lessons to be learned from this table.

First, the greatest gains in influence capacity come from the five power sources with very high potential impact: network, knowledge, reputation, character, and expressiveness. So you should focus on building these power sources first. Character and expressiveness are relatively easy power sources to build, and they have very high potential impact, so they are powerful levers for building influence. Learn to speak well and ensure that you manifest sound character. Knowledge requires a bigger investment on your part, but the payoff is huge. Reputation will take care of itself if you steadfastly work and behave in ways that build your reputation.

I'm reminded of a managing partner in a large management consulting firm whom I had the privilege to meet at a conference. He was speaking to a group of young associates, and one associate asked what someone had to do to advance in the firm. The managing partner's answer was illuminating. "You have to create demand for yourself," he said, "and you do that by doing good work." That's how reputations are built. You consistently do good work. People will notice. The word will spread. And you will be in demand by those senior people who want only the best people on their teams. Sometime in your career you may have worked with or known people who aspired to be promoted to managers but were doing no more than a mediocre job in their current roles. Would it make sense to promote such a person to a more responsible position? No. In organizations, reputation is built on consistent character, contribution, teamwork, loyalty, and commitment.

History power is relatively easy to build, but table 8-1 shows that it has low potential impact. This is because history power operates between you and the people you know well, which is likely to be a small number of individuals. However, your influence effectiveness with those individuals is likely to be enormous. So don't neglect history power. Getting to know the right people very well is a significant way to build your influence. Role, network, and information power are relatively difficult sources to build, but the rewards, in terms of influence capacity, are great.

The bottom line is that to become more influential, you need to build your sources of power. Some are easier to build than others. If you have a choice, focus on the ones that have the greater potential impact, even if they are more difficult. The one power source not shown in table 8-1 is *will power*. This is the most powerful source of all. It's based on your desire to be more powerful, the courage to exercise your will, and the actions you take to make it happen. You can become more influential if you *choose* to be more influential. It's up to you to make it happen.

IMPROVING YOUR RELATIONSHIPS AND POSITION

People are often less influential than they might otherwise be because they don't have good relationships with the people they are trying to influence or they aren't well positioned with the influencees. The rule of thumb on influence is that you are likely to be more successful if the influencees know you, like you, respect you, and trust you.

Being Known

It is significantly easier to influence people you know than people you don't. So go out of your way to make yourself known. If you work in a business or professional organization, increase your visibility throughout the organization. Introduce yourself to people. As you get to know them, let them know who you are. My research shows that people who are highly skilled at being friendly and sociable with strangers and building close relationships are more than twice as influential as those who lack this skill. People around the world instinctively understand this skill, which is why socializing is one of the most frequently used influence techniques globally. If you aren't naturally good at socializing, then this is a key skill to build.

Being Liked

Sometimes, you know the influencee but aren't as influential as you'd like to be with that person because of bad chemistry. Many years ago when I was younger and single, a friend introduced me to a young woman, and she and I dated for a while. She was a nice, attractive person, and we tried to be a couple but it just didn't work. Somehow, we got on each other's nerves and whatever either of us said or did was somehow wrong. There was no chemistry between us, and it wasn't her fault or mine. We just weren't a good match for each other. So it goes. In my three decades in business I've had similar situations with some colleagues and clients. Despite everyone's good intentions, the plain fact is that there's something about the other person that each of you just doesn't like.

Attraction can be a significant source of power, and it's based in part on the psychological principle of liking. We are more inclined to say yes to people we like than to people we don't. So to be more influential, you should do what you can to be more likable to the people you want to influence. Of course, we each have whatever physical gifts (or challenges) we were born with, but you should do the best you can with what you have. Good grooming, posture, dress, and manners go a long way toward making you more attractive. In business, as well as many other walks of life, these things matter. The same is true with interpersonal behaviors that annoy people: Being too pushy, arrogant, boastful, self-centered, rude, disrespectful, and so on will be a turnoff to people. Personality is a key component of likability.

Being Respected and Trusted

Trust and respect are largely about character, credibility, and confidence. You build character through courage, integrity, reliability, and other character traits; you build credibility through your knowledge, access to information, role, and reputation (of which work ethic, results, and contributions are a significant factor); and you build confidence by behaving self-confidently, achieving consistently superior results, making good decisions, and exercising sound judgment. If you are a member of a business or professional organization, people will also trust and respect you more if you are actively involved, engaged, and committed to the enterprise. To become highly influential, it helps to be well-liked, well-regarded, and as indispensable as possible.

CHOOSING THE RIGHT INFLUENCE TECHNIQUES

Some people tend to overuse a few of the influence techniques, which makes them less influential in the long run because they aren't using the full toolbox. Engineers, scientists, and technicians often rely too much on logical persuading, for instance. Although it's a useful technique, logic does not work in many influencing situations. To maximize your capacity to influence others, it is important that you use the right techniques in the right circumstances. In the research on power and influence, I learned that most people tend to rely on three or four of the ten positive influence techniques. Because they used them so often, they became more skilled at using those techniques. Conversely, they were less skilled at using the techniques they used less often, and this became a self-reinforcing cycle. You aren't good at a technique, so you don't use it very much; because you don't use it very much, you don't develop the skill; and so on. To increase your influence capacity, then, you may need to improve your skill at using the techniques you are less familiar with and less skilled at. Table 8-2 shows what the research revealed about the difficulty of becoming highly effective at each of the influence techniques as well as the technique's potential impact.

INFLUENCE TECHNIQUE	TYPE	DIFFICULTY	POTENTIAL IMPACT
Alliance building	Social	High	Very high
Exchanging	Rational	Very high	Very high
Legitimizing	Rational	Very high	Very high
Appealing to values	Emotional	High	Very high
Modeling	Emotional	Moderate	High
Consulting	Social	Moderate	High
Appealing to relationship	Social	Very high	High
Socializing	Social	Low	Moderate
Logical persuading	Rational	Low	Low
Stating	Rational	Low	Low

► Table 8-2. Influence technique difficulty and potential impact.

What this table shows is fascinating. The five influence power tools—the ones used most often and most effectively around the world—are the five listed at the bottom of the table (consulting, appealing to relationship, socializing, logical persuading, and stating). The four techniques that have very high potential impact are used much less frequently and are not as effective *on average* as the five power tools. Why? Because they are not used as often, so the average person is less skilled at using them. However, the people who are rated highest in effectiveness at alliance building, exchanging, legitimizing, and appealing to values are also rated as being more influential overall than people who don't use these techniques as often or as well. In short, if you learn to use these techniques well, your ability to influence others will increase dramatically.

Here's the key lesson: The best influencers have a full toolbox. They are skilled at using each of the ten techniques and know when to use them. Moreover, if one technique isn't working, they will switch to another technique rather than continue doing what hasn't been working. Albert Einstein said that insanity is doing the same thing over and over again and expecting a different result. Yet that's often what people do when their repertoire of influence techniques is limited. In the preceding chapters, I noted when it was most appropriate to use each of the ten positive influence techniques. You will be more influential if you use the right techniques at the right time and are skilled at using each of them.

DEVELOPING YOUR INFLUENCE SKILLS

In my research on power and influence, I measured how effective subjects were at twenty-eight skills related to influence effectiveness. I grouped related skills into four clusters: *interaction, assertiveness, interpersonal,* and *communication and reasoning,* as shown in the skills table in appendix A.

An interesting finding from the research on influence skills is that interaction skills like resolving conflict and negotiating have the greatest potential impact but are also among the most difficult to develop. Resolving conflicts is not an easy skill for the average person to perfect, but people who do become expert at resolving conflicts have a substantially greater capacity to be influential. Why? Many people are conflict averse, so they don't develop the skills and finesse necessary to resolve conflicts effectively. However, the principal reason may be that conflict resolution is a complex set of skills and it involves influencing more than one person at once. This is true of most of the interaction skills, so they represent high skill difficulty but also high potential impact.

It would be worth identifying in appendix A which of these skills you are best at and which you aren't. An obvious way to build your capacity to influence others is to develop the areas where you are less skilled, particularly the ones with the highest potential impact. However, it is important not to ignore the skills with the lowest potential impact. In the right circumstances, they can make the difference between success and failure. As I noted previously, people who are highly rated on being friendly and sociable with strangers are twice as influential overall as people who lack this skill, although this skill has low potential impact. As in the case of all influence skills, *low* is a relative term.

LEVERAGING PEOPLE'S DECISION-MAKING BIASES

I have already observed that we are not the rational creatures we imagine ourselves to be. We are irrationally swayed by first impressions, we are fooled by the placebo effect, we assume that beautiful people are smarter and kinder than others just because of their looks, we look to other people in crowds to determine how to think and behave, and we are loathe to change our minds once we have made a commitment. In the past few years, a number of books have been published that explore the psychology of persuasion and the often-irrational factors that bias human decision making.[1] If you understand these biases you can sometimes take advantage of them to influence others, although, in candor, the people who are most concerned about these biases are marketers. Nonetheless, you can increase your influence effectiveness in some situations if you are aware of the following:

► *Liking and similarity.* We are more likely to say yes to people we know and like. This is the psychological basis for history power and the reason why appealing to relationship is such a powerful influence technique. If you can get people to like you or feel a connection to you, your capacity to influence them will increase.

► *Commitment and consistency.* People have a deep need to appear consistent, so once they have made a commitment, they are internally driven to keep that commitment. If you can get an influencee to make even a small commitment, this psychological bias will work in your favor as the person strives to appear consistent. It's best if the commitments are in writing or are publicly made.

► *Social proof.* People need to feel that their thoughts and actions are compatible with others' and with society's, so they look for social proof about how to think and behave. You can call it peer pressure, but other popular expressions for this bias include *following the crowd, jumping on the bandwagon, being a good team player, being cool or hip,* or whatever the current slang term is for knowing and doing what's socially acceptable to the group one identifies with. You can take advantage of this bias by pointing out what everyone else is doing or by building an alliance. In organizations, once people are leaning in a particular direction, it's difficult for people to oppose that direction because of the power of social proof.[2]

▶ *Authority.* From 1960 to 1963, Stanley Milgram, a psychologist at Yale University, conducted a series of famous experiments in which people were told to administer increasingly greater electrical shocks to subjects (actually fellow researchers) when they answered questions incorrectly. The majority of people continued to administer the shocks even when the subjects appeared to be in pain (they were acting).[3] When some people objected, the experimenters (who were playing the role as the authorities) told them it was necessary to continue—and most did. The Milgram experiment showed that most people tend to respect and obey authority, even when it goes against their moral sense and better judgment. The influence technique of legitimizing is based on this psychological bias. You can be more influential if you invoke authority; however, it can be challenging to use authority effectively. Using authority without appearing heavy-handed is a difficult skill to master.

▶ *Sunk cost bias.* Most people are loss averse, so they will continue to pursue a course of action (like an investment decision) because of sunk costs and despite the low probability of future success. Gamblers some-times fall for this fallacy. Once they've contributed enough money to the pot, they are inclined to "protect their bets" by continuing to call raises, even though their odds of winning are negligible. Once people have gone down a path, they are reluctant to change course or admit defeat. You can sometimes influence people by pointing out what they have already invested or how much of a stake they have in the out-come. If they bow out, they forfeit the chance to recoup their losses.

▶ *Reciprocation.* People are conditioned to reciprocate gifts, favors, and considerations. If they don't reciprocate, they risk being ostra-cized by others, so reciprocation is related to social proof. Conse-quently, you can influence others by doing them small favors or giving them some special consideration. Then they will feel obligated to reciprocate. Interestingly, it also works if you ask someone for a favor. If they grant it, they will feel kindlier toward you and will be more likely to say yes to you in the future.

► *Scarcity.* People place more value on things that are scarce, even if they don't need them. Marketers use this principle when they advertise something as a "limited" offer, and retailers use it every time they have a sale. When people think that something is available for just a limited time or that only a limited number of something exists, they will place more value on it. Artists take advantage of this principle when they create an original painting, for instance, and then offer a limited number of prints (copies) of the original. Numbering the prints (99/150, for instance, to indicate it is number 99 out of an edition of just 150) increases their perceived value. So, in the right circumstances, you can be more influential by making what you are offering more scarce.

► *Anchoring.* People are highly influenced by first impressions and by the first value they associate with something. Anchoring is a psychological bias that occurs, for instance, when a negotiator says, "The normal price for this item is $1,000." That figure becomes the anchor for the price negotiations that follow, with every subsequent figure being compared to that anchor. Research shows that anchors are powerful ways of influencing how people think about value, so you can be more influential by being the first to set an anchor. Similarly, research shows that people are significantly influenced by their first impressions of others. So, to be more influential, you need to make a very good first impression—or ensure that what you want will be favorably perceived the first time that influencees encounter it.

These are just a few of the psychological factors that affect how people make decisions. Being aware of them can help you be more influential; however, I have not elaborated upon them in this book for two reasons. First, most people can become considerably more influential by building their power base, understanding the ten positive influence techniques, and building their influence skills—without having an intimate knowledge of the psychological biases in human decision making. Second, becoming too facile at using these psychological factors to your advantage can run dangerously close to manipulation, which is discussed in chapter 10. Bernard Madoff, who conned investors out of billions of dollars, was an expert at using authority, scarcity, social proof, and liking to his advantage. This is not to say that taking advantage of human decision-making biases is unethical— but it can be when the influencer's purpose is to manipulate and deceive.

ADAPTING YOUR APPROACH TO PEOPLE'S OPERATING STYLES

It would be fair to assume that people with different operating styles would respond to the influence techniques differently—and my research bears this out. To identify operating styles, I used the familiar Myers-Briggs Type Indicator (MBTI). This instrument, which is available from Consulting Psychologists Press, is among the best known and most used operating-style preference indicators in the world. I will assume that readers are familiar with this framework.[4] I studied the extent to which people with each of the sixteen operating styles responded to the ten positive influence techniques. The results are shown in table 8-3a and table 8-3b.

These tables show, for example, that INTJs (the MBTI designation for introverted, intuitive, thinking, judging people) like to be asked; they don't like to be told. They are usually highly responsive to consulting, logical persuading, and appealing to values, but it is generally not best to use alliance building, legitimizing, or modeling (in the sense of teaching/coaching) with them. INTJs are among the most independent of types, are highly self-confident, and have little regard for authority. By contrast, ENFPs (extroverted, intuitive, feeling, perceiving people) will respond best to consulting but can also be influenced by appealing to relationship, socializing, appealing to values, exchanging, and alliance building. They have less regard for logical persuading and normally react adversely to stating.

These tables are obviously most useful if you know the MBTI and are skilled at reading people's operating-style preferences. If you are not, then use common sense: Use logical persuading with people who are logical or technically educated; use legitimizing with people who have shown respect for authority; use appealing to values with people who are more emotional or values driven; use socializing with everyone, but particularly people who are more outgoing and social by

	ISTJ	ISTP	ESTP	ESTJ	INTJ	INTP	ENTP	ENTJ
Legitimizing	◕	◕	◕	◕	○	○	○	◑
Logical Persuading	◕	●	◕	●	◕	●	◕	●
Appealing to Relationship	◑	◑	◑	◑	◑	◑	◑	◑
Socializing	◑	◑	◑	◑	◑	◑	◑	◑
Consulting	◑	◑	◕	◕	●	◕	●	◕
Stating	●	◕	◑	◕	◑	◕	◑	◕
Appealing to Values	○	○	○	○	◕	◕	◕	◕
Modeling	◑	◑	◑	◑	○	○	◑	◑
Exchanging	◕	◕	●	◑	◑	◑	◑	◑
Alliance Building	○	◑	◕	◑	○	○	◑	◑

LEGEND

○ Not likely to be effective under normal circumstances

◑ A **good** approach, but probably not your best choice

◕ A **better** approach to people of this type

● The **best** influence approach under normal circumstances

► Table 8-3a. Eight MBTI operating styles and their responsiveness to the ten positive influence techniques.

nature; use stating with people who are inclined to respond positively to assertive people; use exchanging with people who are inclined to negotiate for cooperation or who expect something in return for cooperation; and so on. The most effective influencers adapt to the preferences, personalities, and responses of the people they are trying to influence.

	ISFJ	ISFP	ESFP	ESFJ	INFJ	INFP	ENFP	ENFJ
Legitimizing	●	◕	◕	●	◐	◐	◐	◐
Logical Persuading	◐	○	○	◐	○	○	○	○
Appealing to Relationship	◕	●	◕	◕	◕	◕	◕	◕
Socializing	◕	●	◕	◕	◕	◕	◕	◕
Consulting	◐	◐	◐	◐	◕	◕	●	●
Stating	◐	○	○	◐	○	○	○	○
Appealing to Values	◕	◕	◕	◕	●	●	◕	◕
Modeling	◐	◐	◐	◐	◕	◕	◐	◐
Exchanging	◕	◕	◕	◕	◕	◕	◕	◕
Alliance Building	◕	◕	●	◕	◐	◐	◕	◕

LEGEND

○ Not likely to be effective under normal circumstances

◐ A **good** approach, but probably not your best choice

◕ A **better** approach to people of this type

● The **best** influence approach under normal circumstances

► Table 8-3b. Remaining eight MBTI operating styles and their responsiveness to the ten positive influence techniques.

ADAPTING TO CULTURAL DIFFERENCES

Just as you should adapt to the operating-style preferences of the people you are trying to influence, you will be more influential if you adapt to differences between your culture and the culture of the people you are trying to influence. In my research I focused principally on country cultures, but company or organizational culture also plays a significant role in how people influence one another and respond to influence attempts.

Culture refers to the values, norms, attitudes, and beliefs shared by people and groups in organizations that influence how they act toward one another and toward people outside the culture. Culture often affects how decisions are made, who makes them, what matters in decision making, and who influences the decision makers.

Among the most prominent thinkers on organizational culture are Geert Hofstede, Edgar Schein, Terrence Deal, and Allan Kennedy.[5] These writers typically characterize organizational cultures based on such factors as the concentration of power and authority, the flow of communication, the level of formality or informality in the culture, the level of competitiveness, the tolerance for risk, the amount of feedback in the environment, and the degree of trust among members. It would be beyond the scope of this book to elaborate on models of corporate culture and how they affect influence. Suffice it to say here that to be most influential within an organization, you must understand and adapt to how the organization works, how power and authority are distributed among members of that organization, what roles people play, who makes or contributes to various kinds of decisions, and what matters most to organization members (in other words, what the culture values and how those values are reinforced).

It should be clear from this brief discussion that organizational culture is a complicated topic, but we don't need to complicate how you adapt to organizational culture as you try to influence people in an organization. It boils down to two of the ten laws of influence discussed in chapter 1. Remember, law 7 says that people respond best to the influence techniques they use themselves, and law 8 says that if you are observant, people will reveal what they find most influential. To adapt to different cultures you need to respect cultural differences and appreciate that those differences matter. Then you need to be observant as you enter or work in the culture, noting how people interact with each other; how they access and use information; what they consider important as they evaluate alternatives, solve problems, and make decisions; and, mostly, how they influence one another. The influence techniques they use with each other—and with you—are likely to be the ones they will respond best to. You don't need to be an expert on organizational culture. You just need to be sensitive to differences and then observe, listen, and adapt.

For further information on what the research revealed about cultural differences in the use of power and influence, see appendix B and also www.terryrbacon.com or www.theelementsofpower.com.

PREPARING THOUGHTFULLY FOR IMPORTANT INFLUENCE CHALLENGES

Finally, one powerful lever for increasing your influence effectiveness—and impact—is to prepare thoughtfully for key influence attempts. Obviously, you would do preparation work in advance of making an important proposal presentation, having a key discussion with your boss, entering a critical meeting with a customer or donor, or attending some other event where the stakes are high and you need to be as influential and persuasive as you can be. In such circumstances, the following questions will help you analyze the situation and develop the approach most likely to succeed:

1. What am I trying to accomplish in this influence attempt? What is the ideal outcome?

2. Whom am I trying to influence? How well do I know them, and how well do they know me? Do I have history power with them? Do they feel any reciprocal obligation toward me? Do they "owe me one," or vice versa?

3. What is my relationship with them? How close or distant are we? What do they think of me or the subject I'm approaching them about? Do they like me? Respect me? Trust me? If not, what could I do about that now? How can I best position myself in their eyes?

4. Do they have the latitude to say yes? If not, who does? Am I sure I'm talking to the right people?

5. Is it in their best interests to say yes? Is it consistent with their values? If not, how could I overcome that obstacle?

6. What are the answers to the simple test: *Why* might they say yes or say no? What's in it for them if they say yes? What would they lose or gain by saying no? (The key in successful influencing is to swim with the current, not against it. But if you do have to swim upstream—in other words, if saying yes would be disadvantageous to the influencees—then it is better to know that beforehand and prepare for it.)

7. Have I worked with them before and been able to influence them in the past? What worked and what didn't? What's different now?

8. How do they try to influence other people? What techniques do they typically use? What do they respond to? What does their work environment tell me about them? What do their operating styles indicate about how best to influence them?

9. What does their country or organizational culture suggest about how best to approach them and what techniques to use? What to avoid?

10. What influence techniques would seem to be the best choices given all that I know? If those don't work, what are my alternatives?

11. Depending on my choice of influence techniques, do I know everything I need to put together a good case? Here are some further questions to ask:

   ✓ *Logical persuading.* What arguments would be most compelling to the people I hope to influence? Do I have the facts or information I need? What proof or evidence would best support my ideas? Do I need supporting graphs, charts, tables, or other visual tools?

   ✓ *Legitimizing.* What types of authority do they most respect? How can I invoke those authorities without being heavy-handed?

   ✓ *Exchanging.* If they are open to an exchange, what currencies of exchange do I have to give and what are they likely to offer? What would likely be an equitable exchange from their perspective?

   ✓ *Stating.* Would they be responsive to assertiveness and stating? What ideas would be most appropriate for stating?

   ✓ *Consulting.* What would be the most insightful or thought-provoking questions I could ask? How can I use questions to get them to contribute to the solution and then support it? How can I help them feel ownership of the solution?

   ✓ *Appealing to relationship.* Do I know them well enough to rely on our mutual history? What's appropriate to ask for, based on our existing relationship?

   ✓ *Socializing.* Are they open to socializing? Is it part of their culture? What kind of socializing would be most appropriate in this situation? What do we have in common that would make socializing desirable?

   ✓ *Alliance building.* Do they have a history of working with or being part of alliances? What kind of alliance would work best in this situation? An alliance with whom? How could I bring the right people together? And how would I use such an alliance?

   ✓ *Appealing to values.* Do they have a values culture? What values are important to them? How do they manifest their values in action? What values would I appeal to?

   ✓ *Modeling.* What role models are revered in their culture? Whom do they look up to? What behaviors or ways of thinking would need to be modeled? And who is best to do that?

12. What objections could they raise to what I am asking for or proposing? How can I best respond to those hypothetical objections?

13. Am I asking too much? Too little? How big a deal would this request

be to them? Can I get them to commit to some smaller or lesser portion first?

14. Am I prepared to make my best case? If not, how could I improve it?
15. If I encounter resistance, am I prepared to explain why the upside is greater than any downside?

All of these questions will help you gain clarity in your own mind about whom you want to influence and what you want to accomplish.

As this chapter shows, there are many levers you can use to increase your influence with other people and your impact in your organization. Influence effectiveness is a function of power, technique, skill, and thoughtful adaptation to the people you want to influence and the circumstances in which you are trying to exercise power. You won't succeed every time, but using these levers will help you succeed more often than you have previously.

INFLUENCE EFFECTIVENESS SELF-ASSESSMENT

How effective are you at influencing others? This self-assessment is designed to help you gauge your effectiveness in using the ten positive influence techniques. As with any self-assessment, the more honest you are about yourself, the more accurate your results will be. As you respond to these forty statements, be as realistic as you can.

For the items that follow, indicate on a scale of 1 to 10 how accurately each statement describes you. Circle "1" if the statement is *not at all true of you,* and "10" if the statement is *very true of you.*

RATIONAL INFLUENCE TECHNIQUES

Logical Persuading

1. I am a very logical person. I think logically and excel at providing sound reasons for my conclusions or requests.

(not at all true of me)   1   2   3   4   5   6   7   8   9   10   (very true of me)

2. I am nearly always able to convince people to go along with me by explaining what I want and why I want it.

(not at all true of me)   1   2   3   4   5   6   7   8   9   10   (very true of me)

3. I am excellent at putting together the evidence or proof I need to substantiate my ideas, conclusions, and proposals.

(not at all true of me)   1   2   3   4   5   6   7   8   9   10   (very true of me)

4. I am highly skilled at creating compelling charts, graphs, and other kinds of visual aids to support my arguments and presentations.

(not at all true of me)   1   2   3   4   5   6   7   8   9   10   (very true of me)

Logical Persuading total _____

Legitimizing

5. Most of the people I know and work with have a lot of respect for authority.

(not at all true of me)   1   2   3   4   5   6   7   8   9   10   (very true of me)

6. I am highly skilled at citing authorities to legitimize what I want and can do so without making people feel pressured or insulted.

(not at all true of me)   1   2   3   4   5   6   7   8   9   10   (very true of me)

7. I find that most people respond positively when they know that my decisions or requests are supported by management.

(not at all true of me)   1   2   3   4   5   6   7   8   9   10   (very true of me)

8. I am one of those people who has an aura of authority, and when I say that what I want is authorized or approved, most people go along with it.

(not at all true of me)   1   2   3   4   5   6   7   8   9   10   (very true of me)

Legitimizing total _____

Exchanging

9. I am an experienced and skilled negotiator.

(not at all true of me)   1   2   3   4   5   6   7   8   9   10   (very true of me)

10. I do a lot of favors for my friends and colleagues, and they do a lot for me.

(not at all true of me)   1   2   3   4   5   6   7   8   9   10   (very true of me)

11. I am very good at bargaining and trading. I am usually successful at striking a deal that works for everybody.

(not at all true of me)   1   2   3   4   5   6   7   8   9   10   (very true of me)

12. I believe that you get as good as you give, so I try to be helpful and collaborative with everyone, and I find that when I want or need something, people usually come through for me.

(not at all true of me)   1   2   3   4   5   6   7   8   9   10   (very true of me)

Exchanging total _____

Stating

13. I am very good at asserting my views without overwhelming people or making them feel like they can't disagree with me.

(not at all true of me)   1   2   3   4   5   6   7   8   9   10   (very true of me)

14. People see me as a very self-confident person, and they generally accept what I have to say without challenging it.

(not at all true of me)   1   2   3   4   5   6   7   8   9   10   (very true of me)

15. I enjoy sharing my ideas and telling others what I think. If they disagree with me, that's fine.

(not at all true of me)   1   2   3   4   5   6   7   8   9   10   (very true of me)

16. I am in a position of authority in my organization, and if I simply tell people what I want them to do, they will do it.

(not at all true of me)   1   2   3   4   5   6   7   8   9   10   (very true of me)

Stating total _____

SOCIAL INFLUENCE TECHNIQUES

Socializing

17. I am very outgoing, and it's easy for me to engage in casual conversation with people I've just met.

(not at all true of me)   1   2   3   4   5   6   7   8   9   10   (very true of me)

18. I am an excellent listener. When people talk to me, I am fully engaged with them and remember not only the key things they've told me, but also details about themselves.

(not at all true of me)   1   2   3   4   5   6   7   8   9   10   (very true of me)

19. It is easy for me to make friends. I like people and enjoy talking to them and discovering what we have in common.

(not at all true of me)   1   2   3   4   5   6   7   8   9   10   (very true of me)

20. I am most comfortable in meetings when we spend some time socializing before getting down to business. I prefer knowing whom I'm dealing with and having them get to know me.

(not at all true of me)   1   2   3   4   5   6   7   8   9   10   (very true of me)

Socializing total _____

Appealing to Relationship

21. If my closest friends or family members need anything from me, all they have to do is ask.

(not at all true of me)   1   2   3   4   5   6   7   8   9   10   (very true of me)

22. I feel a special bond with anyone who belongs to the same clubs or groups I belong to or who shares my interests.

(not at all true of me)   1   2   3   4   5   6   7   8   9   10   (very true of me)

23. I know that if I ever need anything or have a serious problem, my closest friends will be there for me.

(not at all true of me)   1   2   3   4   5   6   7   8   9   10   (very true of me)

24. I and the people I feel closest to tend to think alike and have shared interests. We agree with each other much more often than we disagree.

(not at all true of me)   1   2   3   4   5   6   7   8   9   10   (very true of me)

Appealing to Relationship total _____

Consulting

25. I am very good at asking people the kinds of probing questions that get them to think about an issue or a situation differently.

(not at all true of me)   1   2   3   4   5   6   7   8   9   10   (very true of me)

26. Rather than give people the answers, I often use questions to lead them through a problem-solving process so that they figure out the answers themselves.

(not at all true of me)   1   2   3   4   5   6   7 .8   9   10   (very true of me)

27. I am very effective at building support by engaging people in the problem-solving process and having them feel some ownership of the solution.

(not at all true of me)   1   2   3   4   5   6   7   8   9   10   (very true of me)

28. When people ask me for coaching, I greatly prefer to ask them questions and have them figure out what's best for themselves rather than tell them what I think they should do.

(not at all true of me)   1   2   3   4   5   6   7   8   9   10   (very true of me)

Consulting total _____

Alliance Building

29. I am an experienced team builder and an excellent team leader.

(not at all true of me)   1   2   3   4   5   6   7   8   9   10   (very true of me)

30. When I'm not confident that I can influence someone by myself, I have always been able to find supporters to help me accomplish my goal.

(not at all true of me)   1   2   3   4   5   6   7   8   9   10   (very true of me)

31. I am highly skilled at resolving conflicts among people and building consensus.

(not at all true of me)   1   2   3   4   5   6   7   8   9   10   (very true of me)

32. I have been very successful at bringing people together to accomplish goals I consider important.

(not at all true of me)   1   2   3   4   5   6   7   8   9   10   (very true of me)

Alliance Building total _____

EMOTIONAL INFLUENCE TECHNIQUES

Appealing to Values

33. I am known as a passionate and committed person who brings a lot of energy to any discussion about issues I feel strongly about.

(not at all true of me)   1   2   3   4   5   6   7   8   9   10   (very true of me)

34. I have an intuitive understanding of what people value, and I know how to talk to them about those values in ways they find authentic and engaging.

(not at all true of me)   1   2   3   4   5   6   7   8   9   10   (very true of me)

35. I am an eloquent and inspirational speaker.

(not at all true of me)   1   2   3   4   5   6   7   8   9   10   (very true of me)

36. Many people would consider me to be a charismatic person.

(not at all true of me)   1   2   3   4   5   6   7   8   9   10   (very true of me)

Appealing to Values total _____

Modeling

37. Many people in my group or organization consider me a positive role model.

(not at all true of me)   1   2   3   4   5   6   7   8   9   10   (very true of me)

38. I am an experienced and successful coach, mentor, or teacher.

(not at all true of me)   1   2   3   4   5   6   7   8   9   10   (very true of me)

39. I am widely considered to be an expert in my field, and people frequently seek my opinions or advice.

(not at all true of me)   1   2   3   4   5   6   7   8   9   10   (very true of me)

40. I am well known because of my publications, speeches, presentations, or public appearances.

(not at all true of me)   1   2   3   4   5   6   7   8   9   10   (very true of me)

Modeling total _____

SCORING

In the blank lines on the next page, record your influence technique scores and then multiply each score by the indicated weights and total the result. The factors reflect the relative strength of each of the power sources based on the research. The highest possible score is 880.

Rational Influence Techniques

Logical Persuading (× 4) = _____

Legitimizing (× 1) = _____

Exchanging (× 1) = _____

Stating (× 2) = _____

Subtotal rational techniques _____

Social Influence Techniques

Socializing (× 4) = _____

Appealing to Relationship (× 2) = _____

Consulting (× 3) = _____

Alliance Building (× 1) = _____

Subtotal social techniques _____

Emotional Influence Techniques

Appealing to Values (× 3) = _____

Modeling (× 1) = _____

Subtotal emotional techniques _____

TOTAL _____

Interpreting Your Self-Assessment Score

Clearly, the higher your total score, the more influential you can be in your company or organization. Your total score is important, but so is your mix of scores. Many people excel at one or two influence techniques and tend to use them much more frequently than anything else—and they are less effective overall than people who have moderately high capabilities in a broader range of techniques. Think of these influence techniques as tools in your toolbox. You'll be more effective at influencing more people if you are good at using six or seven of the techniques than if you excel at using only one or two.

The five global *influence power tools* are logical persuading, socializing, stating, appealing to relationship, and consulting. If you do not have at least moderately high capability in these five influence techniques, then you should work toward developing the ones you are weakest at. On average, these are the techniques you will need to use most often and the ones that will give you the greatest chance of success.

The remaining five influence techniques are important depending on your situation. If you are a politician, senior executive, religious leader, or other kind of public figure, then you should develop your skills for appealing to values. This emotional appeal will be one of your most important influence techniques. If you do not have a lot of role or positional power, then you will probably need to be competent at exchanging (it's how peers influence each other and gain cooperation from the people they need to work with). If you frequently need to influence people who are considerably more powerful than you, then alliance building will be a key technique for you to master.

The weights assigned to these influence techniques reflect their relative importance in your overall influence effectiveness based on the research. In real life, these weights may depend on the situations you face in trying to lead and influence other people. If you must frequently negotiate with people for cooperation, then exchanging might be weighted higher than it is here. If you never need to appeal to people's values, then appealing to values might have a lower weight than it does in this baseline assessment, and so on. As you reflect on your scores, ask yourself these questions:

1. Which influence techniques are most important for your role in your company or group or for the types of situations in which you typically need or want to influence others? You might want to apply your own weighting scheme so that it better reflects your leadership and influence challenges.
2. Are you less effective than you should be in any of the more important influence techniques you identified? These are the techniques you should focus on in your development plan.
3. If you aspire toward positions of greater responsibility in your organization, look ahead. Which influence techniques will be most important as you are promoted to those positions? Building your skill at using these influence techniques should become part of your long-term development plan.

In March 1823, the *Kennersley Castle* neared the Caribbean coast of South America carrying 200 Scottish settlers who were bound for St. Joseph, the capital city of Poyais, a small but prosperous country located along the Mosquito Coast. Many of the settlers carried a 350-page guidebook written and published by Captain Thomas Strangeways entitled *Sketch of the Mosquito Shore, Including the Territory of Poyais, Descriptive of the Country*. They were following another group of settlers who had left London four months earlier aboard another ship, the *Honduras Packet*. Some of these intrepid souls had secured positions in the Poyais civil service; others had purchased commissions in the Poyais army. Most had exchanged their British pounds for Poyais currency, and they were excited to be arriving in a tropical paradise that Strangeways said had been settled by British sailors in the 1730s—a land of fertile soil, rich mines of gold and silver, lush forests, a teeming port, and boundless opportunity for those adventurous enough to make the New World their home.

Yet as the *Kennersley Castle* neared shore, the ship's captain was unable to locate the port. Thinking the maps must be inaccurate, the captain sailed along the South American coastline until, quite by chance, he and his crew located the survivors of the *Honduras Packet*, which had left its passengers on the beach and then departed, only to sink in a storm off the coast. After off-loading their worldly goods and joining the survivors, the *Kennersley Castle* emigrants were stunned to learn that the maps were accurate; they had gone to the right location—only there was no teeming port, no city of St. Joseph, no gold mines, and no country by the name of Poyais. There was only an abandoned stockade; miles of swamp and jungle; humidity; scorching sun; and the godforsaken mosquitoes, which continually tormented them and gave many of them tropical diseases. Their Poyais currency was worthless (it had actually been printed in Scotland), and there was no Captain Thomas Strangeways (his lengthy book about Poyais had been an elaborate work of fiction).

The perpetrator of this massive and costly fraud was Gregor MacGregor, a Scottish soldier and vagabond who had fought, he claimed, in many of the South American wars for independence from Spain. Born in 1786, he joined the Royal Navy when he was seventeen. In 1811, he arrived in Venezuela as a colonel and, some years later, captured the town of San Fernandina on Florida's Amelia Island from the Spanish. It's not certain that he was involved in other substantive military engagements, but in 1820 he returned to Britain, full of pomp and bluster, with the title of *cacique* (prince) of Poyais. The British Isles were ablaze with the spirit of opportunity now that Spain had lost its grip on South America, whose markets were ripe for British plucking. MacGregor became the talk of the town. Investors and prospective settlers were enthralled by his tales of plenty. In 1822, he introduced Captain Strangeways's book (which MacGregor, of course, had written) and then sold £200,000 in bearer bonds purportedly issued by the Poyais government. Later that year, the ill-fated voyages of the emigrants began. Fewer than fifty of the nearly 300 settlers returned to Britain; the rest died of tropical diseases, malnourishment, suicide, or other misfortunes.

When news of the fraud broke, MacGregor skipped to France, where he again tried to perpetrate the Poyais fraud. This time, his associates were sent to prison, although MacGregor was tried but acquitted. Afterward, he returned to London, once more trying to sell interests in his fictional paradise, but by then investors were wary of him. Still, despite a police investigation of his schemes, he was never charged. Eventually, MacGregor returned to South America, applied for and received a military pension from the government of Venezuela, and died peacefully there in 1845. Gregor MacGregor is a prime example of someone who exerted an extraordinary amount of influence through unethical means. A con man, a fraud, a liar, and a cheat, he beguiled people through his ability to fulfill their insatiable need to believe his stories of Eden in the New World. It would be comforting to believe that people are more sophisticated in the twenty-first century than they were in the nineteenth, that a fraud as fantastic as Poyais could not take place today, but then there's Bernie Madoff, who makes Gregor MacGregor look like a clown prince.

Clearly, there are unscrupulous ways to influence people. You can lie to them, pressure them, bully them, threaten them, deceive them, and play to their baser natures. You can intimidate them with your superior size, rank, credentials, authority, wealth, and assertiveness. You can paint a picture of destruction, telling people what will happen if they fail to concede to you. You can turn crowds against them or employ thugs to investigate them, violate them, and harm them if they don't comply. To a greater or lesser extent, all these tactics work. They will influence people, although *influence* is hardly the right word to use. These tactics will *force* people to accede to your wishes, whether they like it or not. Or they will *deceive* people into thinking that they are acting in their best interests, when in fact they are acting in yours. When we remember that influence is getting others to believe something you want them to believe, think in a way you want them to think, or do something you want them to do—all of which Gregor MacGregor accomplished—then it's clear that influence has a very dark side.

Dark-side influence tactics take away people's legitimate right to say no, force them to comply with something contrary to their wishes or best interests, mislead them, or make them act when they would otherwise choose not to.

I include in "the dark side" any influence tactic that is unethical—that takes away the influencees' legitimate right to say no, that forces them to comply with something contrary to their wishes or best interests, that misleads them or forces them to act when they would otherwise choose not to. There are four common negative or unethical influence techniques: *avoiding, manipulating, intimidating,* and *threatening.*

Avoiding Forcing others to act, sometimes against their best interests, by avoiding responsibility or conflict or behaving passive-aggressively. It is the most common dark-side technique. In some cultures, trying to preserve harmony may be mistaken for avoiding.

Manipulating Influencing through lies, deceit, hoaxes, swindles, and cons; disguising one's real intentions or intentionally withholding information that others need to make the right decision.

Intimidating Imposing oneself on others; forcing people to comply by being loud, overbearing, abrasive, arrogant, aloof, or insensitive. It is the preferred technique of bullies.

Threatening Harming others or threatening to harm them if they do not comply; making examples of some people so others know that the threats are real. It is the preferred technique of dictators and despots.

In this part of the book, I describe these techniques more fully, give examples of their misuse, offer suggestions on how to defend yourself against them, and discuss what you can do differently if you find yourself turning to any of these negative influence techniques.

CHAPTER 9

I WOULD PREFER NOT TO

Avoiding

Before we invented carbon paper and photocopiers, important documents had to be copied by hand. In the nineteenth century, the people who did this laborious and meticulous work were called scriveners, and in one of Herman Melville's classic short stories, we meet an odd and difficult character named Bartleby the Scrivener. The story is narrated by the elderly lawyer who has employed Bartleby:

> At first Bartleby did an extraordinary quantity of writing. As if long famishing for something to copy, he seemed to gorge himself on my documents. There was no pause for digestion. He ran a day and night line, copying by sun-light and by candle-light. I should have been quite delighted with his application, had he been cheerfully industrious. But he wrote on silently, palely, mechanically.
>
> It was on the third day, I think, of his being with me, and before any necessity had arisen for having his own writing examined, that, being much hurried to complete a small affair I had in hand, I abruptly called to Bartleby. In my haste and natural expectancy of instant compliance, I sat with my head bent over the original on my desk, and my right hand sideways, and somewhat nervously extended with the copy, so that immediately upon emerging from his retreat, Bartleby might snatch it and proceed to business without the least delay.
>
> In this very attitude did I sit when I called to him, rapidly stating what it was I wanted him to do—namely, to examine a small paper with me. Imagine my surprise, nay, my consternation, when

without moving from his privacy, Bartleby in a singularly mild, firm voice, replied, "I would prefer not to."

I sat awhile in perfect silence, rallying my stunned faculties. Immediately it occurred to me that my ears had deceived me, or Bartleby had entirely misunderstood my meaning. I repeated my request in the clearest tone I could assume. But in quite as clear a one came the previous reply, "I would prefer not to."

"Prefer not to," echoed I, rising in high excitement, and crossing the room with a stride. "What do you mean? Are you moonstruck? I want you to help me compare this sheet here—take it," and I thrust it towards him.

"I would prefer not to," said he.[1]

Astonished at Bartleby's behavior but unsure what to do about it, the lawyer continually tries to get Bartleby's compliance, but to no avail. With a humane acquiescence, he comes to accept that his employee will not do anything he would prefer not to do, and then one day Bartleby announces that he will do no further copying. Unwilling to forcibly remove Bartleby from his office, the lawyer is eventually forced to resolve the matter by moving his practice to a new location—while Bartleby remains in the old office, unwilling to vacate even when the new owners take possession. They notify the police, who take Bartleby to prison, where he languishes and later dies—all to the lawyer's consternation.

"Bartleby the Scrivener" is an interesting tale that illustrates one of the dark sides of influence—influencing by avoiding. By refusing to do what his employer wants him to do, Bartleby is able to influence the elderly lawyer to accommodate his odd wishes, redistribute work to other scriveners, offer him money if Bartleby will leave, and move his practice to new offices. In real life, no employer would accept this degree of defiance and noncompliance from an employee, but in the fictional world of this tale, Bartleby's strange behavior is an amusing and perplexing example of avoiding taken to an extreme. Although we would be unlikely to encounter actual Bartlebys in business today, we do see them in defiant teenagers, societal dropouts, and those rare recalcitrants who refuse to pay taxes or go along with other of society's rules and traditions. However, avoiding in less extreme forms is the most commonly occurring form of the dark side of influence—and most of us have, at one time or another, used avoiding as a way to influence others.

In the children's game "hot potato," players stand in a circle and toss a beanbag back and forth while music is playing. When the music stops, the player left holding the bag is eliminated. Musical chairs is a variation of this party game, as are other games of elimination. In organizational game playing, the hot potato is a responsibility or task no one wants: firing for nonperformance an employee who is well liked by his peers, dealing with an irate customer, identifying employees to be laid off during a downturn, and other such odious duties. To skirt the responsibility for unpopular decisions or the unpleasantness of emotional confrontations, some managers influence by avoiding—by passing the buck, procrastinating until someone else takes care of it, or working behind the scenes to force someone else to take the hot potato.

THE THREE TYPES OF AVOIDING

Avoiding is influencing by indirection, and there are three typical ways it is done. First, there are the responsibility avoiders. These are the people who don't want to be blamed for unpopular decisions, so they try to shift the responsibility for the decision to someone else. Then there are the conflict avoiders—people who don't mind accepting the responsibility for unpopular decisions; they just don't want to be there for the confrontation with those who don't like the decision. These people hate conflict and will do whatever they can to avoid it. Finally, there are the passive-aggressive avoiders. They won't say what they really think to someone's face. Instead, they go behind the person's back and try to influence indirectly by politicking and manipulating others. This last form of avoiding may be the most insidious, but all three are ways of influencing other people indirectly.

Responsibility Avoiders

People who avoid responsibility typically either want to be liked or don't want to be blamed. Their goal is to never be stuck with the hot potato. Here are three examples:

1. One spouse or friend says to another, *Where do you want to go for dinner?* The avoiding spouse answers, *Oh, I don't know. Where do you want to go?* (By forcing the other person to make the decision, the avoider is no longer responsible if dinner isn't good.)

2. A manager and a supervisor in his unit are discussing another employee whom the manager wants fired:

MANAGER: *John, I don't like the way Hanratty handled that sales meeting. Get rid of him. I don't care what excuse you use, just do it.*

JOHN: *I hear you, but Hanratty's a good guy. And he's a solid performer.*

MANAGER: *And I'm sure you'll find someone equally good to replace him.* (As Hanratty is cleaning out his desk, this responsibility-avoiding manager will drop by and commiserate, saying that he didn't agree with the decision but has to give his supervisors the latitude to run their groups. This boss wants to be liked and doesn't want to be blamed, which are often two sides of the same coin.)

3. Another employee and her boss are discussing how to resolve a problem:

KELLY TO HER BOSS: *I've looked at our three options, as you asked, and I think Option B is probably the best solution. But I want to know what you think.*

BOSS: *It's your call, Kelly.*

KELLY: *I know, but you're the boss. I don't want to move forward without your approval.* (If her boss falls for it, Kelly will have done a great job of upward delegating. If Option B doesn't work, Kelly can say that Option B was what her boss wanted, so she can shift the blame.)

Conflict Avoiders

If you ask people whether they like conflict, the vast majority will say no, but when conflict happens most people will face it head-on and deal with it as best they can. Some people, however, would rather eat dirt sandwiches than be in direct conflict with someone. For some, the emotional toll of conflict is more than they care to tolerate. For others, avoiding conflict is a way of buying time. They hope the conflict will go away by itself or the other person will calm down and acquiesce. For still others, avoiding conflict is a way of preventing loss. They need to prevail in situations, and if they are forced to deal with the issues they might have to admit error or acquiesce to the other person, both of which they don't want to do, so they avoid the conflict as a way of saving face. Finally, conflict avoidance is often a strategy people employ to conceal their real feelings (even from themselves) and thus maintain harmony with other people (it's a false harmony, but that doesn't matter to them as long as the appearance of good will remains). Here are three examples of influencing by avoiding conflict:

1. The managing director of a business unit has this exchange with an associate director:

   DIRECTOR: *Henri, as you know, I am in Zermatt next week with my family.*

   ASSOCIATE DIRECTOR (ALARMED): *Our quarterly earnings announcement is next week, and our results are well below what the analysts projected.*

   DIRECTOR: *Yes, I know. I'd like you to make the announcement and handle the analysts' meeting. This is a good opportunity for you to assume a larger role in investor relations.* (Actually, it's a good way for the director to avoid conflict. Managers like this one often put buffers between themselves and people who are likely to be angry or upset. In the "good cop, bad cop" game, these managers are always the good cops, and their buffers are typically the bad cops. When the initial conflict has died down, this director will step back in and take over.)

2. A salesperson says to a peer, *Monika, I've got a really irate customer on line three. Could you please talk to her? I just can't deal with this today.* (At least this conflict avoider is honest about it.)

3. Two working parents receive a call from the police that their school-age son has been picked up for truancy. The conflict-avoiding parent claims to have an important meeting, which forces the other parent (who really doesn't want to be the only family disciplinarian) to pick up their son and confront him about his behavior. The conflict-avoiding parent will likely find an excuse to stay away from home until the storm has passed.

Passive-Aggressive Avoiders

The American Psychiatric Association (APA) classifies passive-aggression as a personality disorder. According to APA, "These individuals habitually resent, oppose, and resist demands to function at a level expected by others," and this behavior occurs most typically at work. "The resistance is expressed by procrastination, forgetfulness, stubbornness, and intentional inefficiency, especially in response to tasks assigned by authority figures."[2] A person exhibiting passive-aggressive behavior is agreeable and supportive in face-to-face dealings, but then demonstrates opposi-tional behaviors behind the person's back. Passive-aggressives often feel powerless and won't challenge or confront the person they disagree with or resent when they are in that person's presence. Later, however, they influence the situation and express their true feelings by delaying, forget-ting to do what was asked, failing to do a complete job, or sabotaging the effort—usually in a way they can't be blamed for. Here are two examples of passive-aggressive avoiding:

1. An employee, Sam, says to his manager, *I absolutely agree. I'll get right on that.* (When he returns to his desk, though, he is consumed by a hundred other priorities and never gets around to what his manager asked. Later, when asked why he didn't get it done, he says he was overwhelmed by some key customer problems that had to be resolved quickly and that took all his time.)

2. Two colleagues, Martin and Sara, are discussing bringing up an idea with their boss:

    MARTIN: *So what do you think of my idea?*

    SARA: *I think it's a great idea. I don't know why we didn't think of it before.*

    MARTIN: *Do you think our boss will like it?*

    SARA: *I can't say. But I think you should present it to her.*

    MARTIN: *Would you support me on it?*

    SARA: *I don't know why anyone wouldn't be supportive. It's a really interesting idea.* (Of course, Sara doesn't support the idea. You can tell because she wouldn't answer his question directly. She may be envious because she didn't think of the idea, or she may be jealous because she resents anyone looking better than her in their boss's eye. In any case, she won't say how she really feels. Later, however, she will mention Martin's idea to another colleague, someone she thinks is her ally, and degrade it. She'll do what she can behind the scenes to shoot it down before Martin presents it to the boss.)

As I said previously, passive-aggressive avoiding is the most insidi-ous of the three types, and this is true because you often think some-one supports you or your idea—only to discover later that the person doesn't or else has become "too busy" (which is usually an excuse). All three forms of avoiding are tactics for influencing people in indirect ways. They force others to accept responsibility, handle a crisis or confrontation, or modify what they are doing because of the influencer's unwillingness to act or be open about his true feelings. They are unethical influence techniques because the influencer is not open about his true motives or intentions and because they force others to do things that may not be in their best interests. Moreover, they are cowardly ways of behaving. That said, it's important to acknowledge that we all use the avoiding influence tactics now and then. One of the ways we cope with stress and difficulty is to avoid conflict or responsibility from time to time. It's problematic when it becomes a behavioral pattern and one of the primary ways you influence others.

INSIGHTS ON AVOIDING

In my research on power and influence, I measured how frequently people used the four negative influence tactics and correlated the frequency of their use with overall influence effectiveness, power sources, skills, and the frequency and effectiveness of the ten positive influence techniques. Here are the key findings for avoiding:

▶ There is a high price to pay for avoiding. People who receive the lowest frequency rating on avoiding (these are the "nonavoiders") had an overall influence effectiveness rating of 4.07 on a 5-point scale. The same rating for those who scored highest in avoiding frequency was 2.59. The gap between these numbers is more than four standard deviations. In other words, it is a highly significant difference. High avoiders are substantially less influential overall than nonavoiders.

▶ Interestingly, high avoiders tend to rely on stating, legitimizing, and appealing to relationship as their positive influence techniques, whereas nonavoiders rely on logical persuading, consulting, modeling, and appealing to values.

▶ Nonavoiders were judged to be very high in character, history, attraction, and reputation. In contrast, the high avoiders had resources, role, and information as their highest-rated power sources. In other words, the high avoiders had to rely on structural clout (role and resources) whereas nonavoiders relied on personal power and the esteem with which they are held by others (reputation).

▶ The strongest skills of people who did not regularly practice avoidance were building rapport and trust, logical reasoning, supporting and encouraging others, speaking conversationally, listening, behaving self-confidently, and showing genuine interest in others, and in these areas they were judged to be significantly more skilled. Among high avoiders, their most highly rated skills were persisting, behaving self-confidently, and showing a willingness to ask others for favors. Their lowest-rated skill was resolving conflicts and disagreements among others (no surprise there). It's intriguing that behaving self-confidently was among the top-rated skills for both nonavoiders and high avoiders. This indicates that avoiding is not about a lack of confidence. It's about an unwillingness to be open and direct with people and to accept responsibility for your thoughts and behavior.

DEFENDING YOURSELF AGAINST AVOIDING

It's important to recognize that avoiding is a tactic people will sometimes use to influence you. They'll use this technique as a way to get you to solve a problem for them, to force you to make a decision they should be making, to make you responsible for an outcome, or to take responsibility when it should actually belong to them. The first step in defending yourself against avoiding is to recognize when it's happening, which isn't always easy. Most of us don't interact with another person and scrutinize that interaction simultaneously. We are too busy dealing with the subject at hand and engaging with the other person. Avoiding can be subtle. We may not immediately become aware that the other person is avoiding responsibility or conflict. Of course, sometimes it's blatantly obvious, but often it's not. Because everyone uses avoiding at some point, it may become apparent to you only when a person habitually tries to influence you this way, or when someone offers support and encouragement to your face but tells a different story behind your back (which you hear about from other people).

Once you become aware of what's happening, you need to decide whether to challenge it. For instance, it may be advantageous for you or the organization if you do accept the responsibility or handle the conflict. Maybe you are better prepared for it. Maybe it would lead to a better outcome. However, if you can't or don't want to catch the influencer's hot potato, then the best approach is not to catch it. A good first step is to help these types of influencers to see what they're doing. Sometimes, people are legitimately unaware that they are trying to avoid responsibility or conflict. When you point it out to them, in a gentle way, they may stop doing it. Then, you need to say no. Say it in a gentle, nonconfrontational way, but be clear that this is a situation the would-be influencer needs to handle himself. If necessary, push back harder, and persist. When the person discovers that you won't accept the hot potato, he will either take it back and deal with it or try to find someone who's more compliant than you. Here are some ways you might respond to the eight examples of avoiding I cited earlier:

RESPONSIBILITY AVOIDERS

1. Tell your spouse or friend who doesn't want to choose a restaurant: *Thanks, but I chose the restaurant last time. It's your turn.* If that doesn't work, cross your arms (in most cultures, this gesture reflects stubbornness) and say, *No. I keep making these decisions, and that's not fair to you. So I'm not choosing this time. It's your call.*
2. When asked to fire an employee, John, who is the unit supervisor, might reply to his responsibility-avoiding manager: *I'm not comfortable doing that, partly because I think it's the wrong decision. If you'd like, I can pull Hanratty into a meeting with the two of us, but I think he needs to hear from you what you didn't like about how he handled the sales meeting.*
3. The boss might prevent his responsibility-avoiding employee from upward delegating a task to him by saying, *I will support whatever you decide, but I delegated the responsibility for this to you, and you need to make the call.*

CONFLICT AVOIDERS

1. The associate director of a business unit can tell his conflict-avoiding managing director, *I appreciate the vote of confidence, but the analysts aren't going to be happy just hearing from me. More important, I think corporate is going to be looking at how we handle this. With all due respect, I think you should consider flying back from Zermatt for this meeting.*
2. The salesperson asked to handle a difficult call by her conflict-avoiding peer can reply, *Sorry. I've had my quota of irate customers for the day,* or else she can shift to coaching mode: *Hey, I know how you feel, but just stay calm and you'll be fine. Be a good listener and then do what you can for them. Unfortunately, dealing with upset customers is part of the job. We all have to do it, and you've done it very well before. I've heard you. Don't worry. You'll be fine.*

3. For the parent who is expected to be the sole family disciplinarian, it's probably time to be adamant and firmly say to the other parent: *I don't think either one of us should go to the police station by ourselves. We need to show our son that this is not acceptable behavior for either of us. If you have to finish a business meeting first, then please call me when it's over, and I'll meet you at the station.*

PASSIVE-AGGRESSIVE AVOIDERS

1. In handling the passive-aggressive employee, it's important, first of all, to establish accountability. The manager can tell his employee, *Sam, when you said you'd get right on it, I took that as a commitment to getting the job done as quickly as possible.* (Sam will offer excuses, so it's also important not to accept them.) *The other things that came up may have been important, but so was this. And if you had a question about which was more important, or if you needed help getting everything done, then you should have come to me, and I would have helped you sort it out. That's what I always expect you to do in the future.* (It's important to drive a stake in the ground so that you eliminate more excuses for avoiding in the future. The manager needs to get Sam to complete the job and be very specific about the requirements and expectations.) *I'd like you to put everything else aside and get this job done. Can you do that?* (The answer needs to be yes. If not, problem-solve.) *When can you have it done? . . . That's great. Then I'll expect you back here tomorrow at 9 a.m. Please don't get distracted by anything else. This is an important assignment.* (Another strategy might have been for the manager to try to uncover the reason why Sam was not fully invested in doing this task. However, I've taken a tough but respectful position in this dialogue because with passive-aggressives you have to. If you give them an inch, they will take a mile, so it's important to be assertive, direct, and clear.)

2. When Sara wouldn't answer Martin's question directly, he should have clarified it right then, saying, *I hope others will be supportive of my idea, but I'm asking if you will support it.* (If she's hesitant at all, he should probe further.) *You seem hesitant for some reason. Is there something about it you don't like? It's okay to be completely candid with me. I'm looking for an honest opinion.* (These last statements give Sara permission to say what she really thinks.)

IF YOU USE AVOIDING HABITUALLY

Everyone uses dark-side influence tactics from time to time. It's part of human nature to avoid some conflicts, to shed some responsibility now and then, to be less than truthful sometimes. However, few of us go to the manipulative extremes of an investment scammer like Gregor MacGregor or his modern-day counterpart Bernie Madoff. So if you occasionally use avoiding, you are like most other human beings. It's the frequent or habitual use of avoiding that is problematic.

It's most important to recognize that chronically avoiding responsibility and conflict is a career showstopper. If you work in an organization and are ambitious, then avoiding is a disastrous strategy to adopt. Once people recognize that you frequently avoid conflict and/or responsibility, they will lose trust and confidence in you and respect for you. If that happens, it may be best to leave the organization and start over somewhere else. You may never be able to change people's minds about what they would see as a fundamental character flaw. That's how important it is.

So what do you do about it? The short answer is to accept responsibility and learn to face conflict, no matter how challenging that may be for you. First, recognize when you are avoiding conflict or responsibility. Try to understand why that's happening. Avoiding is about fear, so try to understand what you are afraid of. With responsibility, it is best to take small steps forward. Seek and accept responsibility for increasingly challenging tasks and assignments. It may be difficult to do, and you may hate it, but the only way to overcome fear is to face it head-on and learn to deal with it. Most people discover that there was little to be truly afraid of. Once they learn that, it becomes much easier. Learning to confront conflict may be more difficult because conflict is between people and it's untidy. It can end badly. It can bruise feelings and cause ill will for serious lengths of time. There are some good educational programs on conflict management, and one of them may be appropriate for you.

If you are behaving passive-aggressively, then again it is best to recognize what you are doing and why. Passive-aggression usually occurs because people feel powerless. Acting behind the scenes is the way they try to gain power. The internal reasoning goes like this: "I don't dare confront the boss directly because he is too powerful and may harm me. So I'll undo what he wants behind his back. He won't know I did it, so I'm safe, and this will make me feel more powerful." Of course, this misdirection will eventually fail, but it mitigates the feeling of powerlessness in the meantime. If you find yourself doing this, know it for what it is and then try to build the courage to be honest and forthright with the person you are being passive-aggressive with. Surfacing the real issues and trying to deal with them candidly and directly is the most courageous and psychologically healthy path forward.

If you are a leader or manager and are avoiding responsibility or conflict or are behaving passive-aggressively, my honest advice is to knock it off. Whether you intend it or not, your employees are picking up on the behavior you are modeling (see chapter 7). Eventually, your subordinates will take their cues from the boss and behave as you do, and you'll have a dysfunctional organization.

KEY CONCEPTS

1. There are four common negative or unethical influence tactics: *avoiding, manipulating, intimidating,* and *threatening.* These tactics take away influencees' legitimate right to say no, force them to comply with something contrary to their wishes or best interests, mislead them, or make them act when they would otherwise choose not to.
2. Avoiding is influencing by indirection, and there are three ways this is done: avoiding responsibility, avoiding conflict, and avoiding through passive-aggression.
3. People who avoid responsibility typically either want to be liked or don't want to be blamed.
4. People avoid conflict to buy time, prevent loss, avoid unsettling emotions, save face, or conceal their real feelings.
5. Passive-aggressive behavior occurs when people resent, oppose, or resist demands, usually from an authority figure, but do it indirectly—by procrastination, forgetfulness, stubbornness, and intentional inefficiency. In passive-aggressive avoiding, people are typically agreeable to your face but sabotage you behind your back.
6. People pay a high price for avoiding. Those who frequently use avoiding are substantially less influential overall than people who rarely use avoiding as an influence strategy.

CHALLENGES FOR READERS

1. Unfortunately, life is full of examples of people who try to influence others through unscrupulous means. In your own experience, where have you seen this happen? Where have you seen someone try to influence others by avoiding? Manipulating them? Intimidating them? Threatening them?

2. Why do you think people use these dark-side tactics to influence others? Do these negative tactics succeed? At what cost to the influencees? To the influencer?

3. Do you know people who are habitual avoiders? What do they gain from it? What do they lose? Do you agree with my assertion that this is a career showstopper?

4. Which is worse—avoiding responsibility or avoiding conflict? Why?

5. Passive-aggression is a way of coping when people feel powerless. Have you ever had anyone behave passive-aggressively toward you? Have you encountered people who are pleasant and supportive to your face but derogatory behind your back? When you discovered what they were doing, what did you do about it?

CHAPTER 10

THERE'S A SUCKER BORN
EVERY MINUTE

Manipulating

On Saturday, October 16, 1869, William "Stub" Newell hired two men to dig a new well on his farm in Cardiff, New York. Around 11 a.m., the two men struck something solid, likely a large boulder. As they removed the dirt around it, however, they discovered that it was shaped like a human foot—except it was two feet long and composed of very hard stone. Amazed, they told the farmer what they had found and kept digging until they uncovered the nearly intact body of a naked man who measured more than ten feet tall. The men were convinced they'd found the petrified remains of a Native American giant. By Sunday morning, the word had spread and Newell's farm was overrun by curiosity seekers, gawkers, and reporters. Before long, Newell was charging admission for those who wanted a glimpse of the "Cardiff Giant."

Although some scientists declared it a fake, interest in the giant grew to such proportions that a syndicate headed by David Hannum offered to buy the petrified remains, which Newell sold to Hannum for more than $37,000—a grand sum in those days. Hannum put the giant on tour, and it drew such large crowds that master showman P. T. Barnum wanted to buy it. Hannum refused to sell, however, so Barnum had a copy of it made and began exhibiting it himself as "the real Giant." Noting that people were lining up to pay for a look at Barnum's giant, Hannum scoffed, "There's a sucker born every minute," an expression commonly but incorrectly attributed to Barnum himself. Of course, both giants were fakes. The Cardiff version had in fact been made by New York merchant George Hull, who had wanted to prove that giants had in fact once walked the earth. Cardiff farmer Stub Newell was his cousin. Before the Cardiff Giant was revealed to be a hoax, hundreds of thousands of people had paid to glimpse it and Barnum's fake of a fake.[1]

Frauds, con artists, swindlers, grifters, imposters, hoaxers, and manipulators try to influence others by creating the illusion of reality, and although deception has an unsavory aspect it has nonetheless played a large role in human history, often a celebrated role. One of the greatest battlefield commanders of all time, Alexander the Great, would march his army into the proximity of his enemy and make camp the night before battle. To convince the enemy that his army was larger than it actually was, Alexander would order his generals to build hundreds of additional campfires beyond the army's camp. The enemy troops, convinced they were confronting a far larger force, would alter their plan of battle, sometimes by defending areas Alexander had no plans to attack and sometimes by keeping too many forces in reserve. When the battle came, enemy troops would be on the verge of defeat, reeling, morale lost, even before they could commit additional forces. Alexander won a number of battles by thus deceiving his enemies. As Sun Tzu observed in *The Art of War,* "All war is based on deception."

During World War II, the Allies perpetrated one of the grandest and most successful deceptions in the history of warfare. At the start of 1944, the Allies were planning the invasion of Europe. The closest point between England and France was at Pas de Calais, and this was the logical choice for a seaborne invasion of France. Normandy, the actual site of the D-day landings, was farther away and would pose greater difficulty. Norway was also a possible invasion site because it was lightly defended by the Nazis and could have allowed the Allies to attack from the north into Europe through Scandinavia. General Dwight Eisenhower and his planners knew that the invasion might fail if the Nazis concentrated their forces at Normandy or moved reserves to the area before the Allies established a secure beachhead, so they hatched a plan to convince Hitler that the invasion would come through the Pas de Calais.

This plan was called Operation Fortitude. One of the primary deceptions was the creation of a fictional army called the First U.S. Army Group, whose commander was General George Patton. To convince German agents in Britain that this army was real, the allies constructed buildings and other infrastructure needed for an army group and deployed inflatable rubber tanks and wooden replicas of landing

craft and artillery pieces. They also simulated the amount of radio traffic the Germans would expect of an army group, had some double
agents feeding misinformation to their German handlers, and leaked
misinformation through diplomatic channels. This elaborate deception enabled the Allies not only to establish a foothold in the conti-
nent but also to build the ports needed to bring in additional troops,
equipment, and supplies.

---

*Manipulators try to influence others by creating the illusion of
reality, and although deception has an unsavory aspect it has
nonetheless played a large role in human history, often a celebrated role.*

In war, deception is often practiced on a grand scale, but socially
acceptable forms of deception occur in many avenues of everyday life.
The art of poker, for instance, includes betting and bluffing in ways
that deceive other players and influence them to make poor decisions.
In American football, offenses run plays designed to deceive the
defense (and vice versa). The finest quarterbacks can disguise their
intentions until the moment before they pass the ball to a receiver,
and the best defenses can disguise a blitz until the ball is snapped.
Companies spend billions of dollars in advertising annually to shape
consumers' impressions of their products, and the fashion and cos-
metics industries are largely about helping people manage others'
impressions of them. Film, theater, and literature are other ways we
allow ourselves to be deceived. Nineteenth-century poet Samuel Taylor Coleridge argued that audiences could accept and enjoy literature
with fantastic elements only because they willingly suspended their
disbelief—a notion that applies to the stage and screen as well. When
we cry at a sad movie or are frightened by a thriller, we know at some
level that we are being manipulated but we allow it because we are
entertained (an implicit agreement between us and the artist that
Coleridge called "poetic faith").

Manipulation is about creating an illusion of reality, and a magic
show is a perfect example of our willingness to be deceived. When the
magician saws someone in half or pulls a rabbit out of an empty hat,
we are baffled by how he did it but delighted to be fooled because we

know it's a trick. What makes this an ethical deception is that we agree to it. We are not being taken advantage of. The magician isn't stealing from us or deceiving us into doing something harmful or otherwise against our wishes. Manipulation is unethical when the lie causes us harm or otherwise dupes us into doing something we would not want to do if we knew the truth. Bernard Madoff was also a magician, but his sleight of hand was to convince investors that he was trustworthy and market savvy and could consistently make more money for them than anyone else could. Like a modern Houdini, he also played into his victims' willing suspension of disbelief, but he did it for self-serving and wholly ignoble reasons.

THE BERNIE MADOFF MAGIC SHOW

To understand how Bernie Madoff became the Harry Houdini of investment advising, it's important to know that he was born in Queens, New York, an ordinary kid in an ordinary family. He was street-smart but an undistinguished student, graduating with a degree in political science from Hofstra College. He regretted later that he hadn't gone to a prestigious tier-one business school like Wharton or Stanford, but it's doubtful that he would have been admitted to one of those institutions. He earned money working as a lifeguard and a lawn sprinkler installer. He lacked money, connections, and privilege—in a time and place where those things mattered. What he did not lack was ambition fueled by a burning desire to be somebody. In this respect he was like the cabana boy played by Matt Dillon in the movie *The Flamingo Kid*, except he lacked that character's moral compass. To Madoff, being somebody meant having power, wealth, and respect, and to him the end justified the means.

In 1960, while working in his father-in-law's accounting firm, he started a penny stock trading firm and then an investment advisory firm. Thanks to his father-in-law, who referred his friends and their families to Madoff, his fledgling enterprises grew. He couldn't compete with the stock traders on the New York Stock Exchange, where he was too small to be registered, so he experimented with computerized stock trading, an innovation that led to the founding of the NASDAQ stock exchange in 1971. NASDAQ is undoubtedly the crowning achievement of his career (and his only legitimate one). He was named the nonexecutive chairman of that exchange in 1990, a position he held for three years. By that time, he was making tens of millions of

Timothy A. Clary/AFP/Getty Images

► Master manipulator Bernie Madoff
conned thousands of investors, including
close friends and family members, out of
billions of dollars.

dollars a year and had earned the recognition and respect he'd craved as a young man—but by then it was not enough, and like Alice in Wonderland, he may already have gone too far down the rabbit hole to return. It's not clear when Madoff started defrauding investors, but government investigators believe it may have been as early as the 1970s. Whenever it started, he created one of the most elaborate and longest-running Ponzi schemes in history. In a feat of magic even Houdini could not have pulled off, Madoff the Magnificent waved his wand and made $50 billion disappear. How he did it is a case study in power and influence.

Madoff's Sources of Power

To understand Madoff's extraordinary ability to influence others, we need first to examine his sources of power. Early in his career, Madoff's power sources were relatively low—with three important exceptions. Although he rated low to neutral on knowledge, expressiveness, character, role, resources, information, and reputation, Bernie had high history power with his father-in-law, Saul Alpern, through his wife, Ruth, who had been his high school sweetheart. Like most fathers-in-law, Alpern did what he could to help his daughter and son-in-law, and as an accountant, Alpern had enough connections to steer clients to Madoff in the early 1960s. Alpern's connections gave Madoff an important source of network power, which he parlayed into enough business to establish his stock trading and investment advisory firm. Moreover, Bernie was charming and soft-spoken. People liked him. He inspired trust. So he had attraction power working for him.

> *Manipulation is unethical when the lie causes us harm or oth-*
> *erwise dupes us into doing something we would not want to*
> *do if we knew the truth.*

If we fast-forward to the 1980s, we see a much different picture. Madoff's firm had steadily grown, largely through referrals from his network of friends and family members and feeder funds (other mutual funds that funneled investor money to him). By this time, his market-maker division was one of the most active on the New York Stock Exchange, and he was able to inflate the volume of his trades through the questionable but legal practice of paying brokers to execute customers' orders through his brokerage. Feeder funds and legal kickbacks were two of the principal strategies he used to accelerate the volume of money flowing into his firm. In effect, he increased his own network power by piggybacking on the networks of others. By 1990, he'd been active in the National Association of Securities Dealers (NASD), which was a self-regulatory organization that oversaw the operation of NASDAQ and the over-the-counter markets. At one point, Madoff was chairman of NASD and served on its board of governors. Now his power sources were considerable.

KNOWLEDGE—Madoff had become very knowledgeable about the markets and was recognized for it. He knew this and used it to his advantage by implying not only that he knew a great deal, but that he knew *more* about trading than anyone else. He said he could provide consistent returns in the 10 percent to 18 percent range no matter what the market conditions—something no one else could do. The people who thought they were getting those consistently good returns did not want to question him, and to those who did question him, Madoff would answer that how he did it was his "secret sauce," in effect. Those who questioned Madoff's dealings, like financial analyst Harry Markopolos, could not get anyone to listen. In Madoff's magic act, then, one of his early tricks was to convince people that he knew more than everyone else and what he knew was a secret. In short, he convinced people that he had superior knowledge power.

EXPRESSIVENESS—Madoff was understated and soft-spoken. Eloquence was never one of his great sources of power—but it didn't need to be.

One of his friends, model Carmen Dell'Orefice, said, "Bernie was quiet, not a storyteller, not a conversationalist. I often thought he was perhaps bored. He was just Bernie, pleasant and polite."[2]

ATTRACTION—Madoff always was charming when he needed to be, especially when he was in front of friends or investors and needed to wear his public mask. Behind the scenes, without the mask, he was reportedly a different person, arrogant and imperial, a man who ruled his family by fear.[3] He had many of the characteristics of the narcissistic personality disorder, which include exaggerated self-importance; need for excessive admiration; fantasies of success, power, and brilliance; arrogant or haughty behaviors; a sense of entitlement; and a belief that he is unique and deserves special treatment or privileges. According to the American Psychiatric Association, people with this disorder often take advantage of others and lack empathy.[4] Although it's an act, sociopaths are often clever and charming. They know how to behave toward others to increase their interpersonal attraction, and Bernie came across as a wise, grandfatherly figure people could trust. So his attraction power was quite high and was enhanced, of course, by the apparent ease with which he made money for his friends, family, and clients.

CHARACTER—Ironically, Madoff projected strong character. He publicly advocated greater transparency in trading, and he congratulated the Securities and Exchange Commission (SEC) for its effective oversight of the markets—at the same time he was duping their investigators. Mostly, however, he got his character power by borrowing it from others, especially two close friends and father figures, Norman F. Levy, a New York real estate tycoon, and Carl Shapiro, founder of women's clothing manufacturer Kay Windsor, Inc. Both men treated Bernie as a surrogate son and vouched for him with their friends, especially those in the wealthy Jewish communities in New York and Palm Beach. Part of Madoff's genius was to ingratiate himself with powerful and respected people whose own character seemed above reproach. Then he not only gained network power from them, he gained character power as well. He did not exclusively target wealthy Jewish communities, but many of his victims came from those communities because he had an affinity with them, and vice versa. People tend to be more influenced by people who are similar to them, and Madoff took advantage of this fact.

HISTORY—Madoff had enormous history power with people like Levy and Shapiro, and many others who served with him on boards or were close country club friends. He had also developed close relationships with the directors of numerous feeder funds, like Walter Noel, who ran the Fairfield Greenwich Group, which funneled billions of investment dollars to Madoff, and Robert Jaffe, of Cohmad Securities, who was Carl Shapiro's son-in-law. There were numerous others in this close-knit network of friends and family ties, all of whom, after the fact, say they were unaware that Madoff was anything but what he appeared to be. The best shills a magician can have are respected people in the community who have extensive networks of their own and are vocal advocates for the trickster.

ROLE—By the 1990s, Madoff had extraordinary role power as the head of Bernard L. Madoff Investment Securities LLC. His role not only gave him the power and authority to direct the firm's people and operations (and perpetrate and hide a massive fraud), it also gave him legitimacy and a platform to represent himself as the most knowledgeable and successful investment adviser of all time. With his success and his role came extraordinary *resource* power. He had significant personal assets but also controlled hundreds of millions of dollars of other people's money.

INFORMATION—Of course, as the head of an investment advisory firm and a well-connected leader in financial services, Madoff had access to an enormous amount of information. More to the point, however, was the presumption by many people that because of his extraordinary track record, he must have had access to privileged information no one else had. How else could he achieve consistently high returns, month after month, year after year?

NETWORK—This had been an early source of power for Madoff, and it grew substantially as he attracted more feeder fund managers, banks, and wealthy investors who would recommend him to their friends. Madoff did not have to do much of any marketing himself. He had rich devotees who spread the word for him.

REPUTATION—Throughout the 1990s and beyond, Madoff's reputation as a market wizard grew, largely through the viral marketing created by word of mouth from investors and feeder fund brokers who were delighted to still be earning excellent returns (or so it seemed on their monthly statements) despite the dot-com meltdown and the recession in 2002. Madoff enhanced his reputation by making clever use of the principle of scarcity, a decision-making bias I described in chapter 8. He did not accept everyone who wanted to invest with him. He made it an exclusive club, which increased people's appetite to be among the chosen ones. To his investors, Madoff was the goose laying the golden eggs. His returns were so consistent, even in horrible market conditions, that many of them not only invested everything they had with him, they actually mortgaged houses they had owned, debt free, and then invested that money with Madoff. It was too good to be true, but they didn't question it, blinded as they were by the magnificent façade he'd created and their own sense of entitlement in the good fortune they were privileged to be part of. They willingly suspended their disbelief.

Madoff's Influence Strategies

At the time of his arrest in 2008, Madoff had more than 3,000 clients, including many banks (Banco Santander reportedly lost $3.1 billion) and charitable institutions (the Elie Wiesel Foundation for Humanity lost $37 million in the fraud). How was Madoff able to influence so many people to invest with him, including institutions that routinely perform due diligence? How was he able to hoodwink the SEC, which cleared him of wrongdoing multiple times? The quick answer is that he manipulated them. He lied, concealed the truth, and practiced an elaborate deception that convinced people they were seeing something that wasn't there. Clearly, manipulation of this kind is unethical, but he also used some of the positive influence techniques as well.

LOGICAL PERSUADING—Had he not concealed the truth about what he was doing with people's money, the logical persuading he used would not have held up to scrutiny. So he refused to disclose how he achieved his remarkable returns, and most people accepted his reticence because they didn't want him to turn them away. Even SEC investigators, faced with contradictions when they questioned him, failed to press for the clarifications that might have unmasked the fraud because of Madoff's veil of authority. He'd been a Wall Street fixture since 1960. He'd been chairman of NASDAQ. Intimidated by his stature, they accepted his assurances and let it go.

LEGITIMIZING—Madoff frequently used this influence technique. He relied on his authority as a Wall Street veteran and a former chair of

NASDAQ, and his presumed financial genius. He used the trappings of his offices on the top floors of the Lipstick Building in New York, and he used the authority of friends like Levy and Shapiro to legitimize his operations. Ironically, he also used the fact that the SEC had investigated and cleared his firm to legitimize his firm and its practices. This kind of influencing was very persuasive with some investors. Before his arrest in December 2008, he'd been investigated numerous times by the SEC, and the agency had never found him at fault. What greater authority could an investor want?

STATING—This was one of Madoff's core influence techniques. Backed by the façade he'd developed and the authority others granted him, he simply told people how it was—and they believed him.

EXCHANGING—It's not clear that Madoff did much active exchanging, but he created a seductive virtual exchange that was influential with the brokers and feeder funds that sent him clients. He paid them what amounted to a commission to refer clients to him, and he did not charge fees for his money-management services, which is unusual. "Indeed," wrote Erin Arvedlund in *Barron's Online*, "while fund marketers like Fairfield Greenwich rake off a 1.5 percent from investors, none of that goes back to Madoff. Nor does he charge a fee on money he manages in private accounts."[5] This arrangement made it highly lucrative for fund managers to funnel investor money to Madoff. So the exchange was implicit: "You can become fabulously wealthy by funneling your clients' money to me." Many fund managers did, and some of them invested all their money with Madoff, too.

SOCIALIZING—He was by all reports charming and pleasant when he needed to be, but Madoff was not known as a great socializer. But remember that the socializing influence technique is about creating commonality. Madoff did that by targeting wealthy Jewish investors, people like himself, including close friends and family members, many of whom were victims of his scheme, including his sister and one of his sons. This is known as *affinity fraud*—scamming people with whom you have many similarities. By the time his Ponzi scheme reached epic proportions, Madoff often refused to meet with individual investors, which enhanced his image as a magisterial wizard running an exclusive club.

APPEALING TO RELATIONSHIP—Because he had no qualms about bilking those closest to him, he used this influence technique frequently.

ALLIANCE BUILDING—Madoff shrewdly built alliances with brokers and feeder fund managers, as described previously. He also made effective use of social proof. Ponzi schemes will fail unless new money keeps rolling in, so he continually needed to attract new investors. To convince people that investing with him was both safe and lucrative, he cited the fact that other notable people had their money invested with him, people like Carl Shapiro and Norman F. Levy. His investors included HSBC, Access International, Fortis Bank, Tremont Capital, Union Bancaire Privée, Royal Bank of Scotland, Yeshiva University, and numerous foundations.[6] Although Madoff insisted that funds and investors not list him as their financial adviser, word of mouth spread, and this was powerful social proof.

In the end, Madoff's house of cards collapsed in the wake of the recession of 2008. The deepest financial downturn in decades led overextended investors to withdraw money from their investment accounts to cover other losses. What began as a mild panic turned into a stampede as the housing market collapsed and the recession deepened. On December 10, 2008, Madoff confessed to his sons that it had all been a big lie. They notified an attorney, and the next day Bernie's magic show ended with his arrest by the FBI.

Manipulators like Bernie Madoff influence others by deceiving them. The big lie usually paints an attractive picture—in this case of consistent double-digit financial returns. Madoff enhanced that mirage by invoking the principle of scarcity and making the supposed gains exclusive. That exclusivity not only inflated his own sense of self-worth, it fed the narcissism of some of his investors, who felt it an honor to be among the privileged few Bernie would accept as a client. It was too good to be true, but they were blinded by the glittering picture the magician showed them, which highlights an important fact about manipulation as an influence tactic: The lies the influencer tells are often ones the influencees want very much to believe. That's why they willingly suspend their disbelief. As Machiavelli noted, centuries ago, "Men are so simple and so much inclined to obey immediate needs that a deceiver will never lack victims for his deceptions."

COOKING THE BOOKS

When executive bonuses and compensation are tied to company performance—as they should be—there can be a terrible temptation among unscrupulous executives to manipulate earnings so that the company appears to be performing better than it actually is. Cooking the books is a way to inflate earnings per share, so the company's performance keeps Wall Street and the board of directors happy, entices new investors, generates bonuses and pay increases, and protects the jobs of senior leaders. Executives can influence the company's various stakeholders through accounting mechanisms such as capitalizing expenses that should be recorded as operating expenses, overstating revenues, or overbudgeting for nonrecurring expenses.

The lies manipulative influencers tell are often ones their influencees want very much to believe. That's why they willingly suspend their disbelief.

Peregrine Systems was forced into bankruptcy after it was discovered that senior executives there had falsified sales figures and hidden losses as goodwill costs related to acquisitions. Ten of Peregrine's senior leaders, including the CEO and CFO, were sent to prison for that fraud. Similar scandals at Enron, Tyco, WorldCom, Polly Peck (a U.K.-based textile company), Waste Management Inc., Computer Associates, BCCI, Adelphia, and many other companies have resulted in losses to investors, bankruptcies, and indictments of company executives. Cooking the books is usually the result of a conspiracy to manipulate because one executive can't do it on his own, so it's common to see both the CEO and CFO indicted for the crime (e.g., Enron and Tyco). Businesses are also guilty of influencing by manipulation when they do the following:

► Misrepresent their products or pull a bait-and-switch
► Fail to disclose hidden fees or surcharges
► Put important disclaimers or notices in the fine print
► Add fillers to their products without disclosing the fact
► Use inflated or inaccurate price comparisons in their advertising

► Manipulate photos so that the person or product shown is more attractive than in reality

Governments manipulate when they spread disinformation or propaganda. Scientists and researchers manipulate when they falsify research results to get product approval or additional research funding. Politicians manipulate when they promise constituents something they have no intention of delivering. And so on. In every area of human endeavor, people sometimes manipulate the facts and distort reality in order to paint a picture that is more favorable to them or less favorable to someone else, and those lies are intended to influence others in various ways. As an influence tactic, manipulation is appealing to the unscrupulous because it is expedient. The Bernie Madoffs of the world would not be able to influence others as they'd like if they had to tell the truth. To them, lying is more expedient and more successful (at least some of the time).

FALSE FLATTERY AND OTHER FORMS OF INGRATIATION

Everyone lies, even if just a little bit. You don't want to embarrass Aunt Sally by telling her what you really think of her dress, so you tell her you like it. The dog did not eat your homework, but you're ashamed to admit that you forgot about it. You don't want to risk telling your boss how dumb you think her idea is, so you say the idea is "interesting" or "provocative" or "worth looking into." We recognize the need for these small departures from the truth and excuse them by calling them "white lies." These, too, are attempts to influence by manipulation, but they are clearly more benign than the colossal fraud perpetrated by Bernie Madoff. Manipulation is less benign when people use false flattery or ingratiation to curry favor or gain an unfair advantage, as in these examples:

► An ambitious employee is very solicitous toward the boss, always agreeing with what he says and complimenting him publicly for his ideas and leadership. Privately and among other employees, this person is more guarded but still says good things about the boss (knowing that a contrary word might get back to the boss).

► An upwardly mobile young professional takes up golf because the managing director plays golf and then starts pursuing other interests the director enjoys. She pays attention to where he and his wife eat, what shows they see, and so on, and goes to the same places and does the same things. During informal hallway chats, she mentions a show they both saw or a restaurant she recently went to that she knows he likes; she takes every opportunity to point out how similar she is to him. He is unaware of her motives, but when a promotion becomes available he gives it to her because he likes the way she thinks.

► The communications director for a public official carefully screens all the information coming into the office and ensures that the official sees only what the director wants her to see. The communications director insists on previewing all presentations people want to make to this official so that the impression she receives is what he wants. In this way, the director influences the public official's opinion on some issues where he has a vested interest in the outcome. Privately, he tells friends that he's the real power behind the throne.

► The director of a laboratory receives a study report indicating that one of the ingredients of a product the lab produces could pose a health hazard. Before publishing the report, he questions the study team and orders it to substitute the word *risk* for the word *hazard* because, he argues, their studies were not comprehensive enough to warrant the more alarming term. The company never makes the report public or notifies past users of the product that it may pose a serious health problem.

Lying, covering up, and manipulative ingratiation are attempts to influence people by creating a false impression or painting a rosier picture than actually exists. People use this negative or unethical influence tactic not only because it's an expedient way to get what they want—it's often the only way they can do it. A con artist manipulates his victims because otherwise they would not comply. A spin doctor manipulates the facts because otherwise people wouldn't believe what he wants them to believe. A dictator calls his army's actions "ethnic cleansing" instead of genocide because he can't admit the truth without mobilizing world opinion against him. Let's face it: People use manipulation because it often works. However, when the people they are trying to influence discover that they are being manipulated, the downside of this negative tactic is as strong as the upside, and the influencer will lose substantial power as his reputation and perceptions of his character are tarnished.

INSIGHTS ON MANIPULATING

My research on power and influence reveals some fascinating insights about people who make high use of manipulation to influence others:

► People who score high on manipulation are significantly less influential overall than people who score low on manipulation. Although manipulators may succeed for a time with some people, in the long run they are considerably less influential than those people who influence ethically.

► High-score manipulators use the following influence techniques most frequently: stating, legitimizing, appealing to relationship, alliance building, and then socializing. This profile is remarkably like Bernie Madoff's. These manipulators use stating significantly more often than any other influence technique, but of course what they are stating is often a lie. Then they will try an appeal to authority to legitimize the deception, or rely on existing relationships. They may, like Madoff, find allies who perhaps unwittingly help them manipulate others.

► Although they are most effective at using stating, their second-most effective influence technique is logical persuading. They may lie or manipulate the facts, but they know how to make arguments and present cases that sound logical.

► Their four strongest sources of power are resources, role, information, and network. Manipulators like Madoff often control resources or have roles with legitimate authority. They often have good access to information (which they use selectively to manipulate their victims' views of reality), and they typically have good networks.

► The research shows that manipulators are skillful at persisting, asking others for favors, behaving self-confidently (it's essential to the façade they are creating), asserting, using assertive nonverbals, behaving authoritatively, speaking conversationally, and being friendly and sociable with strangers. This is a portrait of a con artist: confident, assertive, and persistent, on the one hand, and easygoing and sociable on the other.

► High-score manipulators are significantly less skillful at the interpersonal skills that we have seen are associated with highly effective ethical influencers: showing genuine interest in others, building rapport and trust (although good con artists are able to do this well), showing sensitivity to other people's feelings and needs (a manipulator typically lacks empathy), resolving conflicts and disagreements among others, and building consensus. The latter two interaction skills are complex social skills that require an insightful understanding of other people and a genuine desire to promote harmony and cooperation.

DEFENDING YOURSELF AGAINST MANIPULATING

A very clever manipulator can be difficult to detect, but here are some thoughts on how to defend yourself against unscrupulous influencers:

1. Remind yourself that if it looks too good to be true, it probably isn't true.
2. Don't trust appearances. Bernie Madoff came across as a kind, wise grandfatherly type, and sociopaths are often clever at disguising themselves, their motives, and their true natures. Exercise healthy caution until you get to know someone well enough to trust his intentions.
3. Beware of people who are too friendly, too complimentary, or too ingratiating. They are likely playing a game and manipulating the principle that people tend to like others who like them. Although it may feel good to have someone dote on you, it's probably insincere.
4. When someone presents a case that seems entirely too positive, consider that she may be manipulating the facts to suit her purpose. Before buying her miraculous weight-loss pill, surefire cure for hair loss, or investment strategy with guaranteed high returns, take a very close look, talk to the skeptics, and try to get a balanced view of reality. Con artists often lack subtlety. When they craft their tales they think any contrary information may make potential victims leery, so the picture they paint is too rosy.
5. Don't suspend your disbelief. This is what the manipulator wants. People suspend their disbelief because they want badly for something to be true. It's wise to step back and ask yourself if your needs are clouding your judgment.

6. Be wary of a deal coming your way because you are so special. Madoff used exclusivity to great advantage while perpetrating his fraud. His victims bought into it because they wanted to feel special. If someone is working hard to make you feel special, beware.

I know this advice sounds like that paranoid slogan—Trust no one—that readers may know from the television series *The X-Files*. It would be unpleasant to go through life distrusting everyone you meet. It's better to assume that most people have benign intent and will act according to the Golden Rule—and for the most part this is true. But before you commit your life savings to a wise grandfather type, no matter what his credentials and reputation, remember that if it's too good to be true, you are probably being beguiled by a magician. Beware.

KEY CONCEPTS

1. Manipulation is influencing through lies, deceit, hoaxes, swindles, and cons, where the influencer creates an illusion of reality.
2. Manipulation has an unsavory aspect, but it has played a large role in human history, often a celebrated role.
3. For manipulation to succeed, the victims or influencees must willingly suspend their disbelief, a concept originated by poet Samuel Taylor Coleridge. The lies manipulative influencers tell are often ones their influencees want very much to believe.
4. Corporate fraud often involves cooking the books, or making earnings per share appear greater than they actually are.
5. As an influence tactic, manipulation appeals to unscrupulous people because it is expedient. Moreover, lying may be the only way they can accomplish their goals.

CHALLENGES FOR READERS

1. Have you ever been influenced by someone who manipulated the truth in order to convince you to do something? How did you discover the truth? How did you feel afterward? How did you feel about the person who manipulated you?
2. Have you ever known or seen people who tried to get their way

through false flattery? Did it work? If they were discovered, what impact did it have on them afterward?

3. I claim in this chapter that everyone lies, even if just a little bit. Do you agree? Have you ever lied or deceived someone in order to influence him to do something or believe something? Were you ever caught in the lie? If so, what was the consequence? Assuming that there is a scale of deceptive practices from least to most harmful, which do you consider least harmful? In your view, are these practices unethical? Which ones are most harmful?

4. Reflect on the people you've known who used manipulation to influence others. How did they do it? What lies did they tell? What tricks did they use? What were the instruments of their deception? How long did they get away with it? How were they discovered? What harm did they do?

5. If you were asked to create a corporate ethics policy, what would you write about manipulation? How would you define it? What is manipulative or what isn't? How would you help people recognize manipulative behavior and take appropriate action if they saw it at work in your company?

6. Should people in different professions be held to different ethical standards? If so, which professions should be held to the higher standard? Which professions should be held to the lower standard? Why?

CHAPTER 11

WINNING THROUGH INTIMIDATION

One of the bestselling nonfiction books in the 1970s was Robert J. Ringer's *Winning Through Intimidation*. It's a catchy title, although Ringer wasn't actually advocating that readers try to win through intimidation; he was arguing that the world is full of predators, and *they* will try to win through intimidation. The world doesn't work the way we'd like it to, Ringer argues, and it's dangerous to assume that people are fair, honest, and aboveboard. The unscrupulous will take advantage of you if they can, so you need to be on your guard. Ringer is correct. When people try to lead or influence others through intimidation, they are trying to tip the scales in their favor. They don't want you to feel like you have safe alternatives to doing what they want. Instead, they want you to acquiesce through fear, anxiety, discomfort, and/or self-doubt.

People influence others through intimidation in a variety of ways: bullying, dominating, being verbally abusive, taunting, making derogatory comments or lewd propositions, being condescending, touching someone inappropriately or offensively, interfering with someone's work or access to or egress from an area, and rebuking or embarrassing someone publicly. The intimidation can be intellectual, psychological, emotional, or physical. One of the conditions of ethical influence is that the influencee has the right to say no and can do so without being punished. When people influence others through intimidation, they attempt to deny others the right to say no; therefore, intimidation is a strategy of dominance and control. Intimidators may use this strategy as an expedient (it works quickly), a fail-safe (they are more confident in intimidation than in any ethical technique), or a default (it works well enough for them to have become their standard approach to influencing).

HOW INTIMIDATION IS INFLUENTIAL

Intimidation influences people through fear or discomfort. When people feel intimidated, they place the safer bet rather than the riskier bet; they choose path B rather than path A; they heed warnings rather than ignore them. Intimidation alters their behavior, constricts their choices, makes them reluctant, paints them into a corner. Or it may make them too compliant, too willing to say yes, too trusting when they ought to be wary. Some of Bernard Madoff's clients were intimidated by him—an effect he used to manipulate them. Some of Michael Jordan's opponents were intimidated, too. At the height of his career, Jordan was so talented that the prospect of playing against him was intimidating to some of the average players he faced on the basketball court. Any star athlete—or chess champion, award-winning actor, acclaimed architect, or renowned business leader—can have this effect. It can even be intimidating to be a member of a supper club when one of the other hostesses is an extraordinary chef and you are merely a good cook. And this raises an important point about influence through intimidation: The intimidation may not be intentional.

Passive Intimidation

Passive intimidation occurs when the influencer does not intend to intimidate others but is simply doing the best she can do. My supper club example is a real one. My wife and I are part of a group of couples who meet monthly for dinner at someone's home. The host and hostess are responsible for preparing the dinner and providing the wine. One of our members, Michelle, was a Washington, D.C., hostess who used to prepare gourmet meals for groups as large as fifty or more. Whenever it's their turn to host, Michelle and her husband create a dining experience that puts the rest of us to shame. So it is intimidating when it's our turn to host and we are trying to prepare a meal that others will favorably compare to what we have all experienced at Michelle and Robert's home. Michelle is not the sort of person who would purposefully intimidate the rest of us, but in doing her best as a chef and hostess, she is nonetheless intimidating. Here are further examples of passive intimidation:

▶   One student in a class consistently outperforms the others. He doesn't have an arrogant or know-it-all attitude; he's just very bright, applies himself more than anyone else, and has parents who take an active role in his education and ensure that he excels. But some class-mates are reluctant to answer questions when he's in class because they fear being wrong and looking dumb compared to him.

▶   One member of a consulting team has far more experience than other members, and she works hard to ensure that her analyses are thoughtful, accurate, and thorough. The work she presents in her cli-ent presentations is noticeably superior to the work other team mem-bers produce, no matter how hard they try. Some people enjoy working on teams with her because the competition elevates their performance and they learn from her, but others avoid teaming with her because whatever they produce is never good enough.

▶   One member of a country club is accomplished enough to have been a professional golfer, but he chose another career. When he plays golf with other club members, however, he is so much better than they are it intimidates some of them, who would rather not join his foursome. They would rather play with people who have similar skills so that they can joke about an occasional flubbed shot and not feel like they have to compete. It's intimidating when doing your best never measures up to someone else whose exceptional performance appears effortless.

▶   One student in flight school is a natural flyer. She's smart and has all the right instincts for piloting an aircraft. Whatever she tries, she does well, and she has a very carefree and self-confident attitude that intimidates others who are less skilled and have to work much harder to accomplish what she does.

People can be intimidating and strike fear in others simply because they are smarter, better prepared, more agile, more athletic, more tal-ented, more accomplished, better positioned, better looking, better dressed, wealthier, more courageous, or more knowledgeable. They can be intimidating because of their role, title, experiences, wealth, fame, or self-confidence. And they can be intimidating because they are already members of a club and someone else isn't. Seniors can be intimidating to freshmen; generals to privates; executive vice presi-dents to clerks; queens to commoners; bishops to laypeople. However, this is passive intimidation if the influencers are simply being who they are and do not intend to force others to comply or choose something they otherwise would not choose.

When people influence others through intimidation, they attempt to deny others the right to say no; therefore, intimidation is a strategy of dominance and control.

Active Intimidation

Active intimidation is quite different. People who consciously try to influence others through intimidation know what they are doing and use it as a strategy for getting what they want. Passive intimidation is not a dark-side influence tactic because it is not intentional, but active intimidation is squarely on the dark side. The influencer intends to deny the influencee the right to say no, and use of this tactic is likely to damage the relationship between them. Here are examples of active or dark-side intimidation:

► A physically imposing person butts in line and glowers at anyone who challenges him. His behavior may not intimidate everyone, but it will intimidate most people.

► The lead attorney for a defendant in a medical malpractice case assigns a large number of associates to the case and has them sitting behind him in court when the trial begins. The plaintiff's attorney has only one old lawyer friend on his side and feels very overmatched. (Watch *The Verdict* with Paul Newman and James Mason.)

► A woman goes to a customer service representative demanding her money back (even though she didn't buy the item at that store). The representative asks for her receipt, but the woman claims she lost it. She is loud, stands too close to the representative, and complains bitterly about the store and its people. She continues her barrage until the representative gives in.

► In an executive team meeting, one executive dominates the discussion. He cares only about his business unit and lobbies hard for everything that will improve his unit's performance, regardless of the cost to the company as a whole. He is the proverbial "squeaky wheel" who looks after himself and his interests first. He believes that his career depends solely on him looking good, no matter how the rest of the company performs. His boss wants to encourage competition among the business units, so he lets this executive get away with it, which teaches other executives to look out for themselves first—everyone else be damned—if they want to survive in this cutthroat environment.

► In a high school, a group of popular, good-looking girls from wealthy families form a clique and put down other girls who don't have their advantages. Or a group of jocks hang together and laugh at the nerds. Or a group of smart kids are cavalierly critical of students who aren't as academically accomplished and facile as they are. And so on.

► A team of negotiators from one culture comes to the negotiating table having done meticulous preparation. During the negotiation, they frequently have side conversations in their native language (which the other side doesn't understand). They appear to change their minds based on conversations with their home office and frequently renegotiate a point the other side thought was settled. They treat anyone not on their side with dismissal or contempt and don't care if they ruin relationships with their opponents. They use these and similar tactics to unsettle the other side, thereby gaining the advantage in the deal. Their only aim is to win.

► One of the older Realtors in a community positions himself with potential clients by bragging about his successes and his knowledge of the market while disparaging other Realtors, none of whom, he says, are as accomplished and capable as he is. He is unquestionably successful, but his self-portrayal implies that no other Realtors can get buyers as good a deal as he can (despite much evidence to the contrary if clients bother to check). Other agents know how he operates, and some are intimidated when they learn that potential clients are also talking to him. Fearful about making a bad first impression, they become anxious before meeting potential clients and sometimes do as badly in these meetings as the conniving veteran hopes they will—

particularly when they try to match his bravado without the guile and conviction to pull it off.

Active or conscious intimidating can take many forms, such as verbal taunting or abuse, intimidating body language, emotional manipulation, bullying, inappropriate touching and personal space violations, visual intimidation, and physical interference.

VERBAL TAUNTING OR ABUSE—Two players from opposing American football teams line up across from each other before the ball is snapped. One defensive end taunts his opponent—bad-mouthing him, his team, his ability, his heritage, and anything else that might rattle the other guy. The verbal abuse continues throughout the game, getting worse and worse, until the offensive player pummels the end after a play is over and commits a personal foul. As the referee walks off the penalty yards, the defensive end smiles to himself—that's exactly what he wanted. Verbal taunting is common in sports, where the aim is to intimidate opponents and attack their self-confidence so that they'll lose their composure.

It's also common in everyday life. Verbal intimidation occurs when someone swears at other people, calls them names, jokes about them in the presence of others, laughs at them, or puts them down. It occurs at work when a group of men tell off-color jokes about women in the presence of a female coworker. It typically begins in schools with the verbal abuse of someone who is weaker or different, which is why it can be terrifying for high school students to admit that they are gay, not interested in sports, not part of an "in" group, or in any other way out of the mainstream. For the abuser, intimidating speech serves a dual purpose: It demeans and punishes the weaker person while elevating the abuser's own ego and mainstream cultural identity. Verbal intimidation influences by limiting the victim's options, isolating the victim from the mainstream, and forcing the victim to make choices he would not otherwise make.

Verbal intimidation may also come in the form of lewd or suggestive proposals or remarks—the boss who says he appreciates it when one of his single female employees wears a particularly alluring dress, or the director who suggests to an attractive employee that if she wants to get ahead she needs to put in extra hours, or the manager who tells a new hire that he is handsome enough to have been a male model. Generally, inappropriate suggestions or remarks come from a person in a powerful position and are targeted at individuals of lesser power or stature. The intent is to intimidate the less powerful person into compliance or submission, and although this kind of behavior may constitute sexual harassment and incur severe penalties, it nonetheless occurs.

INTIMIDATING BODY LANGUAGE—An aggressive dog's hair stands up, making it appear larger and more menacing; it snarls, baring its teeth, saliva dripping; it advances slowly, eyes focused on its prey, body tensed and ready to spring at any provocation or sign of weakness. Through this body language the dog tries to induce fear, to weaken resolve, to force submission, to intimidate. Gorillas beat their chests; bulls snort and lower their heads, making their horns more prominent; rattlesnakes rattle their tails; crabs rear back and open their claws. All animals have ways of making themselves appear more menacing. In human beings, the physical techniques may differ (only a few of us snarl and drip saliva), but we also have finely developed body language meant to intimidate.

A mother who is unhappy with a misbehaving child glares at him at the supper table; one of the rivals at a competition purposefully ignores the others, as though they are beneath her; a gang member on a street corner who sees rival gang members driving by makes an obscene gesture (at the risk of inciting escalating forms of intimidation in return). People often use offensive gestures, facial expressions (glowering, scowling, frowning, staring, mugging, making faces at someone, sticking out one's tongue), and a tone of voice (harsh, chiding, dismissive, scornful, and so on) to influence others by intimidating them.

Active or conscious intimidation takes many forms, such as verbal taunting or abuse, intimidating body language, emotional manipulation, bullying, inappropriate touching and personal space violations, visual intimidation, and physical interference.

EMOTIONAL MANIPULATION—Playing with someone's emotions can be painfully intimidating and have devastating effects, as the parents of Megan Meier discovered after their daughter hanged herself when her online boyfriend, "Josh Evans," became mean and wrote to her on MySpace that "the world would be a better place without you." Megan, who was thirteen, had been corresponding with Evans for weeks, their conversations becoming increasingly flirtatious. Josh was sixteen and the cutest boyfriend Megan had ever had, and she was thrilled with his interest in her and his affection. Then something happened, and Josh began insulting her, saying that he didn't like the way she treated her friends. The two teens exchanged insults for an hour on MySpace. During that time, other teens following the disintegrating exchange on MySpace jumped on the bandwagon and sent profane and nasty messages to Megan. Distraught, the girl escaped to her room, sobbing. Her mother, Tina Meier, later found her body hanging from a belt in her closet.

Six weeks later, Tina Meier discovered that there never was a boy named Josh Evans. He was the online creation of forty-seven-year-old Lori Drew, a neighbor and the mother of a girl who at one time had been Megan's close friend. Drew thought that Megan had been saying bad things about her daughter and concocted Josh as a way to spy on the girl. Sadly, that plan hemorrhaged into the cruel hoax that led to Megan's death. Despite widespread outrage at Drew's actions, she has not been held legally accountable for her contributions to Megan's suicide. She was found guilty of a misdemeanor for violating the Computer Fraud and Abuse Act, but that conviction was later overturned. However, Drew's actions did cause some jurisdictions to revise their criminal statutes on the use of the Internet for the purpose of bullying.

Drew's actions were clearly manipulative, but I discussed the case here rather than in chapter 10 because emotional manipulation is a form of influencing by intimidation. Praising someone who is vulnerable and then condemning her, or giving someone affection and then withholding it, or supporting someone in need and then abandoning him are forms of emotional manipulation that can be extraordinarily intimidating to the victim. Writing nasty, profane, or insulting messages on someone's Facebook or MySpace page is a way to induce fear and attack the person's self-respect and self-confidence—particularly if she is emotionally immature or otherwise vulnerable—and bullies know this. Unfortunately, the Internet has given them power vastly exceeding their capacity to exercise compassionate restraint, respect, and simple humanity.

BULLYING—Bullying can be done by a single perpetrator, but it is generally a many-against-one form of intimidation. Bullies typically don't like to act alone. Having a gang of confederates behind them embold-ens bullies and gives them the courage to intimidate their victims. Such is the case with Scut Farkus, the fictional bully in the film *A Christmas Story*; Draco Malfoy and his troop of Slytherin thugs in the Harry Potter series; and Conny and his stooges, Martin and Andreas, in John Ajvide Lindqvist's *Let the Right One In*. In these cases, what intimidates the victims is not just the bully's acrimony but the threat represented by the gang—the isolation and helplessness the victim feels (most victims don't have allies of their own to counter the men-ace), as well as the persistence of the threat (it goes on until the victim reaches a breaking point and either capitulates or finds a way to strike back).

Bullying in schools is more common than many people would like to believe and has led some vulnerable teens to take their own lives rather than continue to suffer. Unfortunately, it also occurs frequently enough to be problematic in the workplace. At work, bullying may involve verbal abuse, emotional manipulation, aggressive behavior, mobbing, or sabotaging of the victim's work space or products. In her doctoral dissertation on workplace bullying, Judith Lynn Fisher-Blando stated that "75 percent of [her study's] participants reported witness-ing mistreatment of coworkers sometime throughout their careers, 47 percent have been bullied during their career, and 27 percent admitted to being a target of a bully in the last twelve months."[1] Workplace bul-lies may target someone they perceive as a rival, someone they believe is not a good cultural fit for the organization, or someone whose per-formance they consider unsatisfactory. As in schools, being different in the workplace is often sufficient to bring out the bully in people.

INAPPROPRIATE TOUCHING AND PERSONAL SPACE VIOLATIONS— Although touching another person's shoulder or arm may be an inno-cent gesture of friendliness in some cultures, that is not universally true, and some people use it as an influence tactic. It can be intimidat-ing to be touched in an unexpected or unwanted way, particularly if the person doing the touching is menacing or strange, and even more so if the touching continues after the victim indicates that the behav-ior is unwanted. It's as if the perpetrator is saying, "I can invade your personal space whenever I want, and you can't stop me."

This type of intimidation can occur even without physical touch-ing. The psychological comfort zone that surrounds people varies by culture and individual, but in general, the distance most people like to keep between themselves and another person is about twenty-four inches on the sides, slightly greater in front, and slightly smaller in back. When we are in public, we are most comfortable when other people, particularly strangers, do not come any closer to us than this distance. If a person crowds us by getting too close, it can cause discomfort, anxiety, or even fear. So a person who wants to intimidate someone else can do so simply by standing too close to that person or leaning in too closely. It's especially intimidating if the perpetrator is large and muscular or menacing in some other way.

VISUAL INTIMIDATION—Visual intimidation can take many forms— from the death's head insignia of the Nazi SS to cross burnings by the Ku Klux Klan, from exclusionary signs ("Members Only") to inflammatory posters ("Baby Killers"; "We Will Crush You"; "Death to Pigs"), and from the masks worn by bank robbers to the black lines drawn under football players' eyes. A group of protesters burning a flag is visually intimidating, as is a line of riot police advancing on an unruly crowd. In Nazi Germany, ranks of jackbooted soldiers marching down the street, their arms uniformly raised in the Nazi salute, were meant to be intimidating, as were the lengthy military parades on May Day in the former Soviet Union, with row after row of tanks and missiles rolling past reviewing stands (and cameras broadcasting the spectacle to everyone Soviet leaders wanted to intimidate). Displays of might and power or menace and contempt are intended to intimidate potential adversaries to the point where they either avoid a confrontation altogether or, if they do confront, will be weakened and afraid. Visual intimidation works well, which is why people continue to use it.

PHYSICAL INTERFERENCE—Finally, preventing someone from entering or leaving a place can be intimidating. A gang of boys loiters in front of the entrance to an arcade. Other boys who want to go inside have to pass through them. Some will choose not to, and some will be afraid of a confrontation, especially if they are by themselves. A schoolgirl being bullied by classmates has to go to the restroom, but three of her antagonists have positioned themselves in front of the door, forcing the victim to use a restroom on a different floor. A female worker at an industrial site enters a portable potty. Some of her male coworkers surround it and won't let her out. They tilt and shake the potty and then tip it over, injuring her and covering her in filth.

This last incident was depicted in the 2005 film *North Country*, a fictionalized account of an actual case of sexual harassment at an iron mine in northern Minnesota. The women in this case endured a number of the tactics of intimidation I've described in this chapter. Obviously, women are not the only victims of intimidation. Throughout history, thugs have used these dark-side tactics to intimidate men and frighten them into compliance or submission. Intimidation is the abuse of power for the purpose of control; people use it because it is an expedient method of getting their way. And it's likely that most of us have been victims of intimidation at one time or another in our lives.

JEFFREY AND ANDY BUILD A HOUSE OF CARDS

When Enron collapsed in 2001, it was the greatest corporate implosion in history (until WorldCom collapsed in 2002 and then Lehman Brothers in 2008). At its peak, Enron was the seventh largest corporation in the country and was the darling of Wall Street. In the late nineties, it had record earnings, unparalleled growth, and a highly touted leadership team. But Enron was not, as it turned out, the rock-solid money-making engine it appeared to be, and its collapse is a story of deception, greed, arrogance, and a spectacular case of winning through intimidation.

One of the principal architects of Enron's meteoric rise and fall was Jeffrey Skilling. Born in Pittsburgh in 1953, Skilling was bright, ambitious, and impatient from the start. After graduating from high school in Aurora, Illinois, he received a bachelor's degree in applied science from Southern Methodist University and then applied to the Harvard Business School. When asked during the Harvard admissions interview if he was smart, Skilling reportedly replied, "I'm fucking smart." And he was. Near the top of his graduating class at Harvard, he joined McKinsey & Company, the premier management consulting firm, and became one of the youngest associates in the firm's history to become a partner and later a director. Skilling worked in McKinsey's

► Jeffrey Skilling, former CEO of Enron, following his arrest.

Dave Einsel/Getty Images

Houston office, where he became a consultant to Enron in the late 1980s. He impressed Enron's CEO, Ken Lay, with his brilliance, and in 1990 Lay hired him away from McKinsey to be president of Enron Finance Corporation. In 1991, Skilling became chairman of Enron Gas Services Company, and in 1997, president and COO of Enron. He was named CEO of Enron in February 2001 when Ken Lay stepped down.

Skilling pioneered two concepts that would eventually lead to Enron's demise: an asset-light strategy and mark-to-market accounting. The company was formed in 1985 after the federal deregulation of natural gas pipelines and the merger of Houston Natural Gas and Inter-North, a Houston-based gas utility, and a large Omaha-based pipeline company. Christened Enron by CEO Lay, the company owned and operated pipelines, plants, and other tangible assets. But Skilling believed the company could make far more money if Enron were principally a wholesaler or trader of energy, a middleman between energy producers and energy consumers. He vigorously built the trading arm of Enron while dismissing those who worked in the asset-heavy side of the business—and that strategy appealed to Lay, the Enron board, and Wall Street because the trading operation was innovative and profitable.

Mark-to-market accounting allows a company to book the value of an asset based on current or future perceived market valuations rather than the cost of the asset. Banks and investment firms use mark-to-market accounting for assets that fluctuate in value based on changing market conditions, such as mutual funds or derivatives, but this approach to accounting had not been used in the energy business until Skilling convinced the U.S. Securities and Exchange Commission to allow Enron to use it. To many people, this practice made no sense. It allowed Enron to recognize all the projected revenue from, say, a ten-year gas contract in the first year of the contract, even though the gas had not yet been delivered, the cash from future deliveries had not been received, and the contract could be sold or canceled at some future point.

The effect was to inflate Enron's booked revenues, and this created a monster. Skilling was determined to raise Enron's stock price continually. That was the driving force behind his leadership of the company, his mantra at many internal meetings. To accomplish that goal, the company had to report increasingly favorable numbers—greater revenue, extraordinary profits, and unparalleled growth. And when you were recognizing all of a long-term contract's revenue during its first year (and none of it thereafter), you had to book an exponentially greater amount of business each year—and hide any losses—to create the image of increasing growth. It amounted to a Ponzi scheme the company played on itself.

Skilling's chief collaborator in this looming debacle was Andrew Fastow, a Tufts University graduate in economics who earned an MBA from Northwestern University and worked initially for Continental Illinois National Bank and Trust in Chicago. There, he developed expertise in asset-backed securities, a strategy that allows a financial institution to move risky assets off its balance sheet. Skilling hired Fastow in 1990, and he later became the company's chief financial officer. At Enron, Fastow oversaw a number of questionable financial practices beyond mark-to-market accounting. If an Enron trader, for instance, bought $150,000 worth of natural gas one day and sold it the next for $156,000, Enron would record revenue of $156,000, not $6,000. This practice made the company's revenues look astronomical.

Fastow also created a number of special purpose entities (SPEs) to hide questionable business transactions (e.g., contracts losing money) and to keep losses off Enron's books. To compensate the investors in these SPEs, Enron issued them shares of Enron common stock. As if this weren't dubious enough, Fastow personally led many of the SPEs he created, which put him in the position of negotiating deals where he represented both Enron and an SPE he led. Although this was clearly a conflict of interest, no one called him on it. Skilling later said he didn't think Andy earned much from his participation in these SPEs, but that was not true. In fact, Fastow made tens of millions of dollars by violating that conflict of interest and straddling an ethical fence that was meant to protect investors and prevent fraud.

Bloomberg via Getty Images

► Enron CFO Andrew Fastow, creator of an elaborate shell game to hide losses and project a favorable earnings picture to investors.

Skilling and Fastow prevailed for many years in Enron—and made millions and millions of dollars for themselves—by using intimidation to get what they wanted. Skilling intimidated people through his forcefulness, intellectual arrogance, and expressiveness. To his credit, he was a confident, articulate, and persuasive speaker. When he boasted about Enron's business and its bright future, people believed him. Of course, they wanted to believe the stories he told. The roaring nineties had made a lot of people a lot of money. They were eager for reassurance that the gravy train would keep rolling along, and Skilling was happy to oblige. And it wasn't as if he was deliberately conning everyone. Until the end, until he saw the train coming off the tracks, he believed it himself, because he was so convinced of his own genius and the infallibility of his judgment.

Skilling's intellect, not his values, was the driving force of his life. It defined him and was the source of his arrogance and intolerance of anyone who wasn't in his intellectual league. He was a product of Harvard Business School and McKinsey & Company, a school renowned for attracting top business students and a firm known for hiring only the best and the brightest. Skilling was convinced he was better and brighter than the majority of the smart people passing through McKinsey. At Enron, it appeared that he wanted to re-create the rarified atmosphere of McKinsey by raising hiring standards; recruiting the top graduates of the top business schools; and instituting a draconian performance review system nicknamed "rank and yank," in which the highest-rated traders were rewarded handsomely while those rated in the bottom 10 percent were forced out. In time, Enron's culture developed the same sense of superiority that characterized Skilling. As Bethany McLean and Peter Elkind note in their book on Enron, "There was an attitude that permeated Enron, an attitude that Enron people were simply better than everybody else. At conferences, Skilling would openly sneer at competitors."[2]

Like many intellectually arrogant people, Skilling had no tolerance for others who "didn't get it," or those who dared to question him. During one infamous conference call with analysts, Skilling's intimidating nature was starkly evident. Uneasy about Enron's lack of transparency in financial reporting, Wall Street analyst Richard Grubman was recommending that investors sell Enron stock. At one point during the conference call, he observed that Enron was the only company in its industry that did not provide a balance sheet or cash flow statement with its quarterly earnings announcement. Skilling replied,

"Well, thank you very much. We appreciate that . . . asshole." Among pipeline workers that kind of language might be commonplace, but it was a shocking breach of decorum in a public forum with Grubman's peers present. "It was a form of intimidation," said another analyst on the call. "It was Skilling's message to his long-term shareholders that he wasn't going to acknowledge those types of pressures. He was going to keep saying the story was strong and people like [Grubman] didn't belong on the call and didn't deserve an answer."[3]

If the instrument of Skilling's intimidation was his arrogance, then Fastow's was his position and the power that came with it. As Enron's chief financial officer, he controlled hundreds of millions of dollars' worth of contracts with the company. The bankers, the investment firms, the auditors—all knew that to get or maintain a share of Enron's business they had to placate Andy. According to McLean and Elkind, "Fastow maintained a stranglehold on doling out Enron's extraordinarily lucrative banking and financing work—and he kept score. Ponying up for LJM2 [one of Fastow's SPEs] was the price the banks needed to pay to retain his favor."[4] When Enron collapsed in the fall of 2001, there were thousands of these SPEs—and numerous bankers and investors who didn't know how Enron kept making so much money but didn't want to look too closely because they, too, were on one hell of a joyride and didn't want it to end. Anyone who scrutinized the picture the company was painting risked Skilling's scorn or Fastow's threats. But, as the summer of 2001 rolled on, Skilling was smart enough to see what was happening. He knew Enron was a house of cards, and he resigned in August 2001, citing "personal reasons," and then began selling his shares of Enron stock. Fastow remained but was fired as the house of cards began to buckle and the banks lost confidence in him.

After the collapse, after thousands of retirement funds and individual investors lost billions of dollars, Skilling, Fastow, and other complicit Enron executives were jailed for their part in the disaster. Of course, the executives who built this house of cards were not solely responsible for what happened. As investigative journalist Kurt Eichenwald noted, "Shocking incompetence, unjustified arrogance, compromised ethics, and an utter contempt for the market's judgment all played decisive roles. Ultimately, it was Enron's tragedy to be filled with people smart enough to know how to maneuver around the rules, but not wise enough to understand why the rules had been written in the first place."[5]

From a leadership and influence perspective, the most important lesson to be learned from Enron's collapse is that when people try to win through intimidation, it is because they are bullies or frauds and don't have or don't want to take the time to use more ethical influence strategies. Whenever business leaders, political leaders, or any other kind of leaders resort to intimidation to get their way, it is because they are hiding something and think that leveling with people is less likely to achieve their goals than using their power to push people around. Beware.

INSIGHTS ON INTIMIDATING

The research on power and influence shows that people who use intimidation to influence others are, in the long run, significantly less influential than people who don't use intimidating approaches. This is true in part because intimidators depend primarily on two influence techniques—stating and legitimizing. Either they try to make bold assertions, which they discourage others from questioning, or they try to appeal to authority. These are "push" techniques as opposed to the "pull" techniques of consulting, modeling, socializing, and logical persuading. A push technique tries to force others to comply, whereas a pull technique invites people to agree or smoothes the way for cooperation. Intimidators are bullies, so they are significantly more effective at the influence technique of stating and significantly less effective at social or inspirational influence techniques like socializing, consulting, exchanging, modeling, appealing to relationship, alliance building, and appealing to values.

The strongest power sources for intimidators are role and resources (e.g., Andy Fastow) and information, network, and knowledge (e.g., Jeffrey Skilling). Not surprisingly, their weakest power sources are attraction (the ability to cause others to like you) and history (the power that derives from close relationships). Appendix A has a fuller explanation of all these power sources.

The most highly rated skills of intimidators are persisting, asserting, behaving self-confidently, using assertive nonverbals, logical reasoning, conveying energy and enthusiasm, using a compelling tone of voice, and behaving authoritatively. Taken together, all these characteristics read like a description of Jeff Skilling's operating style. Conversely, the lowest-rated skills of intimidators include displaying sensitivity to others' feelings and needs, using authority without being heavy-handed, resolving conflicts and disagreements among others, listening, building consensus, showing genuine interest in other people, and building rapport and trust. Bullies are not soft touches. If they were, they wouldn't rely on intimidation to get their way.

DEFENDING YOURSELF AGAINST INTIMIDATING PEOPLE

Intimidators are pragmatists. They use intimidation to influence others because it works for them. When it stops working, they typically try something else. So the first step in defending yourself against intimidation is to refuse to be intimidated—which, of course, is easier said than done. Intimidation works because it plays on one of our most primitive emotions—fear. If you are afraid to challenge a brash, self-confident executive whose bill of goods you either don't understand or don't accept, then he wins (through intimidation). If you are afraid to lose business with a CFO who insists that you buy into a deal that is unethical, involves a clear conflict of interest, or otherwise doesn't feel right, then he has won (through intimidation). The answer is to stand up to the bully and refuse to be intimidated.

I admit it may be difficult to do in practice, so if going it alone is impractical or too daunting, you may be able to find allies who can help you stand up to the intimidating person. When the bully is a boss or someone else in a powerful position, you may not have the power to successfully challenge him. However, people who use force to get their way typically respect and respond to force when it is used against them. So an alliance may work where individual efforts would fail. Logical reasoning and appealing to values are unlikely to work with a bully. Typically, the only language that bullies understand is the language they speak, so force must be met with counterforce, and an alliance is often the best and safest way to confront someone who consistently tries to win through intimidation.

IF YOU USE INTIMIDATING TACTICS

If you are consciously and deliberately using intimidation to get your way, recognize that this expedient influence tactic is likely to damage or destroy your relationships with the people you are trying to influence. You will be less successful in the long run if you rely on intimidation instead of using ethical influence techniques. You will eventually pay the price, as all bullies do, for using force and fear to get your way. You may prevail for a while, but the piper will be waiting, and the price you have to pay the piper may be steep. Find other ways to lead and influence people.

KEY CONCEPTS

1. Intimidation can include bullying, dominating, being verbally abusive, taunting, making derogatory comments or lewd propositions, being condescending, touching someone inappropriately, interfering with someone's work, or rebuking or embarrassing someone publicly.

2. Intimidation is an attempt to deny others the right to say no, so it is a strategy of dominance and control.

3. Passive intimidation occurs when the influencer does not intend to intimidate others but is simply doing the best she can do. People who are naturally smarter, faster, more talented, or more successful are going to intimidate some other people.

4. Active intimidation is a conscious attempt to influence others by causing fear, anxiety, discomfort, or self-doubt.

5. When leaders resort to intimidation to get their way, it is because they are hiding something and think that leveling with people is less likely to achieve their goals than using their power to push people around.

6. Intimidation works because it plays on one of our most primitive emotions—fear. The first step in defending yourself against intimidation is to refuse to be intimidated.

CHALLENGES FOR READERS

1. Everyone has felt intimidated at one time or another. Reflect on the times when someone has intimidated you. What was it about the person that you found intimidating? How did the intimidation affect you?

2. Have you known any leaders who used intimidation as an influence tactic? How and why were they successful—or not?

3. Have you ever stood up to someone who was trying to intimidate you? What did you do? How did it feel? What was the result?
4. Have you ever intimidated other people? How? What happened? Was the intimidation passive or active on your part?
5. If you are an intimidating person—for whatever reason—what can you do to be less intimidating to other people?

CHAPTER 12

MAKING AN OFFER THEY CAN'T REFUSE

Threatening

In Mario Puzo's *The Godfather,* Don Corleone uses a threat to convince a bandleader to release Corleone's godson from a contract. While henchman Luca Brasi holds a gun to the bandleader's head, Corleone tells him that either his brains or his signature will be on the contract before they leave. The bandleader signs. Making an offer the guy can't refuse is the godfather's approach to influencing.

In Don Corleone's world, might makes right. His fellow Italian Niccolò Machiavelli understood well the use of force in human affairs and also had a dim view of human nature. Machiavelli believed that men go from one ambition to another. First, they seek to secure themselves against attack and then they attack others. In *The Prince,* Machiavelli argued for whole, rather than half, measures because halfhearted attempts to punish would only invite retaliation. "Men should be either treated generously or destroyed," he wrote, "because they take revenge for slight injuries—for heavy ones they cannot." Threatening people to get them to comply with your wishes is the most extreme "dark side" influence tactic. It may occur less noticeably today than in Machiavelli's era, but we shouldn't deceive ourselves about the efficacy of this influencing technique or the regularity with which it is applied. Threatening is a time-honored means of exerting one's will and forcing others to comply.

Threatening is an expressed or implied intention to inflict harm, injury, or damage to a person or an organization or to the person's or organization's property or belongings. We might argue that threatening is just an extreme form of intimidation, but as a dark-side influence tactic, threatening has quite a different effect than most forms of intimidation. I may be intimidated by someone who is bigger, faster, smarter, richer, more talented, more capable, more powerful, or better looking, but I generally don't worry about them killing or injuring me. A direct threat does more than raise fear; it raises the prospect of imminent harm and possibly violence. My response to intimidation can range from discomfort to heartburn, anxiety, fear, or self-doubt; but my response to a threat is more urgent and stark: fight or flight. Either I defy the person threatening me or avoid the consequences by complying or fleeing. When I feel intimidated by someone, I may imagine what might happen if I don't acquiesce, but when I am threatened by someone, the consequences are generally pretty clear. Here are some examples of threatening:

- ► A parent warns a child that if she doesn't clean her room she will be grounded.
- ► A schoolyard bully tells another child that if she touches the soccer ball again he will hit her.
- ► A parent tells a teenager that if she exceeds her allotted cell phone minutes she'll have to pay for the extra minutes herself.
- ► A teacher gives a student until the end of the week to turn in a late paper or get an F on the assignment.
- ► A sports coach threatens to bench a player if she can't execute plays as well in games as she does in practice.
- ► During a semiannual review, a manager tells an employee that his performance is subpar and he will lose his job if he doesn't improve.
- ► A library warns a patron that if her overdue books are not returned promptly she will be fined.
- ► A labor leader threatens a strike if the company doesn't agree to the demands of the union.
- ► A police officer warns that if I don't step out of my vehicle, he will arrest me.
- ► During an executive meeting, one executive openly criticizes the CEO. At the next executive meeting, that executive is gone, having "resigned for personal reasons." (The threat to the remaining executives is obvious.)
- ► A gang leader threatens to kill a subordinate if he steps out of line.
- ► A boss lets an employee know that he is interested in her and implies that if she doesn't submit he will find a good reason to fire her.
- ► The leader of a country threatens to go to war with another country if that country doesn't give in to his demands. (During another era there was the image of Nikita Khrushchev banging his shoe on a desk during

a speech at the United Nations and screaming, "We will bury you!") Or, as happens even today, a country's leader may order his artillery to shell the target country's border regions to show that he is serious and has the power and the will to make good on his threats.

These types of threats may be familiar to readers, if not because you have experienced such threats yourself, then because you have seen them portrayed in countless movies, television shows, and plays, or have read about threatening behavior in stories, books, magazines, and newspapers. From the time we are babies, we learn that there are rewards for doing what others want us to do and punishments for failing to do what they want. By the time we are grown, we have developed a Pavlovian response to the rewards of acting in one way or the consequences of acting in another. That's why threatening, as an approach to influencing others, is second nature to us, even if we consider the most egregious forms of it disgusting or worse.

The use of threats is an effective means of influencing because of its clarity. Avoiding and manipulating are deceptive techniques. Intimidation is fear-provoking but vague. However, there is nothing ambiguous about a threat. As the previous examples illustrate, the consequences of noncompliance are generally very clear.

INSIGHTS ON THREATENING

The research on power and influence shows that threatening is significantly less effective in the long run than the ethical forms of influence. As with intimidation, people who make threats frequently use stating as an influencing technique the vast majority of the time, followed by legitimizing. They rely principally on the power vested in role and resources—the dual hammers of authority and control of resources—to get their way with other people. Their lowest-rated power sources are, not surprisingly, attraction and reputation. These people are disliked and disrespected, so being threatening has significant disadvantages for those who overuse it. Their lowest-rated skill is using authority without appearing heavy-handed (they *are* heavy-handed, so this outcome is to be expected). They are best at asserting themselves and worst at all of the social skills.

People who are nonthreatening have nearly the opposite profile. They use logical persuading, consulting, modeling, and appealing to values most frequently and effectively as their favored influencing techniques; they are most highly rated in character, history, reputation, and attraction; and their highest-rated skills are logical reasoning, speaking conversationally, behaving self-confidently, building rapport and trust, supporting and encouraging others, and listening. In short, they are well-rounded, socially adept people who are significantly more influential than those who frequently resort to threatening to try to get their way.

DEFENDING YOURSELF AGAINST THREATENING

How you respond to a threat depends largely on who is doing the threatening and how serious the consequences would be to you. I can't offer universal guidelines on defending yourself against threats, but here are some thoughts:

1. If what the influencer wants you to do (e.g., finishing your homework, paying your bills, or doing your work) is something you have already agreed to do and should do, then it is probably best to comply unless you have a compelling reason not to. Explaining that reason may help if the influencer is reasonable.

2. Reduce the threat by trying to find ways to make the consequences less severe or meaningful to you. It's not a threat if you don't care about the consequences. For many battered wives, for instance, the answer is not being dependent upon the abuser. By reducing their dependence, they decrease the abuser's leverage and can more confidently leave the abusive relationship. In fairness, this advice is easier for me to give than for many battered women to take. Depending on the nature of the threat, reducing the severity of the consequences may be difficult.

3. If the person who is threatening you is your boss, try talking to that person if she is approachable. Explain why you find her behavior threatening and how it is affecting your work or level of engagement. This approach may work with some bosses; with others, it would be hopeless. In these cases, try to transfer to another department or find another job. (That's not so easy in this economic environment, but remaining in an abusive job longer than you need to is dehumanizing and demoralizing. You will eventually pay the price for having lived with threats for a prolonged period.)

4. Try to find allies who can help you deal with the threats. If the person doing the threatening is more powerful than you are, then you may

need other people or resources to help you counter the threat. In business, allies may come from an ombudsperson, the human resources group, a coach, a union representative, other employees, or another manager.

5. If the influencer is someone who habitually threatens you and you habitually give in, then his behavior is not likely to change until yours does. It may be difficult to summon the strength to resist, but that may be the only way to stop the cycle.

6. If possible, find some way to threaten back. As I said in the previous chapter, sometimes the only language people know is the language they speak, so fight a threat with a threat. Clearly, this is a riskier strategy, but the person threatening you may not respond to anything else.

7. Threats embolden some people. Threats make them angry and defiant. If that's how you become, then channel your anger in a way that is most likely to eliminate the threats without making you the antagonist.

IF YOU USE THREATENING

All of us sometimes use threats to influence others, but few are guilty of using the most heinous kinds of threats. In general, only about one percent of people worldwide frequently use threatening as an influence strategy. If you are among the minority of people who threaten others to get your way, then recognize that this strategy will weaken or destroy relationships and can cost you whatever power you have when people get fed up and strike back or move out of your sphere of influence. In the end, this is a loser strategy, and it's best to avoid the more destructive forms of threatening (which means it is still okay to threaten to ground your kids if they don't clean their rooms).

KEY CONCEPTS

1. Threatening people to get them to comply is the most extreme "dark side" influence technique, but it is a time-honored method of exerting one's will over others.

2. Threatening is an expressed or implied intention to inflict harm,

injury, or damage to a person or an organization or to the person's or organization's property or belongings.

3. Threatening is an effective means of influencing because of its clarity. Avoiding and manipulating are deceptive; intimidating is fear-provoking but vague; but there is nothing ambiguous about a threat.

4. Threatening is not an effective long-term influence strategy, although all of us use it now and then. The most egregious forms of threatening destroy relationships and will eventually erode the influencer's power and may foment rebellion among those who feel threatened.

CHALLENGES FOR READERS

1. I argued in this chapter that threatening is a common influencing technique, that everyone uses it from time to time. Do you agree?

2. What kind of threats have you made? To whom? For what reason? How effective were they? Were there any negative outcomes from using threatening to get what you wanted?

3. At one time or another, all of us have been threatened. Think about some times when someone has threatened you. What did this person want you to do? In what way was the person threatening? What were the consequences of noncompliance? What did you do? How did you feel about it?

4. Have you ever responded to a serious threat by defying the person threatening you? What happened? Was your defiance successful? If so, how did you change? How did the person doing the threatening change?

5. Threats are common in international affairs. Think of some examples. Who was threatening whom and for what reason? What could the country making the threats have done differently? Why didn't the country's leaders act differently?

DEFINITIONS OF POWER SOURCES, INFLUENCE TECHNIQUES, AND INFLUENCE SKILLS

This appendix provides a comprehensive overview of the frameworks of power, influence, and skills developed through extensive research during the past twenty years and as measured by the Survey of Influence Effectiveness (SIE). For a more comprehensive explanation of the sources of power, see my book *The Elements of Power: Lessons on Leadership and Influence* (AMACOM, 2011). Also see my websites www.theelementsof power.com, www.booksbyterryrbacon.com, or www.terryrbacon.com.

HOW POWER WORKS

Power in people is like power in batteries. The higher the voltage of a battery, the more electromotive force it can deliver and thus the more work it can do. A 1,000-volt battery is far more powerful than a 10-volt battery. Likewise, people with greater sources of power are better able to lead and influence others than people with fewer and lesser sources of power. The more powerful you are, the more influence you will have.

To lead or influence people effectively, you must have a sufficient power base. There are eleven sources of power: five personal sources (knowledge, expressiveness, history, attraction, and character), five organizational sources (role, resources, information, network, and reputation), and one meta-source (will). Here is a brief explanation of each of these power sources:

PERSONAL SOURCES OF POWER

Knowledge   Your knowledge, skills, talents, and abilities, as well as your learning, wisdom, and accomplishments. Power derives from what you know and can do. People rated high in knowledge power are three times more influential than people rated low in knowledge power.

Expressiveness   Your ability to communicate powerfully and effectively in written and oral forms. Power is based on the clarity, energy, conviction, and eloquence of speech. In its most powerful form, expressiveness is an element of charisma. Building this power source will increase your influence effectiveness more than building any other power source. Expressiveness is strongly correlated with three other power sources: character, attraction, and reputation.

History   Specifically, the history you have with the person you are trying to lead or influence. Power derives from cultivating familiarity and trust with another person, and the psychological principles of liking, similarity, and reciprocity are the basis for this power. Between people who know each other well, history can be the most important power source. High ratings on history power are strongly correlated with high ratings on interpersonal skills.

Attraction   The ability to attract others by causing them to like you. Power is based on physical attractiveness as well as authenticity; commonality of values, attitudes, or beliefs; personality; character; wisdom; shared experience; and many other factors. Globally, attraction is one of the strongest power sources. High ratings on this power source more than triple your influence effectiveness.

Character   Power that is based on people's perceptions of your character, including such elements of character as integrity, honesty, fairness, courage, kindness, modesty, and prudence. A significant source of personal power, character is ranked number one globally.

ORGANIZATIONAL SOURCES OF POWER

Role   Power that's derived from your role in a group, an organization, or a community, or the legitimate power and authority vested in a role or position. A person's role can be a significant source of power but can also lead to abuses of power if not used wisely. Role power is strongest when combined with high ratings on character, attraction, knowledge, expressiveness, and reputation power.

Resources   Power derived from your ownership or control of important resources (such as wealth or natural resources) that other people value and need. Typically, resources are not a strong source of power for most people.

Information   Your access to and control of information. This power source has five elements that form the mnemonic RADIO: retrieval, access, dissemination, interpretation, and organization. Together and separately, these capabilities enable people to lead and influence others through the effective deployment of information.

Network   Power derived from the breadth and quality of your connections with other people. Social capital among network members (e.g., reciprocal respect, admiration, favor granting, and collaboration) makes networking a substantial source of organizational power. High ratings on this power source can triple your influence effectiveness and make you twice as inspirational as people with low network power.

Reputation   Power based on an estimation of the overall quality of a person by others in a community (or a team, an organization, or a society) to which the person belongs. Reputation is a significant source of power for people who are well thought of—and a significant power drain for those with poor reputations. High ratings on this power source more than triple your influence effectiveness and significantly increase the likelihood that others will follow you.

WILL POWER (META-SOURCE)

Will	Power based on your desire to be more powerful, coupled with the courage to act. This power comes from within and can magnify every other source of power. It depends entirely on your decision to act; it takes passion and commitment but also energy and action. Will power is different from desire and longing. It comes not from the impulse to act but from acting on the impulse. It is the most important power source of all. Compared to having low will power, having high will power can increase your leadership and influence effectiveness by a factor of ten. In *The Elements of Power: Lessons on Leadership and Influence,* I cite examples of otherwise ordinary people who have accomplished a great deal through the sheer force of their will.

HOW INFLUENCE WORKS

Influence is the application of power to accomplish a specific purpose. Research shows that people typically try to lead and/or influence others using ten positive influence techniques: logical persuading, legitimizing, exchanging, stating, socializing, appealing to relationship, consulting, alliance building, appealing to values, and modeling. There are also four negative or "dark side" influence tactics: avoiding, manipulating, intimidating, and threatening.

Influence can be as complex as forming an alliance of nations to try to influence a rogue country's leadership to change its policies, or as simple as a child smiling and extending his hand in an offer of friendship. Every time we try to affect how other people think, behave, or decide, we are trying to influence them. A smile and a handshake are attempts to socialize, to form a connection with another human being and break down barriers. As people get to know us and like us, they are more likely to say yes to our requests.

RATIONAL APPROACHES TO INFLUENCING

Logical persuading	Using logic to explain what you believe or what you want. Logic is the number-one influence power tool throughout the world and the most frequently used and effective

influence technique in nearly every culture, but it does not work with everyone—and in some circumstances it will not work at all.

Legitimizing   Appealing to authority. On average, it's the least-effective influence technique in the world but will work with some people most of the time and most people some of the time and can result in quick compliance.

Exchanging   Negotiating or trading for cooperation. This technique is most effective when it is implicit rather than explicit. It is used less often globally than any other influence technique but is sometimes the only way to gain agreement or cooperation.

Stating   Asserting what you believe or want. One of the influence power tools, stating is most effective when you are self-confident and can state ideas using a compelling tone of voice. This technique can cause resistance, however, if overused or used heavy-handedly.

SOCIAL APPROACHES TO INFLUENCING

Socializing   Getting to know the other person, being open and friendly, finding common ground. Complimenting people and making them feel good about themselves is a critical technique in many cultures and situations. Socializing is one of the influence power tools and the second-most important one in frequency and effectiveness globally.

Appealing to relationship   Gaining agreement or cooperation with people you already know well. This influence power tool is based on the length and strength of your existing relationships. As an influence technique, it is the third highest rated in effectiveness globally.

Consulting   Engaging or stimulating people by asking questions and involving them in the problem or solution. Consulting is one of the influence power tools and ranks fourth globally in frequency and effectiveness. The technique works well with smart, self-confident people who have a strong need to contribute ideas.

Alliance   Finding supporters or building alliances to help influence
building   someone else; using peer or group pressure to gain cooperation or agreement. This influence technique is not
used often and is not always effective, but in the right circumstances it may be the only way to gain consent.

EMOTIONAL APPROACHES TO INFLUENCING

Appealing to   Making an emotional appeal or an appeal to the heart;
values   appealing to people's strongest values and beliefs. Because
it is one of the principal ways to influence many people at
once and the best technique for building commitment,
this emotional appeal is a frequent technique of religious
or spiritual leaders, idealists, fund-raisers, politicians, and
some business leaders.

Modeling   Behaving in ways you want others to behave; being a role
model; teaching, coaching, counseling, and mentoring. It
is possible to influence people without you being aware
that you are influencing. Parents, leaders, managers, and
public figures influence others through modeling all the
time—positively or negatively—whether they choose to
or not. This influence technique ranks fifth globally in
effectiveness.

THE "DARK SIDE" INFLUENCE TACTICS

There are also four negative influence techniques to be wary of. These techniques are negative because they take away the other person's legitimate right to say no. They force people to comply with some-thing contrary to their wishes or best interests, mislead them, or com-pel them to act when they would otherwise choose not to.

Avoiding   Forcing others to act, sometimes against their best interests, by avoiding responsibility or conflict or behaving
passive-aggressively. Avoiding is the most common dark-

side technique. In some cultures, trying to preserve harmony can be mistaken for avoiding.

Manipulating   Influencing through lies, deceit, hoaxes, swindles, and
cons. Manipulators disguise their real intentions or intentionally withhold information that others need to make
the right decision.

Intimidating   Imposing oneself on others; forcing people to comply by
being loud, overbearing, abrasive, arrogant, aloof, or
insensitive. Intimidation is the preferred technique of
bullies.

Threatening   Harming others or threatening to harm them if they do
not comply; making examples of some people so that others know that the threats are real. Threats are the preferred technique of dictators and despots.

THE INFLUENCE SKILLS

Influence effectiveness is partly a function of the influencer's skill in
using any given influence technique and is measured in the SIE. Like
a skilled craftsman, it takes time and practice to perfect those skills.
The research on power and influence shows that there are twenty-
eight skills associated with influence effectiveness. These skills fall into
four categories: communication and reasoning, assertiveness, interpersonal relationships, and interaction. People who become highly
skilled in these areas can be extraordinarily effective at leading and
influencing other people.

COMMUNICATION AND REASONING SKILLS

Logical reasoning   The ability to think logically, to analyze
problems, and to identify logical solutions to
them.

Analyzing and displaying data visually	Skill at creating charts, graphs, illustrations, and other visuals that clearly convey the relationships among data points and communicate ideas and conclusions.
Finding creative alternatives	Being creative and innovative, and being able to see alternatives and solutions where others haven't; skill at "thinking outside the box."
Probing	Skill at asking insightful questions that lead others to the heart of the problem or issue.
Speaking conversationally	Being able to converse on a number of topics and engage people in casual conversation; being a skilled conversationalist.
Conveying energy and enthusiasm	Bringing energy and enthusiasm to interactions and situations; being naturally energetic and engaged and being able to energize other people.
Listening	Skill at actively listening to others; being engaged with others when they are speaking and accurately hearing and retaining the essence of their thoughts.

ASSERTIVENESS SKILLS

Asserting	Skill at stating an opinion with confidence or force; presenting ideas strongly and affirmatively; maintaining one's position without becoming aggressive.
Persisting	Skill at enduring steadfastly; continuing on one's course despite opposition or resistance; being insistent and tenacious.
Behaving self-confidently	Having faith in one's own judgment, abilities, and rights; projecting firmness and steadfastness in one's purpose, directions, and goals.

Behaving authoritatively	Being able to project authority; behaving as though one has the legitimate right to use authority; clearly stating a decision, conclusion, or course of action.
Using a compelling tone of voice	Having a strong, firm, and resonant voice, so as to command attention when one speaks.
Using assertive nonverbals	Projecting confidence and assurance through all the nonverbal aspects of communication, such as using strong and confident gestures, facial expressions, and body language.
Using authority without appearing heavy-handed	Being able to command others and use legitimate authority without being overbearing, clumsy, oppressive, or harsh, which is a key skill in using the influence technique of stating.

INTERPERSONAL SKILLS

Being friendly and sociable with strangers	Opening up to and engaging with people you don't know; being outgoing and conveying warmth, acceptance, and interest in strangers. A critical skill in the influence technique of socializing.
Showing genuine interest in others	Being authentic in showing caring and concern for, and curiosity about, other people; making others feel important. A critical skill for the influence techniques of socializing and appealing to relationship.
Having insight into what others value	Having a strong, intuitive understanding of other people and what is important to them; being able to discern what others value without them having to say what it is; interpersonal perceptiveness. A critical skill for the influence technique of appealing to values.

Being sensitive to others' feelings	Skill at understanding human emotions and empathizing with them. The effective use of appealing to relationship and socializing depends on this skill.
Building rapport and trust	Establishing trustful connections with other people; skill at building harmonious and sympathetic relationships with others; conveying confidence in other people and causing them to feel that you too can be trusted.
Building close relationships	Creating trusted friendships and close relationships with other people, and sustaining intimate and friendly relationships with others over a period of time.
Supporting and encouraging others	Giving aid or assistance to others; promoting, advancing, inspiring, or stimulating others and encouraging them to forge ahead. This skill involves not only providing practical aid, but conveying an attitude of helpfulness. This skill is critical for the influence technique of modeling.

INTERACTION SKILLS

Convincing people to help you influence others	Skill at building agreement and cooperation and a unified sense of purpose, particularly in approaching others and trying to persuade them as well as enlisting their support and assistance in influencing others. This is the most critical skill in the influencing technique of alliance building.
Resolving conflicts and disagreements among others	Skill at managing conflict; the ability to defuse emotionally charged situations, reduce the tension between people in conflict with each other, and reach the calmest level of acceptance and agreement among them.

Building consensus	The ability to mediate differences of opinion and reach solutions that others can accept; skill at creating harmony and agreement among people who initially disagree.
Taking the initiative to show others how to do things	Skill at coaching, teaching, advising, and helping others in developing their skills and abilities. A strong interest in and desire to teach others is an essential skill in the influencing technique of modeling.
Bargaining or negotiating	Skill at reaching agreement with others over an exchange of things of value; skill at discussing terms and reaching a satisfactory agreement in a settlement, bargain, or deal. Crucial to the influencing technique of exchanging.
Being willing to ask others for favors	The ease and comfort with which you are willing to ask other people for something that's done or granted out of kindness or goodwill. An essential ability in appealing to relationship.
Being willing to do favors for others	Your own willingness to do something or grant something to others out of kindness or goodwill and with no expectation of remuneration. An essential ability in appealing to relationship.

INFLUENCE SKILL DIFFICULTY AND POTENTIAL IMPACT

The following table lists the twenty-eight influencing skills, the difficulty of mastering each skill, and the potential impact each skill can have on leading and influencing others. The skills are ranked according to potential impact and then by difficulty. Bargaining or negotiating, for instance, has very high potential impact but is also a difficult skill to master. Conversely, persisting has low potential impact and is easy to master. In developing your leadership and influencing skills, you will have more leverage with the skills having the greatest potential impact, even though many of them are difficult to master. These rankings are based on twenty years of research on power and influence that was conducted at Lore International Institute, which is now part of Korn/Ferry International.

INFLUENCE SKILL	TYPE OF SKILL	DIFFICULTY	POTENTIAL IMPACT
Convincing people to help you influence others	Interaction	Very high	Very high
Resolving conflicts and disagreements among others	Interaction	Very high	Very high
Using a compelling tone of voice	Assertiveness	Very high	Very high
Bargaining or negotiating	Interaction	Very high	Very high
Using authority without appearing heavy-handed	Assertiveness	High	Very high
Taking the initiative to show others how to do things	Interaction	High	Very high
Building consensus	Interaction	High	Very high
Behaving authoritatively	Assertiveness	Very high	High
Using assertive nonverbals	Assertiveness	Very high	High
Having insight into what others value	Interpersonal	High	High
Probing	Communication and reasoning	High	High
Finding creative alternatives	Communication and reasoning	Medium	High
Supporting and encouraging others	Interpersonal	Medium	High
Building rapport and trust	Interpersonal	Low	High
Building close relationships	Interpersonal	Very high	Medium
Showing genuine interest in others	Interpersonal	Medium	Medium
Conveying energy and enthusiasm	Communication and reasoning	Medium	Medium
Asserting	Assertiveness	Medium	Medium
Listening	Communication and reasoning	Medium	Medium
Behaving self-confidently	Assertiveness	Low	Medium
Logical reasoning	Communication and reasoning	Low	Medium

INFLUENCE SKILL	TYPE OF SKILL	DIFFICULTY	POTENTIAL IMPACT
Willingness to ask others for favors	Interaction	Very high	Low
Being sensitive to others' feelings	Interpersonal	High	Low
Analyzing and displaying data visually	Communication and reasoning	High	Low
Willingness to do favors for others	Interaction	High	Low
Being friendly and sociable with strangers	Interpersonal	Medium	Low
Speaking conversationally	Communication and reasoning	Low	Low
Persisting	Assertiveness	Low	Low

GLOBAL INFLUENCE RESEARCH

Many of the insights I gained about how people build power and use it to influence others is based on a research study I conducted at Lore International Institute (now part of Korn/Ferry International). That research on global power and influence began in 1990 and continues today. It is based on a proprietary 360-degree assessment, the Survey of Influence Effectiveness, which gathers data from the subjects of the study (self-ratings) as well as data from other people who work with them (respondent ratings). Throughout the book, when I cite the research on power and influence, I am referring to this study and to the "self" or "other" ratings the study generated. During the past twenty years, our database has grown to more than 64,000 subjects and over 300,000 respondents, and it has given me and my colleagues insight into the strength of people's power sources, how frequently they use different influence techniques, how effectively they use them, how appropriate those techniques are for their culture, and how skilled they are in twenty-eight areas related to leadership and influence effectiveness. Because this study was global, it has allowed me to identify differences in the uses of power and influence in forty-five countries around the world. This appendix includes some of the insights on global influence gleaned from the research. For further information on the forty-five countries I studied, see www.theelementsofpower.com.

When you seek to influence a customer, supplier, partner, boss, subordinate, or colleague in your own culture, you are generally working with people who have grown up with the same influence conventions you have. You know what is important. You know how people generally respond to different forms of influence, and you know what's been more or less successful for you previously. Consequently, you can moderate your influence techniques, the content of your messages, and the types of communication to best suit the person you are trying to influence.

However, when the people you seek to influence live in another country, when they have a different cultural background and a different set of beliefs and values, then the influence techniques that may have worked for you before may not work with them. The way you have learned to influence others, using the conventions and beliefs you have learned since childhood, probably won't be as effective when you are working with people whose conventions and beliefs are different (often in ways you may not comprehend). Moreover, since the cues they give you will likely be different from the cues you are accustomed to, you may not know how to interpret the way they are responding to you, and you may not know until much later whether your influence attempt succeeded or failed. A case in point is a Westerner trying to influence a customer in Japan. The Westerner, not understanding the Japanese desire to preserve harmony, may mistake the customer's agreeableness for consent and believe that a deal has been made when in fact it has not. Influencing others successfully in business can be difficult enough. Adding cultural complexity to the mix makes influencing global partners, suppliers, and customers very challenging.

GLOBAL DIFFERENCES IN THE USE OF THE TEN ETHICAL INFLUENCE TECHNIQUES

Despite many global similarities in how people operate, power and influence work differently in different countries. If you are involved in global business, you can glean from these research findings some lessons on how to apply influence techniques cross-culturally.

Logical Persuading

Logical persuading is the most prominent influence technique in the world. In the forty-five countries I studied, logical persuading was the most frequently used influence technique (except for in New Zealand, where logical persuading ranks a close second to socializing).

Logical persuading is particularly prominent in many European countries (Portugal, Spain, Greece, the Czech Republic, Italy, Poland, Switzerland, Germany, and Belgium); in Latin America (Brazil, Argentina, Colombia, Chile, Mexico); as well as in India, the United States, and Canada. This influence technique is used somewhat less frequently in Asian countries (Japan, Thailand, Hong Kong, South Korea, Singapore, Indonesia, and China). Influencing through logic is still the most frequently used influence technique even in these Asian countries. However, Asians make greater use of social influencing techniques (especially socializing and appealing to relationship), which reflects the more collective and relational nature of Asian cultures.

It is safe to assume that people in every culture will appreciate hearing logical arguments for why you are asking for what you want, but they still may not be influenced. Remember that for numerous reasons (emotional barriers, psychological biases, cultural prescriptions, and so on) they may not find logical persuasion compelling, even if your logic and facts are sound.

Legitimizing (Appealing to Authority)

Around the world, legitimizing is used most often in the United States, followed closely by Venezuela, Singapore, China, Colombia, India, Pakistan, Turkey, South Korea, Canada, Hong Kong, Peru, Mexico, Brazil, Taiwan, and Chile. So you are most likely to see it used in the Americas and in many parts of Asia. Legitimizing is used significantly less often in the Nordic countries (Sweden, Norway, Finland, the Netherlands, and Denmark) and parts of Europe (the Czech Republic, Austria, Germany, Hungary, Belgium, Italy, Portugal, France, and Greece).

The Nordic countries are more equalitarian and less hierarchical, so appealing to authority is less culturally acceptable than it is in other parts of the world. It may be surprising that legitimizing is used less frequently in Germany than in the United States. Germany is a more formal and structured society than the United States, and therein lies the difference. For Germans, the traditions and rules of behavior are more implicit and well accepted, so they don't need to be cited. In fact, citing the rules may seem overbearing and unnecessary in Germany. In the States, however, people may have less respect for authority and feel less bound by traditions, so citing rules, customs, and traditions may be necessary if an influencer believes they should be followed.

Exchanging

Exchanging is an interesting influence technique because dealing, trading, negotiating, and compromising are deeply embedded in the human psyche. Indeed, had we not developed the ability to gain cooperation by bargaining with each other, we would never have succeeded in creating civilization. So exchanging is ubiquitous in human interactions throughout the world. Nonetheless, the technique is used more frequently in cultures where explicit bargaining is more common: China, Hong Kong, Taiwan, Singapore, India, Australia, Malaysia, Pakistan, and the United States. It is less common in cultures where the bargaining that occurs is more implicit: most of the Nordic countries (Finland, Sweden, Norway, and Denmark) and many European countries (Poland, France, Hungary, Italy, Belgium, and Portugal).

Stating

The frequency of stating varies considerably around the world. Stating is more commonly applied in cultures where people can vigorously argue with each other without seriously being in conflict, where debates can be loud and contentious but still friendly, where interrupting people in meetings or at the dinner table is the only way to be heard. The research shows that stating is used most frequently in these countries: Israel, Greece, Chile, Venezuela, Russia, Turkey, Spain, Italy, Portugal, Poland, Argentina, the Czech Republic, France, Colombia, Peru, and Brazil. Most of these countries are in South America or the Mediterranean region. The countries where stating is used significantly less often include Thailand, Malaysia, Hong Kong, Japan, Sweden, Norway, Finland, Korea, Indonesia, Singapore, Taiwan, the United Kingdom, and Denmark—countries in Asia or the Nordic region. The United States is average in the frequency of the use of stating.

In the Nordic countries, which cultural studies rate as being more equalitarian and less assertive, too much stating would seem contentious and undemocratic. In Asian cultures, which value harmony, being too assertive could appear dishonorable and cause conflict, which Asian cultures typically try to avoid. In Latin and Mediterranean countries, on the other hand, asserting yourself and vigorously joining in the discussion is not only expected, you may lose respect if you are not assertive.

Socializing

Socializing is the second most frequently used influence technique worldwide (after logical persuading). Nonetheless, the research shows that it is used significantly more often in the English-speaking countries (New Zealand, Australia, the United States, Ireland, Canada, the United Kingdom), as well as some Latin American countries (Argentina, Peru, Venezuela, Colombia) and Italy and Spain. Socializing is used less frequently in former Soviet bloc countries (Russia, the Czech Republic, Hungary, Poland); some Asian countries (Japan, Thailand, Indonesia, Singapore, India); and in South Africa, Turkey, and France.

Socializing means finding common ground with people who are strangers or people you don't know well, so it is more commonly used in cultures where "breaking the ice" is a traditional part of social intercourse and people are expected to spend time getting to know one another before getting down to business. It has been said, for instance, that business meetings in the United States are like a hamburger, where the bun represents socializing and the meat represents substance. Americans commonly socialize at the beginning of a meeting, then get down to business, and then socialize at the end (so, like a hamburger, it's bun-meat-bun). In other cultures—notably Germany, the Netherlands, and Finland—socializing in business meetings is typically kept to a minimum.

New Zealand is the only country in the world where socializing is used more often than logical persuading. New Zealanders are a very social bunch.

Appealing to Relationship

Appealing to relationship means influencing through close or strong existing relationships. The research shows that it occurs most frequently in countries in Asia (China, Taiwan, Malaysia, New Zealand, Hong Kong, Singapore, Australia, South Korea, Pakistan) and Latin American countries (Peru, Venezuela, Argentina, Mexico, Colombia, Brazil). This influence technique is used somewhat less frequently in Europe and the Nordic countries (Finland, the Czech Republic, Hungary, Sweden, Austria, Portugal, Germany, France, Belgium, Switzerland, Norway, the Netherlands, and Denmark).

In cultures where family is the core social unit, appealing to relationship is likely to be one of the dominant influence techniques. In China, for example, appealing to relationship is used significantly more often than the global norm and, in particular, stands in contrast to the European tradition. Consequently, Chinese businesspeople working in Europe are likely to overestimate the importance of family ties for their European counterparts. Likewise, Europeans working in China are likely to underestimate the importance of family and clan ties to their Chinese counterparts. Chinese in Europe may rely too much on existing relationships to influence their European customers, while Europeans in China may not recognize the importance of existing relationships in influencing their Chinese customers.

To increase your influence in cultures where existing relationships are more important, you have to devote time to building and maintaining such relationships, although as an outsider you will probably never be as close to or influential with the members of a family as the existing family members are—no matter how well you get to know them. To increase your influence in cultures where existing relationships are less important, you need to rely on other influence methods (such as exchanging, alliance building, logical persuading, or stating).

Consulting

Consulting is more common in cultures where people are less likely to buy into a solution or proposal unless they have participated in its creation or been asked for their opinion. The United States, Canada, and Ireland rank among the world's most frequent users of consulting. In these cultures, it is important to ask rather than tell, to engage people in discussion and solicit their opinions as a way to gain their cooperation. Other countries where consulting is frequently used include Italy, Australia, India, Spain, Brazil, New Zealand, Singapore, China, and South Korea.

Consulting is somewhat less common in cultures that tend to be more direct in their communication, including Russia, Poland, Hungary, Finland, the Netherlands, Austria, Mexico, Japan, Indonesia, the Czech Republic, Sweden, Norway, Denmark, and Germany. Even so, the frequency of the use of consulting in these countries is still high, which means consulting is among the most commonly used influence techniques in the world.

The difference in usage depends to some extent on how a society views authority. In Poland, for instance, bosses are generally expected to have the answers, so a boss who frequently uses consulting to influence subordinates might be considered a weak leader. In the United States, on the other hand, a boss who frequently uses consulting would likely be considered a good leader who knows how to engage a team. Authority is less respected in the United States, so consulting is likely to be a more effective influence technique than in countries where people are more likely to defer to authority.

Alliance Building

Overall, alliance building is a less frequently used influence technique than all the other techniques except legitimizing. Cultures where group or team efforts are as efficacious (or more so) than individual efforts—where people gain power and influence by working together to achieve results and where collaboration is traditional—rely more heavily on alliance building. Although this happens in every country, the research shows that it is more likely to occur in Pakistan, the United States, Canada, China, Chile, Ireland, Argentina, India, South Korea, Australia, New Zealand, Brazil, and the United Kingdom. Alliance building is somewhat less frequently used in some Nordic and Germanic countries (Finland, Austria, Norway, Germany, Switzerland, and Denmark).

Appealing to Values

This influence technique is favored in cultures where people are expressive rather than stoic, emotional rather than pensive, and more likely to act on their values rather than live them quietly. According to the research, such countries include the United States, Greece, Spain, Italy, Ireland, Argentina, Turkey, India, Chile, South Korea, Brazil, Colombia, Pakistan, Malaysia, Australia, Canada, and New Zealand. In contrast, appealing to values is used less frequently in Finland, Russia, Norway, Hungary, the Czech Republic, Denmark, Austria, Sweden, Poland, and Switzerland.

In general, appealing to values is among the influence techniques used less frequently than most others, and the gap between the country with the highest frequency score (United States) and the lowest (Finland) is not substantial. Appealing to values is likely to be effective in every culture throughout the world if you are attuned to the values that matter most to people and can successfully appeal to those values in an influence attempt.

Modeling

The gap between the country with the highest average frequency score on modeling (Spain) and the country with the lowest average frequency (Japan) is only moderate, which indicates that modeling is used about the same amount of time by people in all cultures.

AVOIDING AND CULTURAL DIFFERENCES

The only dark-side influence technique that occurs with any degree of frequency throughout the world is avoiding. I am including the research findings on the frequency of avoiding because they offer interesting cultural insights. The research shows that the frequency of avoiding is highest in two areas of the world: Asia and the former Soviet/Eastern bloc countries. In Asia, avoiding is used most frequently in Japan, Indonesia, South Korea, Thailand, Taiwan, China, New Zealand, and Hong Kong. In the GLOBE study, these are countries that score high in "societal institutional collectivism practices," which means they place a high value on relationship maintenance, people view themselves as interdependent with groups, and extended family structures are important to individuals.[1] These cultures also score moderate to low on assertiveness, which means they value cooperation, face saving, and indirect speech.[2] There is more subtlety and nuance in their communications. Because face saving and harmony with others are so highly valued, people in these cultures will influence each other in ways that are less confrontational. What appears to be avoidance in these cultures is often simply the culturally appropriate way of exerting influence while preserving harmony. In the former Soviet/Eastern bloc countries, avoiding may well have been a self-preservation strategy even though people there are more direct in their communication. They are more direct among themselves, but not necessarily with the government. When it is dangerous to confront authority, people will avoid using the more direct influence techniques, and this is true anywhere in the world or in an organization with autocratic leadership.

Rated lowest on frequency of avoiding were the Germanic (Germany, Austria, Switzerland) and Nordic (Norway, Sweden, Finland) countries, as well as Greece, the United States, Canada, and Ireland. These cultures tend to be much more direct. They value candor over subtlety and are far more individualistic than collectivist; consequently, less value is placed on harmony and saving face. In these countries, avoiding may foster suspicion because it suggests a person has something to hide.

The results of the power and influence research for each country would be too lengthy to include in this book. However, brief profiles of each of the forty-five countries I studied appear on my website at www.the elementsofpower.com. Additional information on power and influence and other topics related to business, politics, and leadership is available at www.booksbyterryrbacon.com and www.terryrbacon.com.

NOTES

INTRODUCTION

1. Timothy C. Brock, Sharon Shavitt, and Laura A. Brannon, "Getting a Handle on the Ax of Persuasion," in Sharon Shavitt and Timothy C. Brock, eds., *Persuasion: Psychological Insights and Perspectives* (Boston: Allyn & Bacon, 1994), 1.

2. John P. Kotter, *John P. Kotter on What Leaders Really Do* (Boston: Harvard Business Review Press, 1999), 100.

3. Jay Conger, "The Necessary Art of Persuasion," *Harvard Business Review Classics* (Boston: Harvard Business Press, 2008), 1–2.

4. Two validation studies (one with a sample size of 4,500 and the other with a sample of 10,700) showed that the Survey of Influence Effectiveness (SIE) is a valid instrument. Using the alpha coefficient (a measure of internal consistency), we found that scale reliabilities ranged from .73 to .90, indicating that the SIE produces reliable and consistent measurements. We established construct validity through factor analysis, which demonstrated that the SIE items form clusters corresponding to the TOPS model for rating influence effectiveness, which is discussed in chapter 2. Criterion validity was established through correlations between the influence clusters and the ratings of influence effectiveness. In the twenty years since the SIE was created and validated, we have assessed the power bases and influence effectiveness of more than 64,000 people, mostly business professionals and managers around the world. In addition to having these people complete a self-assessment of their approaches to influence, we asked them to identify other people they worked with who could provide insights on how they influence others, and our database includes perspectives on those people from more than 300,000 respondents. This rich source of information has given us substantial insights on how power and influence are used globally.

CHAPTER 1: Fundamentals of Influence

1. John P. Kotter, *John P. Kotter on What Leaders Really Do* (Boston: Harvard Business School Press, 1999), 98.

2. Noah J. Goldstein, Steve J. Martin, and Robert B. Cialdini, *Yes! 50 Scientifically Proven Ways to Be Persuasive* (New York: Free Press, 2008), 82.

3. Robert J. House, Paul J. Hanges, Mansour Javidan, Peter W. Dorfman, and Vipin Gupta, eds., *Culture, Leadership, and Organizations: The GLOBE Study of 62 Societies* (London: SAGE Publications, 2004).

4. Ibid., 12. This dimension of assertiveness is similar in some respects to Geert Hofstede's masculinity dimension. Hofstede was one of the first to research cultural differences. More about Hofstede appears in chapter 8.

CHAPTER 2: The Ways and Means of Influence

1. Warren Bennis and Burt Nanus, *Leaders: Strategies for Taking Charge* (New York: HarperBusiness, 1997), 20.

2. Ibid., 37.

CHAPTER 3: Logical Persuading and Legitimizing

1. George Orwell, *Animal Farm* (New York: Harcourt, Brace Jovanovich, 1946), 17–18

2. Ibid.

3. Ibid.

4. Ibid.

5. Ibid.

6. Ibid.

7. Ibid., 18–19.

8. Theodore Levitt, *The Marketing Imagination* (New York: Free Press, 1986), 77.

9. Ed Michaels, Helen Handfield-Jones, and Beth Axelrod, *The War for Talent* (Boston: Harvard Business School Press, 2001), 58.

10. Margaret J. Wheatley, *Leadership and the New Science: Learning About Organization from an Orderly Universe* (San Francisco: Berrett-Koehler, 1994), 20.

11. Terry R. Bacon, *The Elements of Power: Lessons on Leadership and Influence* (New York: AMACOM, 2011).

12. Daniel Goleman, *Emotional Intelligence* (New York: Bantam Books, 1995), 13–29.

13. Robert B. Cialdini, *Influence: The Psychology of Persuasion,* rev. ed. (New York: William Morrow, 1993), 17.

14. A growing body of evidence indicates that we are consistently and often subconsciously influenced by a variety of emotional and psychological factors that make us anything but rational. These works include Ori Brafman and Rom Brafman, *Sway: The Irresistible Pull of Irrational Behav-*

ior (New York: Doubleday, 2008), 17; and Dan Ariely, *Predictably Irrational: The Hidden Forces That Shape Our Decisions* (New York: HarperCollins, 2008), xx. In *Sway,* Ori and Rom Brafman identify some of those factors. They write: "These hidden currents and forces include loss aversion (our tendency to go to great lengths to avoid possible losses), value attribution (our inclination to imbue a person or thing with certain qualities based on initial perceived value), and the diagnosis bias (our blindness to all evidence that contradicts our initial assessment of a person or situation)." MIT behavioral economist Dan Ariely argues that traditional economic theory falsely assumes that consumers behave rationally: "In conventional economics, the assumption that we are all rational implies that, in everyday life, we compute the value of all the options we face and then follow the best possible path of action. . . . [However] we are really far less rational than standard economic theory assumes. Moreover, these irrational behaviors of ours are neither random nor senseless. They are systematic, and since we repeat them again and again, predictable." Ariely observes, for example, that the first price we associate with a particular product becomes an anchor that affects how much we are willing to pay for that product in the future, although the actual future value of the product may be quite different.

15. John P. Kotter, *John P. Kotter on What Leaders Really Do* (Boston: Harvard Business Review Press, 1999), 100.

16. Orwell 33.

17. Orwell 123.

CHAPTER 4: Exchanging and Stating

1. Mark Twain, *The Adventures of Tom Sawyer* (Racine, WI: Whitman, 1955), 26.

2. John W. Gardner, *On Leadership* (New York: Free Press, 1990), 58.

3. Robert B. Cialdini, *Influence: The Psychology of Persuasion,* rev. ed. (New York: William Morrow, 1993), 17–56.

4. John P. Kotter, *John P. Kotter on What Leaders Really Do* (Boston: Harvard Business Review Press, 1999), 104.

5. Gardner, *On Leadership,* 33.

CHAPTER 5: Socializing and Appealing to Relationship

1. Dale Carnegie, *How to Win Friends and Influence People,* special anniversary ed. (New York: Pocket Books, 1998).

2. Gary Yukl, *Leadership in Organizations,* 7th ed. (Upper Saddle River, NJ: Prentice Hall, 2010), 176.

3. Ronald J. Deluga, "Kissing Up to the Boss: What It Is and What to Do About It," *Business Forum* (Summer–Fall 2001), http://www.entrepreneur.com/tradejournals/article/127538894_3.html.

4. John P. Kotter, *John P. Kotter on What Leaders Really Do* (Boston: Harvard Business School Press, 1999), 104.

CHAPTER 6: Consulting and Alliance Building

1. Terry R. Bacon and Karen I. Spear, *Adaptive Coaching: The Art and Practice of a Client-Centered Approach to Performance Improvement* (Palo Alto, CA: Davies-Black, 2003), 166.

2. Terry R. Bacon, *What People Want: A Manager's Guide to Building Relationships That Work* (Mountain View, CA: Davies-Black, 2006), 126.

3. This quote is widely attributed to Bengis. See http://www.worldofquotes.com/author/Ingrid-Bengis/1/index.html.

4. *The Paper Chase*, directed by James Bridges (1973; Beverly Hills, CA: Twentieth Century Fox).

5. Michael Vitiello, "Professor Kingsfield: The Most Misunderstood Character in Literature," *Hofstra Law Review* 33, no. 3 (2005), p. 969; http://www.hofstra.edu/PDF/law_lawrev_vitiello_vol33no3.pdf.

6. Jack Welch quoted in "The Man Who Invented Management: Why Peter Drucker's Ideas Still Matter," *Businessweek*, November 28, 2005, accessed July 24, 2010, www.businessweek.com/magazine/content/05_48/b396 1001.

7. "The Man Who Invented Management," *Businessweek*.

8. Noah J. Goldstein, Steve J. Martin, and Robert B. Cialdini, *Yes! 50 Scientifically Proven Ways to Be Persuasive* (New York: Free Press, 2008), 10.

CHAPTER 7: Appealing to Values and Modeling

1. Robert Cowley, "The Antagonists of Little Round Top," in Robert Cowley, ed., *With My Face to the Enemy: Perspectives on the Civil War* (New York: G. P. Putnam's Sons, 2001), 217.

2. Michael Shaara, *The Killer Angels* (New York: Ballantine Books, 1974), 30.

3. Ibid., 210.

4. Kevin Cashman, *Leadership from the Inside Out*, 2nd ed. (San Francisco: Berrett-Koehler, 2008), 98.

5. J. Peter Burkholder, Donald Jay Grout, and Claude V. Palisca, *A History of Western Music*, 8th ed. (New York: W. W. Norton, 2010), 550.

6. Vince Lombardi Jr., *What It Takes to Be #1: Vince Lombardi on Leadership* (New York: McGraw-Hill, 2001), 157.

7. Ibid., 158.

8. Noel M. Tichy, with Eli Cohen, *The Leadership Engine: How Winning Companies Build Leaders at Every Level* (New York: HarperBusiness, 1997), 57.

9. Ibid., 51.

10. Mary-Kate Olsen and Ashley Olsen, *Influence* (New York: Penguin Books, 2008), 13.

CHAPTER 8: How to Become More Influential

1. See in particular Robert B. Cialdini, *Influence: The Psychology of Persuasion*, rev. ed. (New York: William Morrow, 1993); Dan Ariely, *Predictably Irrational: The Hidden Forces That Shape Our Decisions* (New York: Harper-Collins, 2008); Jonah Lehrer, *How We Decide* (Boston: Houghton Mifflin Harcourt, 2009); Noah J. Goldstein, Steve J. Martin, and Robert B. Cialdini, *Yes! 50 Scientifically Proven Ways to Be Persuasive* (New York: Free Press, 2008); and Ori Brafman and Rom Brafman, *Sway: The Irresistible Pull of Irrational Behavior* (New York: Doubleday, 2008).

2. For a fascinating discussion of the psychological bias of social proof and its effect, see Jerry B. Harvey, *The Abilene Paradox and Other Meditations on Management* (San Francisco: Jossey-Bass, 1988).

3. See Stanley Milgram, *Obedience to Authority* (New York: Harper Perennial Modern Classics, 2009).

4. If you aren't familiar with the Myers-Briggs Type Indicator (MBTI), Consulting Psychologists Press has many publications explaining the framework and its applications. Another excellent resource is David Keirsey and Marilyn Bates, *Please Understand Me: Character and Temperament Types* (Del Mar, CA: Prometheus Nemesis, 1984).

5. For further reading, see Terrence E. Deal and Allan A. Kennedy, *Corporate Cultures* (New York: Basic Books, 2000); Edgar H. Schein, *Organizational Culture and Leadership*, 3rd ed. (San Francisco: Jossey-Bass, 2004); and Geert Hofstede, *Cultures and Organizations: Software of the Mind*, 2nd ed. (New York: McGraw-Hill, 2004).

CHAPTER 9: Avoiding

1. Herman Melville, "Bartleby the Scrivener" (Lexington, KY: ReadaClassic .com, 2010).

2. *Diagnostic and Statistical Manual of Mental Disorders*, 4th ed. (Washington, DC: American Psychiatric Association, 1994), 733.

CHAPTER 10: Manipulating

1. For a full account of the Cardiff Giant, see Scott Tribble, *A Colossal Hoax: The Giant from Cardiff That Fooled America* (Lanham, MD: Rowman & Littlefield, 2009).

2. Mark Seal, "Madoff's World," *Vanity Fair* (April 2009), 129.

3. Ibid., 135.

4. *Diagnostic and Statistical Manual of Mental Disorders*, 4th ed. (Washington, DC: American Psychiatric Association, 1994), 661.

5. Erin E. Arvedlund, "What We Wrote About Madoff," *Barron's Online* (December 22, 2008).

6. "Bernie Madoff's Victims: The List," *Clusterstock* (December 23, 2008).

CHAPTER 11: Winning Through Intimidation

1. Judith Lynn Fisher-Blando, "Workplace Bullying: Aggressive Behavior and Its Effect on Job Satisfaction and Productivity" (doctoral dissertation, University of Phoenix, January 2008), iii.

2. Bethany McLean and Peter Elkind, *The Smartest Guys in the Room: The Amazing Rise and Scandalous Fall of Enron* (New York: Penguin Books, 2004), 241.

3. Robert Bryce, *Pipe Dreams: Greed, Ego, and the Death of Enron* (New York: PublicAffairs, 2003), 269.

4. McLean and Elkind, *The Smartest Guys in the Room*, 200.

5. Kurt Eichenwald, *Conspiracy of Fools* (New York: Broadway Books, 2005), 11.

APPENDIX B: Global Influence Research

1. Robert J. House, Paul J. Hanges, Mansour Javidan, Peter W. Dorfman, and Vipin Gupta, eds. *Culture, Leadership, and Organizations: The GLOBE Study of 62 Societies* (London: SAGE Publications, 2004), 468.

2. Ibid., 410.

INDEX

consulting, 37, 114–125
building ownership in, 119–120
cultural differences in use of,
268–269
difficulty and potential impact of,
166
effective use of, 124–125
frequency and effectiveness of, 42,
43
as influence power tool, 41
insights on, 120–122
limitations of, 122–123
and MBTI types, 172, 173
questions used in, 114–116
as social approach, 49, 253–254
Socratic method in, 118–119
when to use, 123–124
context for influence, 20–24
convincing people, to help you
influence others, 258, 260
cooking the books, 216–217
counseling, 150–154
Cowley, Robert, on Little Round Top,
136
creative alternatives, finding, 256, 260
credibility, 165
cultural differences, 26–27
adapting to, 173–174
learning about, 7
in socializing, 98–99
see also global influence research
curiosity, about people, 116–117

dark-side influence
in modeling, 155
success of, 28–29
tactics used for, 254–255, see also
specific techniques, e.g.: avoiding
Davis, Jefferson, 135
Deal, Terrence, 174
deception, 206–207, 215
decision making
leveraging biases in, 168–171
reason and emotion in, 60–62
Dell'Orefice, Carmen, on Bernie
Madoff, 211
Deluga, Ronald, on ingratiation,
99–100
displaying data, 256, 260
disposition of influencee, 22–23
Drew, Lori, 230
Drucker, Peter, 120–121

on asking questions, 118, 121
on knowledge workers, 5
DuBois, W.E.B., 17

effectiveness in influencing, 38–39, 42
Eichenwald, Kurt, on Enron, 237
Einstein, Albert, 56–58, 167
Eisenhower, Dwight D., 206
Elkind, Peter, on Enron, 236, 237
emotional approaches to influencing,
16, 36, 50, 254
emotional manipulation, 229–230
encouraging others, 258, 260
energy, 144, 256, 260
Enron, 233–238
enthusiasm, 144, 256, 260
ethical influence, 3–4, 27–28, 35, 48,
see also specific techniques
exchanging, 36–37, 77–87
cultural differences in use of, 266
difficulty and potential impact of,
166
effective use of, 86–87
examples of, 79–81
frequency and effectiveness of, 42,
43
insights on, 82–85
limitations of, 81–82
Madoff's use of, 214
and MBTI types, 172, 173
as rational approach, 49, 253
when not to use, 86
when to use, 41, 42, 85–86
explaining, 36, 51–96
by exchanging, 77–87
by legitimizing, 64–73
by logical persuading, 54–64
by stating, 87–94
techniques associated with, 36
expressiveness, 250
and alliance building, 130
and appealing to values, 143
building, 162
impact of, 163
Madoff's use of, 210–211
and modeling, 154

false flattery, 217–218
Fastow, Andrew, 235–237
favors, 259, 260
Feinberg, Kenneth R., 82–83, 90
Feynman, Richard, 149

ABOUT THE AUTHOR

Terry R. Bacon is a senior partner and scholar in residence in the Korn/ Ferry Institute, the research center of excellence for Korn/Ferry International, the world's leading talent-management firm. For more than thirty years he has been a thought leader, innovator, teacher, coach, and consultant to global businesses in leadership, management, business development, and interpersonal skills. In 1989, he founded Lore International Institute, a widely respected executive-development firm that was acquired by Korn/Ferry International in 2008.

Terry is a prolific author and speaker. He has written or cowritten more than 100 books, articles, white papers, and research reports, including *Selling to Major Accounts, Winning Behavior, The Behavioral Advantage, Adaptive Coaching, Powerful Proposals, What People Want, Leading in a Boundaryless Organization, Leading for Empowerment, Leadership through Influence, High-Impact Facilitation, Interpersonal and Interactive Skills, Proposing to Win, Effective Coaching,* and *The Elements of Power.* He has given presentations on such topics as leading in challenging times, balanced leadership, respect, accountability, the life cycle of companies, behavior-based selling, what people want from their managers, leaders developing leaders, the ideological foundations of adaptive coaching, global account management, developing client relationships, behavioral differentiation and the customer experience, and developing the C-suite.

He received a Ph.D. from the American University in 1977 and a BS in engineering from the United States Military Academy at West Point in 1969. He has studied business and management at The Wharton School (University of Pennsylvania), the University of Chicago, Stanford University, and Harvard Business School. In 2007, 2008, 2009, and 2010, he was named by *Leadership Excellence* magazine as one of the "top 100 thinkers on leadership in the world."

For more information about Terry's books, ideas, and research, visit his Facebook page or websites: www.terryrbacon.com, www .booksbyterryrbacon.com, and www.theelementsofpower.com.